CHILDREN, CULTURE, AND ETHNICITY
Evaluating and Understanding the Impact

Maureen B. Slonim

GARLAND PUBLISHING, INC. • NEW YORK & LONDON
1991

© 1991 Maureen B. Slonim
All rights reserved

Library of Congress Cataloging-in-Publication Data

Slonim, Maureen.
  Children, culture, and ethnicity : evaluating and understanding
the impact / Maureen B. Slonim.
      p. cm. — (Reference books on family issues ; vol. 18)
(Garland reference library of social science : vol. 470)
  Includes index.
  ISBN 0-8240-5646-9
  1. Child development—Cross-cultural studies. 2. Child
development—Cross-cultural studies—Bibliography. 3. Ethnicity—
Cross-cultural studies. 4. Ethnicity—Cross-cultural studies—
Bibliography. 5. Children of minorities—Cross-cultural studies.
6. Children of minorities—Cross-cultural studies—Bibliography.
I. Title. II. Series: Reference books on family issues ; v. 18.
III. Series: Garland reference library of social science ; v. 470.
HQ767.9.S55   1991
305.23'1—dc20   91-14314
                                                              CIP

Printed on acid-free, 250-year-life paper
Manufactured in the United States of America

CHILDREN, CULTURE, AND ETHNICITY

REFERENCE BOOKS
ON FAMILY ISSUES
(VOL. 18)

GARLAND REFERENCE LIBRARY
OF SOCIAL SCIENCE
(VOL. 470)

Reference Books On Family Issues

1. Resources for Early Childhood: *An Annotated Bibliography and Guide for Educators, Librarians, Health Care Professionals, and Parents*, Hannah Nuba Scheffler, General Editor
2. Problems of Early Childhood: *An Annotated Bibliography and Guide*, by Elisabeth S. Hirsch
3. Children and Divorce: *An Annotated Bibliography and Guide*, by Evelyn B. Hausslein
4. Stepfamilies: *A Guide to the Sources and Resources*, by Ellen J. Gruber
5. Experiencing Adolescents: *A Sourcebook for Parents, Teachers, and Teens*, by Richard M. Lerner and Nancy L. Galambos
6. Sex Guides: *Books and Films About Sexuality for Young Adults*, by Patty Campbell
7. Infancy: *A Guide to Research and Resources*, by Hannah Nuba-Scheffler, Deborah Lovitky Sheiman, and Kathleen Pullan Watkins
8. Postpartum Depression: *A Research Guide and International Bibliography*, by Laurence Kruckman and Chris Asmann-Finch
9. Childbirth: *An Annotated Bibliography and Guide*, by Rosemary Cline Diulio
10. Adoption: *An Annotated Bibliography and Guide*, by Lois Ruskai Melina
11. Parent-Child Attachment: *A Guide to Research*, by Kathleen Pullan Watkins
12. Resources for Middle Childhood: *A Source Book*, by Deborah Lovitky Sheiman and Maureen Slonim
13. Children and Adjustment to Divorce: *An Annotated Bibliography*, by Mary M. Nofsinger
14. One-Parent Children, The Growing Minority: *A Research Guide*, by Mary Noel Gouke and Arline McClarty Rollins
15. Child Abuse and Neglect: *An Information and Reference Guide*, by Timothy J. Iverson and Marilyn Segal
16. Adolescent Pregnancy and Parenthood: *An Annotated Guide*, by Ann Creighton-Zollar
17. Employed Mothers and Their Children, by Jacqueline V. Lerner and Nancy L. Galambos
18. Children, Culture, and Ethnicity: *Evaluating and Understanding the Impact*, by Maureen B. Slonim
19. Prosocial Development: Caring, Helping, and Cooperating: *A Resource Guide for Parents and Professionals*, by Alice Sterling Honig and Donna Sasse Wittmer
20. Hispanic Children and Youth in the United States: *A Reference Guide*, by Angela L. Carrasquillo

To the loving memory of
Flora Weiss Slonim

ACKNOWLEDGMENTS

To Regina Weiss, Gloria Hunter, and Debbie Sheiman, my sincere appreciation for their invaluable assistance in editing the many drafts of this manuscript.

To my son Mark, special thanks for his patience in teaching me computer usage and word processing skills.

To Phil LoPiccolo, my admiration for his work in Developmental Pediatrics and concern for handicapped children of military families. This book is an outgrowth of the multidisciplinary conference planned by him and Marian McNeil for the 7th Army Medical Command in Germany.

To Inger Sigfridsson Dahlberg, my gratitude for sharing information on multicultural education services in Sweden.

To my daughter Linda, for her enthusiastic support and encouragement of my efforts and endeavors.

To Virginia Florence and Jane Atkinson of the Weston (CT) Library staff, for assistance in obtaining reference texts.

Above all, to my husband Al, a special acknowledgment for his support and love.

CONTENTS

Foreword	xi
Preface	xiii
The Role of Culture and Ethnicity in Personality Development	3
A Family Systems Framework	31
Understanding One's Own Culture	45
A Framework for Assessing Culture and Ethnicity	61
Implications for Health, Education, and Social Services	93
Asian Cultures	121
Hispanic American Cultures	163
Black Cultures	195
European Cultures	223
Author Index	253
Title Index	259
Subject Index	267

FOREWORD

My interest in this topic began when, as a nursing student at a university medical center, I encountered many foreign patients and their families. I was fascinated by the differences in their cultures, and how this influenced their interaction with the health care system, particularly in childbearing and childrearing.

As a graduate student in child psychiatric nursing, my interest increased, along with my knowledge of psychosocial development and family systems. As I learned to evaluate children from a transdisciplinary perspective, an understanding of culture and ethnicity became an increasingly vital diagnostic and intervention tool.

Subsequent work in the development and coordination of programs for handicapped children led to increased recognition of how profoundly culture and ethnicity impact on health, education, and social services. The experience of living abroad then afforded me the unique opportunity to observe firsthand child and family development in other cultures.

Later, a consulting assignment from the U.S. Army Exceptional Family Member Program in Europe transformed my interest into formal research. The Army's multidisciplinary staff of professionals, assigned overseas, was providing services to a large population of racially and culturally mixed families. They requested a continuing education training workshop on "Cultural Differences Pertaining to Handicapped Children and Their Families."

I soon discovered that there is a paucity of literature on the subject. There are a few classical studies on culture and children, primarily in the literature of anthropology. Each discipline—sociology, psychology, child development, mental health, and pediatrics—has contributed a little insight to the knowledge base, but most studies are limited to one or two specific cultures. Family systems, social work, and nursing tend to deal with a more holistic approach to service and have thus provided the most useful resources. Even so, no one discipline seemed to be addressing the total picture.

The purpose of this book is to provide a broad, transdisciplinary look at how culture and ethnicity affect children. It is a resource guide for understanding the culturally different child. A selected annotated bibliography is included at the end of each chapter to provide an additional resource for information. It is my sincere hope that this book will aid in understanding and appreciating children of all cultures.

Maureen B. Slonim, R.N., M.S.

PREFACE

In today's world there is a crucial need for cross-cultural and pluralistic understanding. Such understanding requires emphasizing *how* and *why* cultures differ rather than focusing on the differences themselves.

This work is intended to provide both general and specific information regarding ways that culture and ethnicity affect child development. It focuses on *how* and *why* a child's cultural and ethnic heritage influences the developing personality.

This book is addressed to professionals of all disciplines who work with children from different cultures. The information presented imparts a basic core of theory for practical application; it is transdisciplinary in nature. It is applicable whether one teaches at the preschool or high school level in special or regular education, practices as a nurse, doctor, or therapist, or works in a mental health or counseling capacity. Laypersons, interacting with persons of different cultures, should also find this work of interest.

Professionals are usually aware of the literature generic to their own discipline; they rarely read the publications of other disciplines. Too few human-service professionals of any discipline are exposed to cultural anthropology at either the undergraduate or graduate level. This book draws from the literature of diverse disciplines: anthropology, psychology, child development, education, health, mental health, social work, nutrition, and public policy. It provides a comprehensive approach to the complex subject of multiculturalism.

Family Systems Theory is utilized as a theoretical rationale; a child cannot be understood in isolation from his family and environment. This framework recognizes the influences of past history and tradition and the ways that present experience can modify or change tendencies. Ethnocentrism and ways to overcome it are examined, and guidelines are presented for identifying the culture and ethnicity of an individual child and/or family. Specific examples enable readers to translate general principles into practice and provide points of comparison and contrast in the painting of a "cultural portrait" of a particular child or family.

The book concludes with a series of chapters describing specific cultural characteristics of four broadly defined groups: Asian, Hispanic, black (African American and Caribbean), and European. Emphasis is on those characteristics that are most likely to have implications for health, education, and social service professionals.

Children, Culture, and Ethnicity

THE ROLE OF CULTURE AND ETHNICITY IN PERSONALITY DEVELOPMENT

It is essential for professionals to explore how culture and ethnicity affect child development in general in order to understand their effect on a specific child. To promote such understanding, this chapter defines culture and ethnicity and examines the processes by which cultural and ethnic traditions influence the developing child. Many of these practices are interrelated; most are followed without consideration of origin or purpose.

Culture and ethnicity mean many things to many people. Most definitions vary only in complexity and/or semantics. Basically, culture refers to those value systems that are transmitted from generation to generation and represent an integrated pattern of human knowledge, belief, and behavior. The word "culture" is derived from the Latin root "colere," meaning to till, cultivate, or nurture like a plant.

Before one can comprehend the pervasive influence that culture and ethnicity have on child development, one must first recognize the significant implications of each term. The importance of culture and ethnicity is conveyed in the following definitions:

> Culture is a word used in referring to the totality of learned behaviors in the context of a social system. It exists only within the context of human society. . . . Culture is society's blueprint for behavior.[1]

> Culture is man's medium; there is not one aspect of human life that is not touched by culture. . . . One of the functions of culture is to provide a highly selective screen between man and the outside world. In its many forms, culture therefore designates what we pay attention to and what we ignore. . . . Man needs the experience of other cultures. That is, to survive, all cultures need each other.[2]

> Culture may be thought of as traditional or learned patterns of thinking, feeling, and acting which become established in an ongoing social group and are transmitted from one generation to another. Cultural norms specify what must be done, what ought to be done, what may be done, what must not be done, and prescribe solutions to basic life problems. In this respect, tradition provides stability. At the same time, culture is dynamic in that it is a product of people's responses to changing life situations.[3]

A briefer definition, often cited, is from one of the earliest texts on cultural anthropology:

> Culture is that complex whole which includes knowledge, belief, art, morals, law, custom, and any other capabilities and habits acquired by man as a member of society.[4]

This all-encompassing definition is reflected in a more modern text which states that there are five criteria which define a culture: (1) a common pattern of communication, sound system, or language unique to the group; (2) a common basic diet and method of preparing food; (3) a common pattern of dress; (4) predictable patterns of relationship and socialization between men and women, mother and child, uncle and niece; and (5) a common set of values and beliefs or common set of ethics.[5]

Ethnicity primarily denotes a sense of identification with or belonging to a particular group: the word "ethnic" is derived from the Greek word "ethnikos," meaning people or nation. There is a distinction between the terms culture and ethnicity, yet there is some overlap in how they are defined and used. In many instances the terms (culture and ethnicity) are used interchangeably to describe unique behavioral characteristics:

> While culture deals with symbolic generalities and universals, ethnicity deals with an individual's sense of identification and provides a sense of belonging to a reference group. Ethnicity carries a highly subjective meaning for it is concerned with the sentiment felt by members of the ethnic group, such as "Black is beautiful." Ethnicity is usually displayed in the values, attitudes, life-

> styles, customs, rituals, and personality types of individuals who identify with particular ethnic groups.[6]
>
> Ethnicity patterns our thinking, feeling, and behavior in both obvious and subtle ways. It plays a major role in determining what we eat, how we work, how we relax, how we celebrate holidays and rituals, and how we feel about life, death, and illness.... Ethnicity is a powerful influence in determining identity. A sense of belonging and of historical continuity is a basic psychological need.[7]
>
> Ethnicity describes a sense of commonality transmitted over generations by the family and reinforced by the surrounding community. It is more than race, religion, or national and geographic origin. It involves conscious and unconscious processes that fulfill a deep psychological need for identity and historical continuity.[8]
>
> Ethnicity is more than an influence on events; it is commonly the source of events. Social and political institutions do not merely respond to ethnic interests; a great number of institutions exist for the specific purpose of serving ethnic interests. This in turn tends to perpetuate them.[9]

The culture in which we are raised strongly affects our attitudes, beliefs, values, and, in turn, our behavior. In a sense, to understand culture is to understand learned behavior. Without cultural standards of behavior, it would be impossible for any society to function or to survive.[10]

It is helpful to consider that culture is an adaptive response of people to their environmental and historical circumstances. Cultural beliefs did not develop illogically. Rather, they evolved as practices deemed necessary for survival and represent an organized blend of human effort, feeling, and thought:

> Culture shapes the way of life shared by members of a population. It is the sociocultural adaptation or design for living that people have worked out and continue to work out in the course of their history.[11]

Ethnicity, inextricably interrelated and interwoven with culture, must therefore be considered in the light of a culture's history—its economic, political, and social factors. Culture, like personality, is subject to change; it is constantly evolving.

Childrearing

One way to understand a culture is to identify those values that are emphasized in childrearing. Once identified, it is important to ascertain *how* and *why* those particular values evolved. A scrutiny of childrearing practices can often provide a window upon the traditions and beliefs of a culture. Culture and ethnicity are vital components of child development in general and crucial determinants in personality development.

Clearly, culture is not the sole determinant of personality development in children. Those aspects of personality that are genetically determined cannot be attributed to culture. Heredity and environment *both* affect personality development. Child development in general evolves from an interaction between biological and environmental factors. Culture can only affect *learned* behavior: it impacts on those aspects of personality that are shaped by environmental experiences.

We are all the products of our early family values. Child behavior must therefore be studied within a family and a cultural context. A child's social class, home environment, parental involvement, play patterns, and play materials are ipso facto culturally determined. Even the psycho-socio-biological stages of child development vary from culture to culture. In essence, culture is the basic setting for human development. Yet family environment alone does not constitute a child's culture. Community environment and social norms are also elements of human development.[12]

The environmental demands of a culture can affect childrearing practices. This is evident in the Bedouin culture, where the principal aim of early caretaking practices is to protect the vulnerable infant from a harsh environment. Bedouin infants are traditionally swaddled. Though this restricts mobility and limits stimulation, it does not affect subsequent motor development. Bedouin mothers consider early sitting, standing and walking to be major goals of childrearing and invest much energy in the coaching of these skills. This early achievement of walking enhances independence and increases the chances of survival in a nomadic society.[13] When childrearing practices adapt to environmental conditions, children are more apt to survive and to perpetuate their culture.

Socialization and Social Control

There are two kinds of cultural learning, according to Kluckhohn—technical and regulatory. Technical learning is intended to make the individual "productive, socially useful, and to increase the group's wealth and strength." Regulatory education, on the other hand, is intended to "reduce the nuisance value of the individual within the group as much as possible, to keep him from disturbing others, creating in-group disharmony, etc." In our society, the school is traditionally responsible for technical training, the home and church, for regulatory training. There is considerable overlapping, however.[14]

Cultural learning, whether technical or regulatory, is an individual matter. According to Goodenough, "People learn as individuals. Therefore, if culture is learned, its ultimate locus must be in individuals rather than in groups."[15]

The manner in which a society socializes and controls its young—regulatory training—is instrumental in personality development. Some societies use shame while others use guilt as a means of socialization and social control. Those societies that use guilt teach their members to internalize generalized rules of behavior, which then act as a conscience. Children (and adults) raised in such a society refrain from committing negatively sanctioned acts because they have been taught to feel guilty if they knowingly commit wrongful acts. Their conscience thus functions as a strong inner control for right and wrong. In contrast, other societies use shame, stressing exposure and ridicule as consequences for negatively sanctioned behavior. Societies using shame often teach family or community shame, whereby all are shamed by the action of any one of its members. Family shame is a concept that is useful in understanding cultures which stress "saving face." But childhood discipline alone, as one manifestation of social control, is insufficient to explain typical personality structure. That discipline must be examined in the context in which it was applied—by whom, how, when, and why.

An additional means of social control is provided by cultural myths. Such myths—the stories of how the rules were established—are symbolic expressions of social values that relate current practices to beliefs and events in the distant past. Because cultural myths imply both a promise *and* a warning, they provide an effective means of social control.[16]

Social controls start early in childhood and continue as habits throughout adult life. It should be noted, however, that social rules rarely receive total compliance. There is usually some discrepancy between socially prescribed behavior and actual behavior in any society. In rural communities and in neighborhoods (especially ethnic neighborhoods) where everyone knows everyone else, gossip is often a principal form of social control.

It is important to distinguish between a society and its culture. According to the noted anthropologist Linton, "A society is an organized group of people, a collection of individuals who have learned to work together. A culture is an organized group of behavior patterns."[17] Brown distinguishes between the two as follows:

> The terms culture and society are frequently used interchangeably, and there is usually no great harm in doing so as long as we know what the difference is. In the simplest form, we can say that a society is always made up of people; their culture is the way they behave. In other words, a society is not a culture; it has a culture.[18]

All societies devote a great deal of time and energy to training their younger members in acceptable behavior. Individuals are usually not considered adult until they have learned the acceptable behavior of the society.

The first few years of life are crucial to the development of values, attitudes, and the control of other environmental factors which shape personality. It is during infancy, notes Kluckhohn, that the child develops an "attitude toward life: confidence, resignation, optimism, pessimism." These attitudes are largely determined by the kind and amount of *care* given. Kluckhohn believes that insufficient attention is paid to this connection between child care and personality. The connection is important in two ways: (1) it helps the child develop basic

Role of Culture and Ethnicity in Personality Development

skills which will be useful when the period of indulgence ends, and (2) it helps the child to accept regulatory training when it starts, if he has positive attitudes toward parents and others.[19]

Linton believed that cultural behavior influences the developing personality in two ways: (1) behavior toward the child and (2) behavior by the child. He stressed that culturally patterned behavior *toward* the child from birth was of paramount importance during infancy to insure that children would be reared in traditionally approved ways. Adoption and practice of the behavior characteristics of the particular society, on the other hand, become more important after early infancy.[20]

Linton stressed that a crucial element in a child's value-attitude system was the close and continuous contact with parents and siblings and that personality formation seemed to be mainly one of integration of such experiences.[21] To Linton, culture was the dominant factor in establishing the basic personality type for any society.

A somewhat different viewpoint on socialization and personality development is offered by Orville Brim, a child developmentalist. Brim states the following:

> The functioning of the socialization process is not to produce for society something such as the "dominant" individual or "dependent" person; socialization instead is aimed at producing individuals equipped to meet the variety of demands placed upon them by a life in a society.[22]

Superstitions, Myths, and Folklore

Since early childhood marks a period of extreme malleability, when the developing individual is highly sensitive to accepted and expected mores, as well as the rationale and consequences of those mores, personality development is also influenced and affected by the superstitions and folk beliefs of a culture. These beliefs are inextricably bound to cultural values, health and education practices, food patterns, religious practices, and interpersonal relations. They influence courtship, marriage, childbearing, childrearing, and even death.

Folk beliefs and superstitions are found among people all over the world. Folklore embodies symbolic manifestations of universal themes—birth, life, and death. As such, it provides a socially acceptable way for people to deal openly with the frightening things in life that are not within their control. Folklore provides a window into the psyche and deals with the essence of life in any culture. There are striking similarities in folklore across cultures, with differences in detail reflecting local geography, plants, animals, and weather.

Superstitions, as well, are shared by many societies. Belief in the power of the "evil eye" is found in southern Europe and the Middle East, and in such scattered and diverse ethnic groups as Fijians, Native Americans, and Haitians; each group has a different method of dealing with ill effects of the evil eye. The way in which a superstition is contrived often reveals a culture's fundamental traits. Alan Dundes, a teacher of folklore at the University of California at Berkeley, explains:

> In contrast to the almost structureless folk tale, many superstitions follow the formula: if A then B with an optional C. For example: If you break a mirror, then you will have seven years' bad luck, unless you throw the broken pieces into a moving stream. Or, if you spill salt, then you will have bad luck, unless you throw some over your left shoulder. . . . Fatalistic societies, such as those in Asia and the Middle East, do not have the "optional C" escape clause in their superstitions. If A happens, B follows and there is no way out. Such societies tend to be oriented to the past and use divination techniques to find out why things happened. Meanwhile, folklore in agrarian societies, such as medieval Europe, tends to deal with harvest and calendar cycles.[23]

Customs and folklore affect not only children but ultimately the personality and lifestyle of the adults within a given culture. In Moslem and Hindu cultures, it is customary to seek assistance from the supernatural for solving life's problems.[24] Traditionally, children in India have been encouraged to continue to live in a mythical, magical world for a long time. This may explain the proclivity for Indians to believe in spirits or astrology and to be particularly sensitive to the nonverbal nuances of others, the so-called inner eye. It is further speculated that these conditions of childhood contribute to an unusual faith in gurus or spiritual leaders of various kinds.

Just as folklore and cultural beliefs are transmitted in the stories told to children, family myths are also passed on by storytelling. Family stories often perpetuate ethnic stereotypes by defining those attributes considered special to the family. These lauded attributes generally focus on interpersonal relations rather than workplace success. Thus, family myths in Italian families are apt to extol expressive emotions and, in French families, lovemaking. Other common themes in family myths are the mother-child bond, sibling rivalry, leaving home, courtship and marriage, family curses, illness, suicide, anger, and violence.

Family myths usually stress that the family can always be counted on for comfort and support, no matter what the circumstances. Through family myths, ancestral figures, especially grandparents of the same sex, often become a major part of a child's imaginative life and may even serve as role models. In fact, adopted children will often cite the need for stories about their family ancestors and experiences. Even though family myths do not always stand up to close scrutiny, they effectively foster a sense of family cohesiveness. This family identity then becomes incorporated into the child's personal sense of identity, an impact that Elizabeth Stone stresses in her book on family stories:

> The family is our first culture, and like all cultures, it wants to make known its norms and mores. It does so through daily life, but it also does so through family stories which underscore, in a way invariably clear to its members, the essentials, like the unspoken and unadmitted family policy on marriage or illness. Or suicide, or who the family saints and sinners are, or how much anger can be expressed and by whom.[25]

Time Orientation

The time orientation of a culture has an effect on the personality and behavior of its children. Time is a value orientation, a temporal focus of human life. There are distinct differences between cultures that are oriented to the past, the present, or to the future. The American middle class exemplifies a future orientation. Americans plan their families, their education, and their careers. Calendars, clocks, and appointment books are constantly consulted. This emphasis on the future places a high priority on youth, novelty, transient fads, and an obsession with change, with what is yet to come, and with conquering new frontiers. Striking examples are "trendy" fashions and toys, computers, election polls, and survey research. Children are taught that promptness is important. An even greater regard for promptness is instilled in children in Germany, Switzerland, and Scandinavia, where punctuality is almost a fetish.

In most Middle Eastern cultures, by contrast, any time consideration beyond a week is categorized as in the future. In such an informally structured time system, children learn that it is pointless to make appointments or any plans too far in advance. To the Arab way of thinking, only God knows the future, so it is useless, even crazy, to talk about it. Traditionally, in Iran, there is an indifference to the present, whereas the past has great importance. Those Far Eastern cultures that practice ancestor worship also put more emphasis on the past than the present.

In Hispanic or Latino cultures, time orientation, traditionally, is to the present, not the future or the past. Time is not an important consideration in childrearing or in other aspects of living. The pace of life is much slower than in Anglo-American cultures—hence the term, "mañana philosophy."

In the Sioux and Navaho cultures, there is no sense of time. The concepts of "being late" or "waiting" are foreign to them. Cross-culturally, children raised in "the culture of poverty" operate in a present time frame, with little or no conception of any future.

Time orientation is a factor in learning the accepted rules of interpersonal relations. In some countries, arriving late is considered catastrophic, and people learn to go to great lengths to avoid such a calamity. In other countries, one would not dream of arriving exactly on time. In still others, arriving early is frowned upon. Different times of day are highly significant in some cultures. Even the hours for dining are often culturally determined. In many cultures, there are specific ways of expressing honor or displeasure with friends or business acquaintances by how promptly they are greeted.

Religion

Religious traditions and ideologies strongly influence personality development. They affect one's values, one's method of social control (shame versus guilt), diet, attitudes toward health and illness, relationships with people and with the environment, family life cycle phases, occupational choices, politics, education, celebrations, even time orientation. In fact, there is hardly any aspect of personality development that is not affected by religion. Religion and culture are closely intertwined.

Within certain religious groups, for example, common behavioral patterns exist. Traditional Catholics are apt to feel guilt about pleasure, the body, and defiance of parental or church authority. Religions such as those of Mormons or Seventh-Day Adventists that oppose the use of alcohol generally produce either teetotalers or people who have problems with alcohol. Jews tend not to become alcoholics, because drinking is generally done in the home (as opposed to bars or pubs), in moderation, and with meals, often as part of a ritual. However, since food is a main part of family and religious rituals, Jews may substitute overeating for over-indulgence in alcohol. Avoidance of excessive drinking among Jews may also be influenced by their traditional devotion to scholarship and abstract thinking with concomitant investment in educational pursuits and career-oriented goals.

Eastern religions, such as Confucianism, Buddhism, and Taoism, are generally based on concepts of conformity, harmony, fatalism, and suppression of emotion. Western religions, such as Christianity, tend to be based on concepts that stress just the opposite—competition rather than conformity and harmony, control of one's own fate versus fatalism, and—increasingly—expression, rather than suppression, of emotion. These philosophical differences may have had religious origins, but they have become deeply ingrained in the culture and, subsequently, in the developing personalities of the various religions' followers.

Parental belief in a religious philosophy cannot in itself affect a child's personality. It is when that philosophy becomes ingrained in their childrearing practices that definitive behavior patterns evolve. Traditionally, children raised in a Catholic family were taught that parental authority was absolute. Parents were responsible for the salvation of their children's souls and were required to teach them a clearly defined "sin-oriented" morality. The Protestant home stressed individualism, emphasis on personal salvation and self-awareness, and the role of the individual layperson (and his conscience) versus absolute church authority. These childrearing patterns were (consciously or not) accepted and continuously reinforced.

Family Values and Life-Styles

Still another influence on personality is family values and life-styles, which are dependent on and reflective of a host of factors, many of which, though not all, are culturally influential. These values often determine whether childhood is prolonged or whether independence is encouraged, whether children are indulged or whether they are valued merely as potential helpers. The rules of etiquette that a child is taught are usually an indication of the family values. A child's play also reflects these values. Is the play structured? Is the child encouraged to incorporate fantasy and/or pretend play? Is competition or skillbuilding fostered? Are the parents involved in the play? Is creativity encouraged? Is messy play tolerated?

The nature of the community, as well as the socioeconomic status of the family, must also be considered, even though these may be at odds with the family values and usual life-style. Social class and place of residence are described as two universal determinants of behavior by Selye in his book on intercultural communication.[26] Similarly, in an extensive cross-cultural study, the Whitings state the following:

> Two independent cultural features—the complexity of the socioeconomic system, and the composition of the household—were shown to be predictive of the social behavior of children.[27]

Communication Style

Communication patterns, especially language, learned in childhood are not easy to change. Social class and place of residence (during childhood) are often indicated through speech patterns. The speech of children in the United Kingdom is strikingly revealing. There are distinct regional dialects (e.g., Cockney, Liverpool, Welsh, or Scottish). There is also a distinct difference in the speech patterns of children who attend "public" or boarding schools and those who attend "private" schools; it is almost a class distinction. (In England, the terms "public" and "private" schools mean just the opposite of the same terms in the United States.)

Role of Culture and Ethnicity in Personality Development

In fact, English accents and their social class implications are the subject of a recent book, *Does Accent Matter?*, by John Honey, which has evoked much controversy. The author, a professor and linguistics expert, advocates a revamping of British education to eliminate regional accents and dialects, which he feels seriously influence children's chances in life. In Honey's view, a person's accent still counts for a lot in Britain, often determining success or failure. Class divisions remain, and accent is the coding, says Honey, who asserts he can pigeonhole the origin and social values of most people "within the first fourteen words out of their mouths."[28]

The communication style of a culture involves more than just verbal conversation. It includes all patterns and aspects of non-verbal communication, especially body language and emotional expression. *How* people say something is frequently more important than *what* they say. Verbal communication includes the content and the context of speech, particularly the intent of words in relation to cultural values. Communication can occur through eye contact, touch, the written word, even music.

If a child grows up in a culture where children are taught that a given form of communication, such as making eye contact with adults in conversation, is impolite, this mannerism may become incorporated into his or her personality. Similarly, if a child learns to avoid confrontation and not express anger or displeasure, then this, too, becomes inherent to his or her communication style. Communication styles, like cultural beliefs, are frequently subject to misunderstanding by those unfamiliar with them.

The actual content or subject matter of communication is usually determined by cultural norms. Children quickly learn which subjects are "taboo" (especially with strangers) and whether sensitive topics are addressed openly or indirectly. They also learn "conversational etiquette," specifying the degree of formality and proper means of addressing others. Edward Sapir, a linguist, theorized that "[l]anguage does not, it would appear, so much *determine* cultural differences as *reflect* cultural concerns that already exist."[29]

Role and Status of Women and Children

The status of children in a culture can sometimes be determined by communication style or by observable indications of how children are valued. As an example, the use of proper forms of address is more important in Europe than in the United States. A German child is called *du* (you) until the age of confirmation, when he or she is presumed to have earned the right of being addressed as *Sie* (the formal form of "you"). Likewise, in Europe, a sense that children are valued and welcome is evidenced by a vast array of benefits to parents (from health supervision to housing) and by the availability of special resources for mothers with baby carriages and strollers ("stair steps" on inclines and access/space on public transportation). "Mothers rooms" or designated areas for nursing and for changing infants are available in many public facilities.

An important aspect of personality—the self-concept of masculinity or femininity—is derived largely from the value that culture assigns to that role. Agrarian-oriented cultures traditionally valued sons more than daughters. They left female newborn infants to die when times were difficult. Other cultures to this day restrict land ownership, even legal rights, to male offspring. Family names and lineage primarily pass through the male side.

The sex-role typing of a culture can ordain the socialization opportunities and experiences of its children and its adult members. A child's gender may determine the quantity and quality of education and the choice of a vocation or future mate. Even rites of passage are different for male and female children. A number of cultures test the strength and skills of their male youth before recognizing them as adults. Female circumcision, an ancient puberty rite, is still common in a number of African countries.

In many cultures today, the primary role for females is limited to having babies and taking care of the household. Childbearing may be more socially approved than education and/or employment for women; there may be intense pressure to marry and have children. Many Islamic cultures have a family-oriented society with traditional attitudes and values regarding women that involves veiling and other socialization restrictions. The role and status of women in the Middle East occurs largely within the framework of Islamic law and seems to be perpetuated within the political, social, historical, cultural, and economic systems.[30]

Birth order, in addition to sex-role typing, can be an influencing factor in personality development. Different cultures assign different obligations to firstborn and later born children. Birth order can affect the relationship between siblings as well as the relationship between child and parent.

Clearly, culture and ethnicity have a profound effect upon those aspects of personality development that reflect learned behavior. Learned behavior is eloquently characterized by the familiar poem *Children Learn What They Live*:

> If a child lives with criticism, He learns to condemn.
> If a child lives with hostility, He learns to fight.
> If a child lives with ridicule, He learns to be shy.
> If a child lives with shame, He learns to feel guilty.
> If a child lives with tolerance, He learns to be patient.
> If a child lives with encouragement, He learns confidence.
> If a child lives with praise, He learns to appreciate.
> If a child lives with fairness, He learns justice.
> If a child lives with approval, He learns to like himself.
> If a child lives with acceptance and friendship,
> He learns to find love in the world.[31]

NOTES

1. Peter Farb, *Humankind* (Boston: Houghton Mifflin, 1978), pp. 351–352.
2. Edward T. Hall, *Beyond Culture* (Garden City, N.Y.: Anchor, 1977).
3. Kazuye T. Kumabe, Chikae Nishida, and Dean H. Hepworth, *Bridging Ethnocultural Diversity in Social Work and Health* (Honolulu: University of Hawaii School of Social Work, 1985), p. 9.
4. Edward B. Tyler, *Primitive Cultures* (London: John Murray, 1871).
5. Louis A. Bransford, Leonard Baca, and Karen Lane, eds., *Cultural Diversity and the Exceptional Child* (Reston, Va.: Council for Exceptional Children, 1974).

6. Kumabe, *Bridging Ethnocultural Diversity in Social Work and Health*, p. 11.

7. Monica McGoldrick, "Ethnicity and Family Therapy: An Overview," *Ethnicity and Family Therapy*, M. McGoldrick, J.K. Pierce, and J. Giordano, eds. (New York: Guilford, 1982), pp. 4–5.

8. Joseph Giordano and Grace P. Giordano, *The Ethno-Cultural Factor in Mental Health: A Literature Review and Bibliography* (New York: Institute on Pluralism and Group Identity, 1977).

9. Nathan Glazer and Daniel Patrick Moynihan, *Beyond the Melting Pot: The Negroes, Puerto Ricans, Jews, Italians, and Irish of New York City* (Cambridge, Mass.: M.I.T. Press, 1963).

10. Ralph Linton, *The Cultural Background of Personality* (New York: Appleton-Century-Crofts, 1945).

11. John Ogbu, "Cultural Influences on Plasticity in Human Development," *The Malleability of Children*, J.L. Gallagher and C.T. Ramey, eds. (Baltimore: Paul H. Brookes, 1987), p. 156.

12. John Ogbu, "Cultural Diversity and Human Development," *Black Children and Poverty: A Developmental Perspective*, D.T. Slaughter, ed. New Directions for Child Development Series, no. 42 (San Francisco: Jossey-Bass, 1988), pp. 11–28.

13. Zipi Karplus, "Cultural Variations in Child Caretaking Practices Among the Negev Bedouins." Paper presented at the Fourth World Congress on Infant Psychiatry and Allied Disciplines, Lugano, Switzerland, 22 September 1989.

14. Clyde Kluckhohn, *Mirror for Man: The Relation of Anthropology to Modern Life, Classics of Anthropology*, Ashley Montagu, ed. (Tucson: University of Arizona Press, 1985), p. 206.

15. Ward H. Goodenough, *Culture, Language and Society*, 2nd ed. (Menlo Park, Calif.: Benjamin/Cummings, 1981), p. 54.

16. Ina Corrine Brown, *Understanding Other Cultures* (Englewood Cliffs, N.J.: Prentice-Hall, 1963), p. 126.

17. Linton, *The Cultural Background of Personality*, p. 56.

18. Brown, *Understanding Other Cultures*, p. 6.

19. Kluckhohn, *Mirror for Man*, p. 217.

20. Linton, *The Cultural Background of Personality*, pp. 139–141.

21. Ibid., pp. 141–151.

22. Orville G. Brim, "Personality Development as Role-Learning," *Personality Development in Children*, I. Iscoe and H.W. Stevenson, eds. (Austin: University of Texas Press, 1960), p. 138.

23. Alan Dundes, quoted in Sandra Blakeslee, "Folklore Mirrors Life's Key Themes," *The New York Times*, August 14, 1985, pp. C1 and C10.

24. Francis L.K. Hsu, ed., *Psychological Anthropology: Approaches to Culture and Personality* (Homewood, Ill.: Dorsey, 1961), pp. 400–456.

25. Elizabeth Stone, *Black Sheep and Kissing Cousins: How Our Family Stories Shape Us* (New York: Times Books/Random House, 1988), p. 7.
26. H. Ned Selye, *Teaching Culture: Strategies for Intercultural Communication* (Lincolnwood, Ill.: National Textbook Co., 1985).
27. Beatrice B. Whiting and John W.M. Whiting, *Children of Six Cultures: A Psycho-Cultural Analysis* (Cambridge, Mass.: Harvard University Press, 1975), p. 128.
28. John Honey, *Does Accent Matter? The Pygmalion Factor* (London: Faber and Faber, 1989).
29. Edward Sapir, "The Status of Linguistics as a Science," *Language* 5 (1929): 207–214.
30. Joyceen S. Boyle, "Professional Nursing in Iraq," *IMAGE: Journal of Nursing Scholarship* 21 (Fall 1989): 168–171.
31. Dorothy Law Nolte, *Children Learn What They Live* (n.p., n.d.).

BIBLIOGRAPHY

Acock, Alan C., and Jeffrey M. Clair. *The Influence of the Family: A Review and Annotated Bibliography of Socialization, Ethnicity, and Delinquency, 1975–1986.* New York: Garland, 1986.

Reviews books, articles, and dissertations dealing with socialization (political attitudes and behavior, educational goals, social attitudes, religious beliefs, and sex roles) and ethnic factors. Emphasis is on how families influence their adolescent children.

Adams, Paul L. "The WASP Child." *Basic Handbook of Child Psychiatry.* J.P. Noshpitz and I.N. Berlin, eds. Vol. I: *Normal Development.* New York: Basic Books, 1979, pp. 283–290.

Describes the cultural distinctiveness of Anglo-Saxon Protestantism and its impact on childrearing patterns. Details the economic and class differences among WASP families and how such traits affect the personal development of their children. Extensive references.

Anderson, Penny P., and Emily Schrag Fenichel. *Serving Culturally Diverse Families of Infants and Toddlers with Disabilities.* Washington, D.C.: National Center for Clinical Infant Programs, 1989.

Presents an overview of the concept of culture and discusses specific cultural issues such as family definitions, roles, relationships and childrearing techniques; health, illness, and disability beliefs and traditions; and communication and interactional styles. Publication highlights proceedings of NCCIP's spring 1988 meeting on this topic. Includes lists of references, recommended readings, and resource programs.

Axelson, John A. *Counseling and Development in a Multicultural Society.* Belmont, Calif.: Brooks/Cole, 1985.

Describes culture as the "total personality" of a people. Explores the dimensions of culture: culture as a social structure; culture as kinship systems; culture as personality; culture as psychological adjustment; culture as ethnic diversity; and culture as socioeconomic status.

Barrett, Richard A. *Culture and Conduct: An Excursion in Anthropology.* Belmont, Calif.: Wadsworth, 1984.

Describes the issues and ideas that intrigue anthropologists and what we can learn about ourselves by studying other cultures. Stresses the importance of "cultural relativism," evaluating people within the context of their own milieu, and "subjective understanding" (the need to perceive issues from the subject's point of view). Discusses emotional attachment to customs and the resultant emotional resistance to change. States that cultural learning is a necessary ingredient in the development of any human being.

Boyle, Joyceen S. "Professional Nursing in Iraq." *IMAGE: Journal of Nursing Scholarship* 21 (Fall 1989): 168–171.

Highlights the problem of women in a culture where they are assigned a low status and restricted in occupational choices. Article chronicles the establishment and subsequent closing (two decades later) of the lone professional nursing program in Iraq. Author attributes the problem to the "government policies made within a traditional context that views women and nursing as occupying an inferior status."

Bronfenbrenner, Urie, and Maureen A. Mahoney. *Influences on Human Development.* 2nd ed. Hinsdale, Ill.: Dryden, 1975.

Cites the effect of ecological factors, such as family size, ordinal position, discipline, and mother-child interaction on human development during childhood. Discusses the sequential pattern by which parental values influence children. This book is divided into five major sections: (I) Scientific Method in the Study of Human Behavior, (II) Nature and Nurture, (III) Infancy, (IV) Early Childhood, and (V) Middle Childhood, with bibliographies for each chapter.

Clark, Ann L., ed. *Culture and Childrearing.* Philadelphia: F.A. Davis, 1981.

A compilation of childrearing traditions of Matrix Americans (the "dominant" American culture), American Indians, American Blacks, Japanese Americans, Chinese Americans, Mexican Americans, Filipinos, Puerto Ricans, and Vietnamese in America. Each chapter is written by a nurse of that culture and includes rich personal and photographic interpretations. The historical background of each culture is chronicled, along with family structure, cultural values, and childrearing patterns for each stage of childhood. Focuses on health care implications, yet includes valuable information on culture in general. Extensive bibliography is included for each chapter.

Comer, James. *Maggie's American Dream.* New York: New American Library, 1988.

Relates the influence of his mother's life on his own childhood and subsequent career. Comer, a professor of child psychiatry at Yale, has developed a process to improve opportunities for academic success for poor, inner city, minority children. His School Development Program is based on parent participation and a synthesis of a child's emotional, social, and psychological needs.

Dixon, Terence, and Martin Lucas. *The Human Race.* New York: McGraw-Hill, 1983.

Examines the relationship of language, humor, sexuality, technology, clothing, architecture, life-style, religion, and art to culture and ethnicity. Explores widely different societies on five continents. Based on the research and images collected for the major television series of the same name.

Edwards, Carolyn Pope. *Promoting Social and Moral Development in Young Children.* New York: Teachers College Press, 1986.

Addresses specific domains of children's social knowledge with theoretical material on gender and sex roles, racial and cultural categories, and family and kinship patterns.

Fogel, Alan, and Gail F. Melson, eds. *Origins of Nurturance: Developmental, Biological, and Cultural Perspectives on Caregiving.* Hillsdale, N.J.: Lawrence Erlbaum Associates, 1986.

Examines research studies on early parenting and its determinants, including cultural contexts and biological influences. Focuses on how caregiving develops in young children and how experiences in childhood often contribute to later parenting and caregiving.

Friedman, W.J. *The Developmental Psychology of Time.* New York: Academic Press, 1982.

Stresses the crucial role of language in the development of temporal order. While notions of the present can be shared without language, past and future can only be shared through verbal language or some recorded communications. Clarifies the role and differences between "physical time" and "social time."

Gallagher, James J., and Craig T. Ramey. *The Malleability of Children.* Baltimore: Paul H. Brookes, 1987.

Provides a multidisciplinary understanding of what influences social, psychological, and intellectual growth. Chapter 13, "Cultural Influences on

Plasticity in Human Development" by anthropologist John Ogbu, is especially relevant.

Geertz, Clifford. *The Interpretation of Culture.* New York: Basic Books, 1973.

Explores what culture is, what role it plays in social life, and how it should be studied. Chapters deal with religion, ideology, politics, art, and the evolution of human mental capacities in a variety of different cultural contexts. Each topic is explored in terms of "Just how important are cultural differences within the human family?"

Gilmore, David D. *Manhood in the Making: Cultural Concepts of Masculinity.* New Haven: Yale University Press, 1990.

Traces the historical, cultural, and social concepts of manliness and male aggression. Identifies the crucial role of society and social structure in gender identity and behavior. Concludes that manliness is a cultural construct that varies according to the circumstances and needs of a society.

Giordano, Joseph. "Ethnicity and Family Life." *Child Abuse, Neglect and the Family Within a Cultural Context.* Washington, D.C.: DHEW Publication No. (OHDS) 78-30135, 1978.

Relates the experience of the author's family in taking in two foster children and the cultural miscues that ensued. Stresses that ethnic roots and family life are so intertwined that you cannot experience one without the other. Giordano and his wife are both professionals in the health care/mental health fields and have written extensively about culture, ethnicity, and families. This article provides a synopsis of the issue and suggests ways for professionals and volunteers to become more aware of the differences in ethnic patterns within families.

Glazer, Nathan, and Daniel Patrick Moynihan. *Beyond the Melting Pot: The Negroes, Puerto Ricans, Jews, Italians, and Irish of New York City.* 2nd ed. Cambridge, Mass.: M.I.T. Press, 1970.

Reviews the influence of ethnic people on a community and vice versa. The book was originally published in 1963; this edition opens with "A View From 1970." Provides a unique look at the relationship between ethnic identity, economic events, religion, and racism within a major city. The authors believe that ethnicity not only influences events, but it often generates those events. They further conclude that many social and political institutions are perpetuated by the ethnic interests they were originally designed to serve.

Goodenough, Ward H. *Culture, Language and Society.* 2nd ed. Menlo Park, Calif.: Benjamin/Cummings, 1981.

Describes the technical systems that comprise language; the evolution, variances, and dialects of language; and the relation of language to culture, the individual, and society. Uses language and linguistics as a means for understanding the content of culture. Extensive bibliography.

Greeley, Andrew M. *Ethnicity in the United States: A Preliminary Reconnaissance.* New York: Wiley, 1974.

Emphasizes that family structure and childhood socialization practices represent the basic mechanisms by which ethnic culture and heritage are transmitted, especially in the early years of life.

Hall, Edward T. *The Silent Language.* Garden City, N.Y.: Doubleday, 1959.

A classic study by this anthropologist and academic, revealing how we communicate by our manners and behavior. To Hall, "silent language" is a way of "talking" to one another without the use of words, an elaborate patterning of behavior which prescribes our handling of time, our spatial relationships, and our attitudes toward work, play, and learning—in short, "the language of behavior." Examples of how these behaviors vary among cultures are vividly presented.

Harrington, Charles. *Psychological Anthropology and Education: A Delineation of a Field of Inquiry.* New York: AMS Press, 1979.

Reviews the state of (the subdiscipline of) psychological anthropology (in 1979) at the request of the National Academy of Education in order to consider the role of anthropology in American education. Explains how psychological anthropology emerged from the subfield of anthropology called "culture and personality" in the 1960s. Defines psychological anthropology as that branch of anthropology concerned with the interface between individuals and their culture. Lists and analyzes contributions to education such as cross-cultural studies in perception, cognition, and socialization. Extensive references cited as well as annotations of additional related sources.

Harris, Marvin. *Our Kind.* New York: Harper and Row, 1989.

Traces the evolution of human life and culture—who we are, where we came from, and where we are going. Weaves fact, research, and speculation into an informative—and entertaining—survey of the origins and role of culture in shaping our lives.

Hite, Shere. *Women and Love: A Cultural Revolution in Progress.* New York: Knopf, 1987.

Explores the cultural traditions associated with sexual identity and roles. States that sex is part of the whole cultural tradition created by social systems and social institutions.

Honigman, John J. *Understanding Culture.* New York: Harper and Row, 1963.

Defines culture as a unique constellation of traits and presents examples of how similar traits exist in diverse cultures. Discusses the evolvement of play and role modeling and the importance of "coming of age" rituals.

Hsu, Francis L.K., ed. *Psychological Anthropology: Approaches to Culture and Personality.* Homewood, Ill.: Dorsey, 1961.

Assesses the gains and the problems of the "culture-and-personality" subdiscipline. The thoughts of 13 anthropology educators on the interaction between culture and personality are included. Of notable relevance is the chapter by Dr. Hsu entitled "Kinship and Ways of Life," which explains the relationship between man and culture. Dr. Hsu describes four basic types of societies, their kinship patterns, and how these patterns affect behavior.

Kluckhohn, Clyde. *Mirror for Man: The Relation of Anthropology to Modern Life.* Classics of Anthropology, A. Montagu, ed. Tucson: University of Arizona Press, 1985.

A classic, written for laymen; an introduction to modern anthropology. Defines anthropology as "an overlapping study with bridges into the physical, biological, and social sciences and into the humanities." To Kluckhohn, anthropology holds up a great mirror to man and lets him look at himself in his infinite variety. Of particular relevance are the chapters "Race: A Modern Myth," "Personality in Culture," "An Anthropologist Looks at the United States," and "An Anthropologist Looks at the World." Originally published in 1949 by McGraw-Hill.

Kobayashi, Noboru, and T. Berry Brazelton. *The Growing Child in Family and Society: An Interdisciplinary Study in Parent-Infant Bonding.* Tokyo: University of Tokyo Press, 1982.

Emphasizes the cross-cultural diversity in child development. Discusses the importance of family childrearing practices in influencing attitudes, coping skills, and other developmental outcomes. Examines multidisciplinary theories and experiences, including medical, biological, anthropological, and educational.

Kumabe, Kazuye T., Chikae Nishida, and Dean H. Hepworth. *Bridging Ethnocultural Diversity in Social Work and Health*. Honolulu: University of Hawaii School of Social Work, 1985.

Examines the psychosocial and cultural factors that influence health and illness behavior of different ethnic groups. Identifies and analyzes variations of response to health, illness, and disability among different ethnocultural groups. This monograph should be of interest to students, educators, and practitioners in human services. Case examples are of Samoan, Hawaiian, and Filipino families yet include principles applicable to other cultures. Extensive reference list included, primarily of publications before 1980.

Lawson, Lauren Valk. "Culturally Sensitive Support for Grieving Parents." *MCN, The American Journal of Maternal/Child Nursing* 15 (March/April 1990): 76–79.

Emphasizes the influence of culture on values, beliefs, behavior, and lifestyle practices. Describes how culture guides people in all aspects of daily life, even attitudes and customs toward grief, death, and funerals.

Lieberman, Alicia F. "Culturally Sensitive Intervention with Children and Families." *Child and Adolescent Social Work Journal* 7 (1990).

Explores the relationship between childhood and culture, concluding that babies become reflections and products of their culture right from birth. Provides examples of adaptive childrearing customs that effectively promote cultural continuity and child survival. Such customs evolve from the survival needs, philosophical outlook, and moral beliefs of a culture. Suggests ways to promote cultural sensitivity. Article is a revised version of a paper presented at the Training Institute of the National Center for Clinical Infant Programs, Washington, D.C., December 1987.

McGoldrick, Monica, John K. Pearce, and Joseph Giordano, eds. *Ethnicity and Family Therapy*. New York: Guilford, 1982.

Focuses on the cultural differences and the influence of ethnicity on human behavior. This book is divided into three sections—a conceptual overview, paradigms, and special issues, with an extensive bibliography for each chapter. The paradigm section contains chapters on American Indians, Afro-Americans, West Indian, Mexican, Puerto Rican, Cuban, Asian, French Canadian, German, Greek, Iranian, Irish, Italian, Jewish, Polish, Portuguese, Norwegian, and British families. A valuable reference source for understanding other cultural and ethnic groups. Its use should not be limited to family therapists.

Norton, Delores G. "Understanding the Early Experience of Black Children in High Risk Environments: Culturally and Ecologically Relevant Research as a Guide to Support for Families." *Zero to Three* 10 (April 1990): 1–7.

Examines the development of a sense of time as one dimension of early socialization. Provides examples from lower socioeconomic black families where the lack of a structured time environment affects children's ability to adapt and achieve in the larger society. Suggests intervention techniques within an anthropological framework.

Nugent, J. Kevin, Barry M. Lester, and T. Berry Brazelton, eds. *The Cultural Context of Infancy*, Vol. I: *Biology, Culture, and Infant Development*. Hillsdale, N.J.: Ablex, 1989.

Explores the interaction of nature and nurture by documenting biosocial influences on newborn behavior, mother-infant interaction in the first year of life, and cross-cultural comparisons. This is the first publication in a series designed to describe the developmental processes of infancy in a wide range of cultural and social environments.

Offer, Daniel, et al. *The Teenage World: Adolescents' Self-Image in Ten Countries*. New York: Plenum Medical Books, 1988.

The published report of a study of 6,000 subjects by a standardized questionnaire, the OSIQ (Offer Self-Image Questionnaire). While the bulk of the book is limited to descriptions of the test and testing procedure, it does provide some interesting data on adolescence in general and on teenagers in Japan, Israel, Hungary, West Germany, Italy, Australia, Turkey, Bangladesh, Taiwan, and the United States. Reviews the evolution of adolescence as a developmental stage. Notable findings are that most adolescents view themselves and their lives as positive and that the larger the proportion of adolescents in a country, the less positive they feel about themselves.

Opler, Marvin K. "Culture and Child Rearing." *Modern Perspectives in Psychiatry*. Vol. 3: *Modern Perspectives in International Child Psychiatry*. Edinburgh: Oliver & Boyd, 1969, pp. 292–320.

Reviews technical theories and data on the relationship of culture and childrearing from the psychiatric, psychoanalytic, and anthropological literature. Concludes that personality is always partly sociodynamic and partly cultural. Views childrearing practices as evidence of cultural evolutionary adaptation in human behavior.

Randall-David, Elizabeth. *Strategies for Working with Culturally Diverse Communities and Clients.* Washington, D.C.: Association for the Care of Children's Health, 1989.

Reviews general cross-cultural principles and definitions. Advocates a holistic view in understanding any cultural system: learning about the broader socioeconomic, political, religious, and cultural context in which health is embedded. Presents guidelines for working with culturally diverse community groups and clients based on this holistic approach, such as understanding cross-cultural variations in nonverbal communication.

Reidy, Joseph. "The Catholic Child." *Basic Handbook of Child Psychiatry.* J.P. Noshpitz and I.N. Berlin, eds. Vol. I: *Normal Development.* New York: Basic Books, 1979, pp. 271–282.

Reviews the childrearing philosophy of the Catholic church and how this affects children at different levels of development. Documents recent changes in church doctrine and resultant impact on child development practices. Includes extensive references.

Roosens, Eugeen E. *Creating Ethnicity: The Process of Ethnogenesis.* Frontiers of Anthropology, Vol. 5. Newbury Park, Calif.: Sage, 1989.

Demonstrates that ethnicity does not always stem from ancient tradition or nationality but can be shaped, modified, recreated, or manufactured in contemporary society. Focuses on ethnic minorities that have successfully preserved or shaped their unique identity in a multi-ethnic society.

Schwartzman, Helen B. *Transformations: The Anthropology of Children's Play.* New York: Plenum, 1978.

A cross-cultural perspective of child-structured play interactions, the role of toys, and parental involvement in child development. Schwartzman reports that children who are required by their parents to work do not give up play but merely restructure it to suit the context of the work situation. Studies find that children from low socioeconomic households are not restricted in imaginative and creative play. Relates how the concept of space is related to childhood play and how the playground movement developed as an effort to encourage "proper" play, even when space was limited.

Selye, H. Ned. *Teaching Culture: Strategies for Intercultural Communication.* Lincolnwood, Ill.: National Textbook Company, 1985.

Promotes the theory that interpersonal communication between people of different cultures requires intellectual skill and emotional appreciation of other cultures. To Selye, folklore provides an anthropologic view of a culture. He believes that people are basically the same the world over. Examines research on "preferred cognitive style," which relates to which hemisphere of the brain is dominant in mental operations and subsequent cross-cultural research on brain-damaged individuals. Includes cross-cultural observations and interpretations on left and right handedness. Extensive bibliography included.

Spindler, George D. *Education and Cultural Process: Anthropological Approaches.* 2nd ed. Prospect Heights, Ill.: Waveland, 1987.

Applies anthropological applications to an analysis of the educational process. Presents examples of how culture is transmitted both consciously and unconsciously. This is the sixth book on the subject (since 1955) by Spindler, considered the "father" of the field of educational anthropology.

Steinberg, Stephen. *The Ethnic Myth: Race. Ethnicity, and Class in America.* New York: Atheneum, 1981.

Challenges commonly held myths about individual and collective ethnicity. Promotes the premise that ethnicity must be considered in the context of history, economics, politics, and social factors. Book deals with three basic issues: (1) the origins of ethnic pluralism in the United States and the viability of ethnic identities now and in the future, (2) rates of mobility and success experienced by different ethnic groups, and (3) social class characteristics of racial and ethnic conflict. Expresses belief that the public schools undermine the capacity of immigrant groups to transmit their native cultures to their children. Extensively critiques commonly quoted studies on ethnicity. Each chapter in this provocative work contains a summary paragraph.

Stone, Elizabeth. *Black Sheep and Kissing Cousins: How Our Family Stories Shape Us.* New York: Times Books, 1988.

Examines the way in which family stories instruct children in norms and mores and convey to them the experiences of their elders. This is one way in which cultural traditions are transmitted from one generation to the next.

Super, Charles M., and Sara Harkness, eds. *Anthropological Perspectives on Child Development.* New Directions for Child Development Series, no. 8. San Francisco: Jossey-Bass, 1980.

Promotes an awareness of the contribution of anthropology to child development theory. States that anthropological research is not to catalog exotica but rather to emphasize culture as a setting for human development. Stresses the need for child development theory to integrate more completely with psychology, psychoanalytic theory, and cultural anthropology. An internationalization of child development is also advocated.

United States Department of Agriculture/Department of Health and Human Services. *Cross-Cultural Counseling: A Guide for Nutrition and Health Counselors.* FNS-250. Washington, D.C.: U.S. Government Printing Office, 1986.

Explores the relationship between family, cultural values, and religion on health and nutritional practices. Outlines the cultural values, health beliefs, and communication styles that affect nutrition. Provides a general and quick reference guide on Asian, Pacific American, black American, Hispanic American, and Native American cultures. A valuable resource for many, not just to health and nutrition counselors.

Wagner, Daniel A., and Harold W. Stevenson, eds. *Cultural Perspectives on Child Development.* San Francisco: W.H. Freeman, 1982.

A compilation of relevant research by leading researchers which provides a broad overview of the subject for non-professional audiences. Gives readers an understanding of why cross-cultural studies are undertaken, sensitivity to methodological problems, and an expanded concept of child development. The 12 chapters cover a variety of topics including affective development, parental speech influences, cognitive development, and moral development. Summaries and bibliographies accompany each chapter.

Whiting, Beatrice B., and John W.M. Whiting. *Children of Six Cultures: Psycho-Cultural Analysis.* Cambridge, Mass.: Harvard University Press, 1975.

Detailed observations and statistical analysis of a landmark cross-cultural survey of children in Taira (Okinawa), Khalapur (India), Nyansongo (Kenya), Juxtlahuaca (Mexico), Orchard Town (New England), and Tarong (Philippines). Children in each culture are evaluated and classified according to twelve behavior types, ranging from "acts sociably" to "assaults."

Young, Michael. *The Metronomic Society: Natural Rhythms and Human Timetables.* Cambridge, Mass.: Harvard University Press, 1988.

Examines the diverse ways in which society thinks about and measures time and the ways concepts of time influence society's patterns. Defines habit, custom, tradition, and culture, and explores each definition in terms of human development. Researches relevant literature in sociology, biology, anthropology, history, and philosophy.

A FAMILY SYSTEMS FRAMEWORK

The theoretical framework upon which this book is based is that of a Family Systems Framework. Basically, this means that a child is not considered as an isolated entity but rather as part of a system, affected *by* and having an effect *upon* his surroundings.

This chapter provides an overview of Family Systems Theory. It is intended to furnish the reader with a theoretical rationale for understanding that a child's behavior is reflective of his unique family and environment, which are strongly affected by culture and ethnicity. When one considers *how* families operate, one gains an appreciation of *why* children unconsciously reflect the cultural and ethnic patterns of their heritage. An understanding of Family Systems Theory is a basic concept in understanding child development; it is an essential concept in understanding the influence of culture and ethnicity on child development.

A family is the basic unit in which a child develops. It is a primary group, intermediate between a child and his environment. To understand a child, it is first necessary to understand the family and the environment in which he is raised. Interaction between a child, his family, and his environment (or community) is simultaneous and transactional. Child, family, and environment/community should be visualized as equal angles of a triangle, connected by two-way, interactional lines as shown in the following figure:

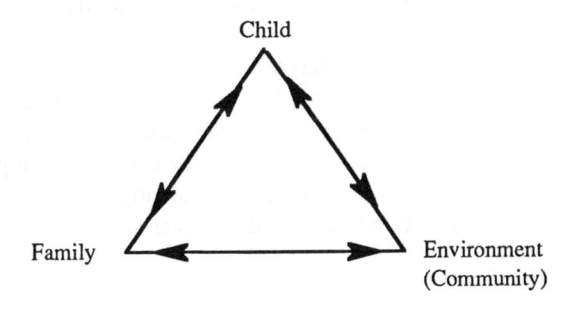

```
                    Child
                     /\
                    /  \
                   /    \
                  /      \
            Family ──────── Environment
                            (Community)
```

A systems approach offers the most appropriate context in which to study families and family interaction. According to systems theory, a family is a social system characterized by the following principles:

- The whole is more than the sum of its parts.
- The whole determines the nature of the parts.
- The parts cannot be understood if considered in isolation from the whole.
- The parts are dynamically interrelated or interdependent.[1]

A family is comprised of many interrelated systems; the larger the family, the more numerous the interactional systems and the more complex the interrelationships. According to Buckley's work on the evolution of systems theory, "[f]amily systems, like all social systems, are organizationally complex, open, adaptive, and information-processing systems."[2]

A family systems approach provides a frame of reference for understanding the impact of culture and ethnicity on child development. Family structure represents a basic mechanism by which ethnic culture and heritage is transmitted; it is also important in determining ethnic identity.[3] Ethnocultural factors are a dominant force in family relations.

The maxim that "to understand family systems is to understand family behavior" is based on the following highlights of family systems theory:

1. A family system is a complex set of interrelated parts, each part affecting the other. Transactional patterns regulate family members' behavior.
2. Family systems seek to maintain homeostasis.
3. All change, whether positive or negative, is stressful because change challenges homeostasis. Family systems resist change.
4. Family systems have boundaries. External boundaries develop between the family and outside systems. Internal boundaries develop between subsystems within the unit.
5. Family systems have a power hierarchy in which parents and children have different levels of authority.
6. Family systems tend to develop triangles, especially when there are crises.

7. Families tend to repeat relationship patterns. "Family ghosts" (unresolved issues) are passed from one generation to another.
8. Family members tend to develop specific roles in the family system; often one member becomes a scapegoat.
9. Families have a family life cycle, passing through a series of developmental stages.

Within a family systems framework, what each person does affects every other person, in essence, setting off a chain reaction. Triangles tend to form in families because of the close, intense relationships. When one person is upset with another family member and cannot settle it with the latter, he tends to bring someone else into the relationship. Parents often use their children to make up for what is lacking between them. Children also involve their parents in triangles by playing one against the other. Sometimes a friend or relative is brought in from the outside to form a triangle.

Every family member gets programmed into a specific role in the family and is labeled accordingly (e.g., peacemaker, troublemaker). Such role labeling serves a need in the family set-up, and each individual gains some identification from it. Each plays a part in assuming his label and continuing it.

The "ghosts" in relationship patterns are passed from one generation to another. Parents tend to assume the same emotional position in their present family as they assumed in their family of origin. They come with prejudices, anxieties, and expectations that are carried over and imposed on the members of their present families.[4]

The concept of family boundaries refers to the way a family (like every system) defines itself in relation to others in its own context. A family "draws its boundaries" by delineating who *is* and who *is not* part of its activity. There are boundaries between the subsystems. The four subsystems operating within a family are: (1) marital (spousal interaction), (2) sibling, (3) parent-child, and (4) extrafamilial (nuclear family interactions with extended family and networks of social/community/professional support).

Family members generally relate to one another in characteristic ways. Diffuse boundaries within families usually indicate too much relatedness. Members are overly involved with one another; privacy, individuality, and autonomy are frequently sacrificed. On the other hand, rigid internal boundaries can indicate a paucity of relatedness—members who are remote and uninvolved with one another. Such families place a premium on privacy, autonomy, and separateness. In families with clear, well-defined internal boundaries, members can interrelate while still retaining their autonomy; such families seem to flourish on diversity.

There are personal boundaries as well. A family member often functions in multiple roles—spouse, parent, and employee—as well as maintaining a personal identity. In most cases, it is optimal for these boundaries to remain distinct yet flexible. It is helpful to think of boundaries as emotional styles which operate on a continuum between rigid and diffuse. When boundaries, especially generational boundaries, are too rigid or are disregarded, the system does not function properly.

A useful framework for conceptualizing family systems is offered by Turnbull, Summers, and Brotherson. Their theoretical perspective includes four dimensions of family dynamics—structure, interaction, functions, and life cycle:

> Family structure consists of the descriptive characteristics of the family in the areas of membership, cultural style, and ideological style. These characteristics are the *input* to the interactional system and can be viewed as the resources shaping the way that the family interacts and the manner in which they carry out their functions. Family interaction, the hub of the family system, is the *process* of individual and group relationships within the family. It includes the different subsystems within the family and the rules by which the subsystems interact. Family functions are the *output* of the interactional system and represent the essential purpose for the existence of families. From a developmental perspective, life cycle interjects *change* into the family system.[5]

What *is* the function of the family? Basically, the family does two things: It insures physical survival and builds the essential humanness of man.[6] Few would argue that the primary—and most crucial—role of the family is to meet the emotional needs of its members. The image of "family" as a refuge of last resort is pictured in Robert Frost's lines, "Home is the place where, when you have to go there, They have to take you in."[7] A list of family functions could be

A Family Systems Framework

expanded to include other categories, such as economic, physical, rest and recuperation, affection, socialization, self-definition, guidance, vocational, and educational.[8] Generally, however, the major functions are:
1. Production of offspring and their care during childhood dependency.
2. Legitimization of offspring and certification of their ability to carry on traditions.
3. Regulation of sexual behavior.
4. Maintenance of economic life.[9]

This list can be further simplified to Reproductive, Educational, Sexual, and Economic.

Cultural traditions—their preservation, modification, and intergenerational transfer—are essential components of the educational function.

The interdependence and transactional relations of child, family, and environment are further attested to by changes in the family's life cycle as well as in society. Families progress through developmental stages or life cycles, just as children progress through stages of development. The stages in a family life cycle are: (1) couple, (2) childbearing, (3) school-age children, (4) adolescence, (5) launching, (6) postparental, and (7) aging.[10]

As families progress from one stage to another, these transitions (e.g., adolescents separating from the family, a child's marriage) *can* be a critical source of stress and family dysfunction. They can also be joyous times, often embellished with traditions of the culture. Each stage in the development of a family is characterized by its own particular stresses and rewards. Each stage presents specific problems and developmental tasks that the family must meet and solve.

In addition to internal changes, there are apt to be external changes affecting the interactive child-family-community triangle. The neighborhood may change, the family may move to a different community, region, or even country. The family may be affected by changes in nature, economics, or politics. The family must accommodate to these changes, whether they occur by chance or by choice.

The structure of a family (i.e., how the family operates) is characterized by its unique cultural style, religion, values, beliefs, and ideological style. Family structure varies from family to family. It may also change, reflecting fluctuations in membership, life cycle, and/or environment. The four subsystems within a family (marital, sibling, parent-child, and extrafamilial) constitute its membership.

Family structure also includes the cultural style and ideological style within the family. Cultural style encompasses ethnicity, race, religion, socioeconomic status, and geographic location. A family's ideological style consists of its beliefs, values, and coping styles. The importance of these aspects of family structure on child development are addressed in Chapter I.

The internal relationship and the importance of each subsystem can vary significantly from one culture to another. For example, in some cultures, the husband-wife relationship is such that the wife's role is inferior and extremely limited. In other cultures, older siblings are expected to care for younger ones and may actually function as a primary caregiver and/or teacher. In cultures where the extended family prevails, all adults may function in a direct parental role. In still others, the extended family structure is such that the extrafamilial subsystem is minimal.

However the composition of the subsystems may vary between cultures, it is the transactional relationship *within* the subsystem and the transactional relationship *between* subsystems that is crucial. It is the emotional impact that family members have on each other that is important, not the physical proximity. These transactional relationships strongly affect a child, both positively and negatively.

For that reason, it is necessary to evaluate closely the role of each subsystem and how it functions in a particular family and in a particular culture; it is not possible to understand child development in terms of parent-child or sibling relationships alone. Child development and child behavior can only be understood in terms of family *and* community—the interaction of all four subsystems—namely, marital, sibling, parent-child, and extrafamilial.

It is both interesting and ironic to note that much of the literature on family systems has evolved from studies of families with problems, that is, families whose children have either physical or emotional problems. There is a paucity of literature on how "normal" families operate—if indeed there exists a "normal" family. Yet an understanding of normal family relationship patterns is a necessary prerequisite for recognizing abnormal patterns. It is analogous to the musician who must first master basic rhythm patterns before he can grasp the intricacies of jazz.

Family systems theory should not be considered a knowledge base only for those who deal in corrective therapies; it should be promoted as a means of understanding human behavior in general. A family systems framework, then, provides a basis for understanding the *whole* child within the *whole* family. As such, it individualizes the meaning of a child's behavior. In addition, family systems theory is in itself an important knowledge base. It enhances and expands the knowledge of child development theory, and thus can improve intervention strategies. A family systems framework can provide a common denominator, a common language among the disciplines concerned with children, proving itself an invaluable aid in recognizing and understanding cultural differences in children.

NOTES

1. Roy R. Grinker, Sr. and Helen MacGill Hughes, eds., *Toward a Unified Theory of Human Behavior* (New York: Basic Books, 1967).
2. W. Buckley, *Sociology and Modern Systems Theory* (Englewood Cliffs, N.J.: Prentice-Hall, 1967).
3. Andrew M. Greeley, *Ethnicity in the United States: A Preliminary Reconnaissance* (New York: Wiley, 1974), p. 312.
4. Peggy Papp et al., "Family Sculpting in Preventive Work with Well Families," *Family Process* 12 (June 1973): 201–202.
5. Ann P. Turnbull, Jean Ann Summers, and Mary Jane Brotherson, "Family Life Cycle: Theoretical and Empirical Implications and Future Directions for Families with Mentally Retarded Members," J.J. Gallagher & V. Vietze, eds., *Families of Handicapped Persons: Current Research, Treatment, and Policy Issues* (Baltimore: Paul H. Brookes, 1986), pp. 45–65.
6. Nathan W. Ackerman, *The Psychodynamics of Family Life: Diagnosis and Treatment of Family Relationships* (New York: Basic Books, 1958), p. 18.
7. Robert Frost, "The Death of the Hired Man" (1914).
8. Gerald Caplan, "The Family as a Support System," *Support Systems and Mutual Help*, G. Caplan & M. Killilea, eds. (New York: Grune & Stratton, 1976), pp. 19–36.

9. Peter Farb, *Humankind* (Boston: Houghton Mifflin, 1978).
10. D.H. Olsen et al., *One Thousand Families: A National Survey* (Beverly Hills, Calif.: Sage Publications, 1984).

BIBLIOGRAPHY

Ackerman, Nathan W. *Treating the Troubled Family.* New York: Basic Books, 1966.

One of the earliest and most widely used books on family psychotherapy. Two chapters, "The Family as a Psychosocial Entity" and "The Breakdown of Healthy Process," are valuable to non-therapists as well. Describes in non-technical terms how a family functions, how it interacts, how it changes over time, and how it varies among cultures. Reinforces the adage that you must thoroughly understand what is "normal" before you can hope to recognize and intervene with variations thereof.

Acock, Alan C., and Jeffrey M. Clair. *The Influence of the Family: A Review and Annotated Bibliography of Socialization, Ethnicity, and Delinquency, 1975-1986.* New York: Garland, 1986.

Reviews books, articles, and dissertations on attitudes and behaviors, goals, beliefs, roles, ethnic factors, and delinquency. Focuses on influence of family on adolescent children.

Anderson, Penny P., and Emily Schrag Fenichel. *Serving Culturally Diverse Families of Infants and Toddlers with Disabilities.* Washington, D.C.: National Center for Clinical Infant Programs, 1989.

Discusses specific issues, such as what constitutes a "family" in various cultures, and how family roles, relationships, and childrearing techniques vary from culture to culture.

Andres, Francis D. "An Introduction to Family Systems Theory." *Georgetown Family Symposium Papers.* F. Andres and J.P. Lorio, eds. Washington, D.C.: Georgetown University Press, 1974, pp. 1–13.

Explains family systems theory with graphs and illustrations, in addition to presenting a theoretical rationale.

A Family Systems Framework

Anthony, E. James, and Therese Benedek, eds. *Parenthood: Its Psychology and Psychopathology*. Boston: Little, Brown and Company, 1970.

Explains the psychodynamic processes and the interpersonal relationships of a family and how these change over time. Utilizes a family systems framework in describing the family as a dynamic system that undergoes changes in subsystem relationships. Describes how every aspect of cultural and socioeconomic change influences the family. Two chapters by Benedek, "The Family as a Psychological Field" and "Parenthood During the Life Cycle," are particularly relevant and informative. Each chapter includes a bibliography. A resource for students and professionals presented from a psychobiologic approach.

Barnsteiner, Jane H., and Joanne Gillis-Donovan. "Being Related and Separate: A Standard for Therapeutic Relationships," *MCN, The American Journal of Maternal/Child Nursing* 15 (July/August 1990): 223–228.

Promotes a systems theory framework to improve professional relationships with chronically ill children and families. Written for nurses but applicable for all human service professionals. Reviews systems theory concepts such as boundary, balance, caretaker relationship, overfunctioning/underfunctioning, and reactivity triangles. Each concept is discussed utilizing examples and suggestions for implementation.

Berg-Cross, Linda. *Basic Concepts in Family Therapy: An Introductory Text*. New York: Haworth, 1987.

Presents a comprehensive overview, along with anecdotal examples, of key concepts of a systems perspective of family dynamics. Each chapter incorporates cross-cultural research studies.

Bond, Lynne A., and Barry M. Wagner. *Families in Transition*. Newbury Park, Calif.: Sage, 1988.

Describes the normative and nonnormative transitions that occur during a life cycle of a family. Emphasis is on strategies to prevent family problems. Addresses the mystique of the "traditional" family.

Bowen, Murray. "Theory in the Practice of Psychotherapy," *Family Therapy: Theory and Practice*. P.J. Guerin, Jr., ed. New York: Gardner, 1976, pp. 42–90.

A classic article by the man considered to be "the father of Family Systems Theory." Presents background on how his theory evolved and explains the concepts. The concept *Differentiation of Self* is a cornerstone of Bowen's theory, defining people according to the degree of *fusion,* or *differentiation,* between emotional and intellectual functioning. This concept eliminates the concept of *normal,* which is difficult to define. Another major concept presented is that of triangles, which to Bowen provides a far more exact way of understanding the father-mother-child triangle than do the traditional Oedipal-complex explanations.

Carter, E.A., and M. McGoldrick, eds. *The Family Life Cycle: A Framework for Family Therapy.* New York: Gardner, 1980.

Underscores the value of utilizing a family systems framework for understanding individual children and families. Explores cultural variations in the family life cycle, including various systems and ceremonies.

Combrinck-Graham, Lee, ed. *Children in Family Contexts.* Foreword by Salvador Minuchin. New York: Guilford, 1989.

Examines a wide range of children (and their experiences) within a family context. Represents a variety of theoretical models. Contents include perspectives on issues such as family life cycle, diverse family structures, and families with problems. Section V, "The Local Community and the World Community," addresses the effects of poverty, immigration, and the nuclear age. A resource for students and professionals.

Dunst, Carl, Carol Trivette, and Angela Deal. *Enabling and Empowering Families; Principles and Guidelines for Practice.* Cambridge, Mass.: Brookline Books, 1988.

Written specifically for practitioners who have insufficient training in family systems assessment and intervention. Blends theory and practice with practical suggestions and case studies. Focuses on mobilizing a family's resources and building their capabilities to cope effectively on their own.

Duvall, Evelyn M., and Brent C. Miller. *Marriage and Family Development.* New York: Harper and Row, 1985.

Outlines the developmental tasks that a family performs at each stage of the life cycle and how these tasks change to meet changing family circumstances such as birth, children growing up, retirement, and aging.

Freeman, David S. "The Family as a System: Fact or Fantasy?" *Comprehensive Psychiatry* 17 (November/December 1976): 735–747.

Addresses some of the major myths that surround the understanding and treatment of family systems, such as family structure being nuclear rather that extended, families being closed systems, and families resisting change. Defines nine "myths" and provides evidence to show that they are actually misconceptions.

Friedman, Alma S., and David Belais Friedman. "Parenting: A Developmental Process." *Pediatric Annals* 6 (September 1977).

Humorously presents the five stages of parent-child development (infant, toddler, preschooler, school aged, and teenager) by listing the parents' developmental task, the child's developmental task (according to Erikson and Spock), and an appropriate Ogden Nash quote. As example, Stage I: Infant:

> Parent Development: Learning the cues
> Erikson: Trust
> Spock: Physically helpless, emotionally agreeable
> Ogden Nash: "Many an infant that screams
> like a calliope
> Could be soothed by a little
> attention to its diope"

Actually an introduction to parenting and parent development with a review and outlines of child and family development.

Galinsky, Ellen. *The Six Stages of Parenthood.* Reading, Mass.: Addison-Wesley, 1987.

Identifies and analyzes six predictable periods of parental growth, contending that parents' feelings and actions are often misinterpreted by professionals. Observations are based on interviews with parents of diverse backgrounds.

Henry, Jules, and Samuel Warson. "Family Structure and Psychic Development." *American Journal of Orthopsychiatry* 21 (1951): 59–73.

Proposes that an understanding of the true relation between personality development and culture must include a total and systematic analysis of culture. Conceives of the family as a field of forces, made up of a complex of interactional systems composed of the individuals in the family, each system affecting the development of personality. A frequently cited reference in family systems theory which incorporates the "field of forces" concept developed by Kurt Lewin.

Jackson, K.T. *Crabgrass Frontier—The Suburbanization of the United States.* New York: Oxford University Press, 1985.

Examines the changes in family structure and family-community interaction in contemporary society.

Kantor, David, and William Lehr. *Inside the Family: Toward a Theory of Family Process.* New York: Harper Colophon Books, 1976.

Constructs a theoretical model that is a descriptive theory of family process. Develops new concepts by describing settings where crucial behavior takes place, by analyzing the behavior family members use in specific situations, by identifying clear-cut family types and member roles, and by discussing marital, sibling, and parent-child relationships.

Kerr, Michael, and Murray Bowen. *Family Assessment.* New York: Norton, 1988.

Presents methodology and techniques for assessing families utilizing a family systems framework.

Kramer, Rita. *In Defense of the Family: Raising Children in America Today.* New York: Basic Books, 1983.

Reviews the changing role of children and families throughout history. Cites the influence of culture, commerce, science, and technology in this evolutionary process. This book does not address family systems per se, yet clearly demonstrates the impact of environment and family patterns on child development. Detailed reference notes are provided.

Lawson, Lauren Valk. "Culturally Sensitive Support for Grieving Parents," *MCN, The American Journal of Maternal/Child Nursing* 15 (March/April 1990): 76–79.

Stresses the impact of cultural influences on family-life patterns, such as lines of authority and family roles, especially as they relate to periods of grief and loss.

Lewis, Jerry M. *How's Your Family?: A Guide to Identifying Your Family's Strengths and Weaknesses.* New York: Brunner/Mazel, 1979.

Focuses on *healthy* families, which Lewis defines as one that does two things well: 1) preserves the sanity and encourages the emotional growth of the parents, and 2) produces emotionally healthy children. Also examines *faltering* families, those who seem competent but experience difficulties in parental relationships, and *troubled* families, those dominated by one autocratic person or value system or characterized by daily conflict. Includes two questionnaires to evaluate your family's functioning and suggests ways to implement change when indicated.

Lieberman, Alicia F. "Infant-Parent Intervention with Recent Immigrants: Reflections on a Study with Latino Families." *Zero to Three* 10 (April 1990): 8–11.

Highlights the value of utilizing a culturally sensitive family systems approach in understanding children. Portrays the unique support system within the Latino family and community and how this affects family functioning. Describes the *comadre* and *madrina* role of Latina women in providing child care, emotional support, and guidance.

Markides, Kyriakos S., and Charles H. Mindel. *Aging and Ethnicity*. Newbury Park, Calif.: Sage, 1987.

Reviews the diverse role and status of the elderly among various ethnic groups. Provides data on demographic and socioeconomic characteristics and on family structure and family relations. Includes references and indexes.

Mercer, Ramona T., Elizabeth G. Nichols, and Glen Caspers Doyle. *Transitions in a Woman's Life: Major Life Events in Developmental Context*. New York: Springer, 1989.

Analyzes the life histories of 80 women (ages 60 to 90) to identify developmental transitions and to corroborate the thesis that motherhood is especially influential. Data analysis identifies five major developmental stages, as well as those factors that were more influential than motherhood in the subjects studied.

Miller, Jean R., and Ellen H. Janosik. *Family Focused Care*. New York: McGraw-Hill, 1980.

Presents a theoretical framework and historical perspective on the family. Describes variations in ethnic families and methods for assessment of family structure and function. Bases family intervention strategies on family systems theory. A comprehensive text for health and mental health professionals.

Minuchin, Salvador. *Families and Family Therapy*. Cambridge, Mass.: Harvard University Press, 1974.

Describes his theories about boundaries and their importance in a healthy family. To Minuchin, generational boundaries are sacred. Enmeshment and disengagement result when boundaries are not maintained.

Seligman, Milton, and Rosalyn Benjamin Darling. *Ordinary Families, Special Children: A Systems Approach to Childhood Disability*. New York: Guilford, 1989.

Utilizes a systems approach to examine the many forms of today's "ordinary families." Explores the complex cultural and ethnic variations of family processes involving childhood disabilities.

Shorter, E. *The Making of the Modern Family*. New York: Basic Books, 1975.

Explores the process by which the modern family has separated from the community as it has developed into a private, intimate, fixed unit. Cites the influence of political, economic, religious, and social forces on family dynamics.

Turnbull, Ann P., Jean Ann Summers, and Mary Jane Brotherson. "Family Life Cycle: Theoretical and Empirical Implications and Future Directions for Families with Mentally Retarded Members." *Current Research, Treatment, and Policy Issues*. J.J. Gallagher & V. Vietze, eds. Baltimore: Paul H. Brookes, 1986, pp. 45–65.

Presents a family systems conceptual framework within which life-cycle concepts are linked to other dimensions of family dynamics, reviews theoretical and empirical literature on the life-cycle needs of families with mentally retarded members, and suggests future research, intervention, and policy directions aimed at strengthening family adaptation over the full life cycle. Although intended for helping families of the retarded, it provides a comprehensive overview of family systems theory that is universally applicable. Extensive bibliography.

UNDERSTANDING ONE'S OWN CULTURE

Our personal experiences provide us with a frame of reference for dealing with other families and with other cultures. Before one can truly understand another family or another culture, one must first look objectively at one's own family and one's own culture. Each of us, in a sense, has a "personal culture," a unique family, as well as a "group culture," a broader ethnic and cultural group membership. This chapter will present several ways of attaining an objective perspective on one's own cultural and ethnic heritage.

It is natural to become so identified with one's own family system that it is not easy to separate our personal point of view from what actually exists; it is difficult to be objective. We all have strong feelings about families and how they should behave. When we encounter families that are different from our own, especially families of other cultures, we usually react by thinking that *they* are strange and possibly inferior. We are even apt to be suspicious, if not fearful, of them. In actuality, we just don't understand them—why they act, look, speak, and dress differently from us. It is human nature to reject and to label as "bad" or "crazy" that which appears different to us. The danger in this attitude is that it leads to ethnocentrism.

Ethnocentrism is the belief that our way of living and doing things is the best way, simply because it is *our* way. Ethnocentrism has been described "as an extension of both egocentrism and stranger anxiety."[1] It is much easier to be ethnocentric than to make the effort to understand other cultures. It is easier to evaluate other cultures than our own; they stand out because of their differences. It is much more difficult to study our own culture, which we take for granted. To understand our own culture, we must analyze it from the perspective of an objective outsider; that is easier said than done. According to the anthropologist Linton:

> The ability to see the culture of one's own society as a whole, to evaluate its patterns and appreciate their implications, calls for a percentage of objectivity which is rarely if ever achieved. Those who know no culture other than their own cannot know their own.[2]

In addition to understanding our own families and culture as a prerequisite to understanding others, it is essential to "see" behavior (of other cultures) within the context of *that* culture, not of ours. Just as family systems theory teaches that a child cannot be evaluated in isolation from his family and environment, judgment about the isolated behavior of an ethnic group member or family lacks validity when viewed ethnocentrically without knowledge of that culture. It is essential to become aware of one's own cultural values as a prerequisite to understanding and appreciating the values and beliefs of other cultures. Such a premise is applicable whether one is looking at the business practices or the daily hygiene rituals of another culture.

For example, much has been written about the rapid economic development in Japan based on technology. An American technical expert who recently spent nine months in Japan investigating this phenomenon reported:

> Technology transfer involves many functional as well as cultural factors. . . . Simply stated, the Japanese have a different language, a different thought process, and different social and business processes than Americans. To attempt to observe technology separately from its environment is to lose sight of this larger picture. I was soon to discover that there are strong cultural elements in the ways the Japanese acquire, evaluate, and transfer new technology.[3]

Consider for a moment some of the habits and rituals of our own daily existence, such as brushing our teeth. To us, this is a perfectly natural routine of dental health. To someone from a totally different culture, it might appear very strange. In an effort to make us conscious of this ethnocentrism, Professor Ralph Linton "created" the culture of the Nacirema (American spelled backward). In "describing" the preoccupation of the Nacirema with their bodies, tooth brushing is described as follows:

Understanding One's Own Culture

> The daily body ritual performed by everyone includes a mouth-rite. Despite the fact that these people are so punctilious about care of the mouth, this rite involves a practice which strikes the uninitiated stranger as revolting. It was reported to me that the ritual consists of inserting a small bundle of hog hairs into the mouth, along with certain magical powders, and then moving the bundle in a highly formalized series of gestures.[4]

A single action, taken out of its cultural/ethnic context, can obviously be misleading. A good deal of ethnocentrism could be avoided if we would question the origin and purpose of a custom rather than just criticize it.

Ethnocentrism can lead to prejudice, even among young children. Indeed, research on children's racial awareness shows that "by four years of age, children in our society have a fairly well-developed conception of race and racial differences."[5] In children, prejudice can be attributed to the attitudes of their parents and other significant adults in their lives. In adults, on the other hand, prejudice or even misconceptions of other cultures and races (not necessarily negative) can be fostered by movies and/or television. Consider for a moment how many people in other countries envision life in America as characterized by "Dallas," "Dynasty," and Disneyland!

Avoiding ethnocentrism, however, doesn't mean ignoring cultural and ethnic differences, nor do cultural stereotypes and generalities necessarily imply ethnocentrism. A sociologist who lectures on race relations has written:

> Stereotype is a dirty word among some intellectuals and others who feel that, when used to describe members of a race, religion or nationality, it indicates prejudices. Perhaps it is time we changed our thinking.

Contending that it is better to defuse the highly sensitive topic by discussing stereotypes openly rather than pretending there are no differences among the groups in the melting pot, Helmreich continues:

> People stereotype one another, for the sake of efficiency. Our environment is so complex that we have to break it down into categories before we can understand it and we adapt by placing people, objects and experiences into general groups. . . . The process of ascribing characteristic traits to others is not entirely arbitrary. . . . While most stereotypes are often highly inaccurate, a good many have quite a bit of truth in them.[6]

In differentiating a stereotype from a prejudice, Axelson states that:

> [a] stereotype is not really a prejudice, since prejudice is a special category of belief based on stereotyping. However, a stereotype and a prejudice are the same in that they both contain elements that are false or inaccurate, evoke emotional feeling, and result from routinized habits of judgment and expectations.[7]

It is possible that stereotypes, prejudice, and ethnocentrism are inevitable in a multi-ethnic, multi-cultural society. If so, they should be recognized as such, and efforts should be made to channel their potentially negative, destructive energy into positive and productive outcomes. Three decades ago, writing on ethnicity and prejudice, Gordon Allport warned, "Ethnocentrism, prejudice, and conflict are natural by-products of group identity and belonging." To Allport, the "iron law of ethnicity" determined that "where there are ethnic differences, there will be ethnic conflict!"[8]

Negative stereotypes can often be traced to situations of economic stress or economic competition. Shaky economic periods such as recessions often heighten intergroup tensions. Economic and political uncertainties can lead to personal insecurities. Ethnic resentments also surface in times of political uncertainties:

> In times of great economic insecurity and political turmoil, people need to affirm a sense of their own value. These things shake your identity. You need to recreate a positive view of yourself and the group you are rooted in. But the very definition of yourself as a member of one group includes enmity towards another group. . . .

Devaluing the other elevates the self: this feeling that I am good is all the more important when you feel your world is out of control.[9]

To consider the cultural context—as well as the economic situation—is, in essence, to recognize the impact of environment on behavior. This is a basic principle of family systems theory.

It is important to recognize how one's cultural values and beliefs influence their attitudes and behaviors. One way to facilitate an acknowledgment of one's own cultural heritage is to consider the following questions:

- What experiences have you had with people from ethnic groups, socioeconomic classes, religions, age groups, or communities different from your own?
- What were those experiences like? How did you feel about them?
- When you were growing up, what did your parents and significant others say about people who were different from your family?[10]

To understand the dynamics of other families, one must first objectively appraise one's own family. One method for accomplishing this is to develop a family genogram. A genogram is a structural diagram of a family's three-generational relationship system, a roadmap of a family relationship system. It uses the following symbols to illustrate these relationships:

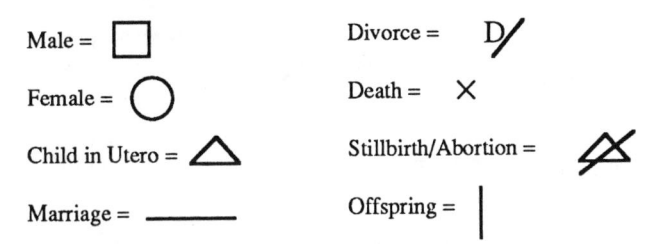

Male = □   Divorce = D╱

Female = ○   Death = X

Child in Utero = △   Stillbirth/Abortion = ⟁

Marriage = ───   Offspring = |

To develop the genogram fill in the names, ages/date of birth, dates of marriages, deaths, divorces, and births for a three-generational look at your family. An example would be:

50 CHILDREN, CULTURE, AND ETHNICITY

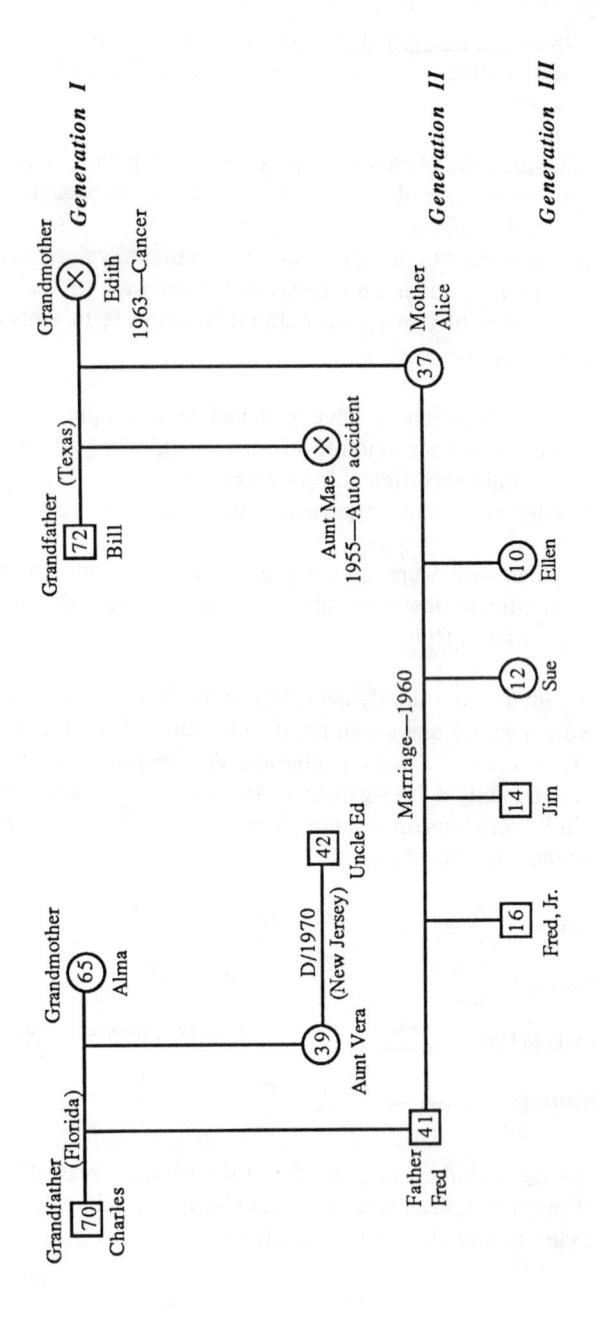

Generation I

Grandmother ⊗ Edith 1963—Cancer

Grandfather (Texas) 72 Bill

Aunt Mae ⊗ 1955—Auto accident

Grandfather (Florida) 70 Charles

Grandmother 65 Alma

Aunt Vera 39

D/1970 (New Jersey) 42 Uncle Ed

Generation II

Mother Alice 37

Father Fred 41

Marriage—1960

Generation III

Fred, Jr. 16
Jim 14
Sue 12
Ellen 10

Understanding One's Own Culture

Once the overall structure is in place, then relationship patterns can be examined. This is accomplished by gathering information about geographical location, frequency and type of contact, universal issues, toxic issues, and nodal events. Geographical location can provide basic information about a family's physical boundaries as well as availability of a support network. Frequency and type of contact identifies who calls, visits, and writes to whom, and how frequently; it should also reveal any pattern of "ritualized family visiting," such as the family *always* having Sunday dinner at grandmother's. Universal issues, such as money, sex, parenting, and children, are often indicative of a family's value system: consider who makes the money, who controls it, and how it is allocated. Also, which side of the family has the greatest influence? Is there a distinction made between what is his, hers, and theirs? Toxic issues include alcohol abuse, divorce, death, religion, and educational level and are often revealing of the "family rules" or the "family image." Nodal events refer to the normative crises and catastrophic events such as marriages, births, divorces, job changes, and moves.

As one recounts these interrelated and emotionally laden issues in his own family of origin, it becomes evident how one's own personality has been influenced by the patterns and expectations of his family. It is also interesting to see how these patterns are repeated in successive generations.

A genogram should not be used superficially. Names, dates, and lines alone provide an impersonal glimpse of one's heritage. It is important to examine closely these relationship patterns. For example, as each family member is added to the genogram, ask yourself what is the most outstanding thing you remember about this particular relative and how has he/she been an influence in your life. With each marriage, ask yourself what is known about the couple's courtship, whether the families approved or not and why, what their wedding was like, and if any family relationships changed as a result of that marriage. With each nodal event, consider the impact on your family system in general and on you in particular.

Taking the time to develop one's own family genogram, then, serves multiple purposes. An understanding of one's own family is a prerequisite to understanding other families. The impact of culture and ethnicity, transmitted via family life-style and values, becomes inextricably clear. As you develop your own family genogram, it is important to be sensitive to the feelings that this process often evokes.

The genogram is one method for analyzing relationship patterns within a family. There are other, less structured approaches to such an exploration. Professionals trained in interviewing, group dynamics, and family therapy utilize techniques involving observation of verbal and non-verbal communication. A home visit, particularly at mealtime, can yield a plethora of information on family relationships to the trained observer.

There are also clusters of questions, usually focusing on specific aspects of family functioning, that can be used to determine relationship patterns. Examples of questions that enable one to think back upon and objectively evaluate one's own childhood are:

- How would you describe your ethnic group?
- Where did your parents and grandparents come from?
- What traditions were important in your family?
- What holidays were celebrated and how?
- Who made most of the decisions in your family?
- Who was responsible for childrearing? for discipline?
- What role did grandparents, godparents, and other relatives play in your family?
- Were the expectations and treatment of boys and girls different? If so, how?
- Did you grow up in an ethnic neighborhood? Did this have any influence on you?
- What practices and beliefs have you adopted from your family? Which have you rejected and/or modified?
- Which family member(s) and event(s) have had the most impact on your life and why?

There are also exercises that can reveal much about ourselves, our families, and our culture. These might involve compiling a written or oral history about one's family or merely encouraging siblings (or other relatives) to recall collectively childhood events or experiences. Each story seems to trigger additional memories.

One can even play the anthropologist game to get an objective perspective on one's culture. To play, one empties pockets, wallet, or purse on a table. Then try to determine the owner's cultural values and

Understanding One's Own Culture

beliefs from the perspective of an anthropologist or a visitor from another planet. One might likewise scrutinize a home, a wardrobe, or a schedule of daily activities.

One way of learning about another culture, albeit unorthodox, is to spend a morning in a supermarket (or neighborhood shopping area) in a foreign country. Observe *who* does the shopping, how purchases are carried, how merchandise is displayed, and what items are purchased. How are the shoppers dressed? How are children involved in the shopping process? Do people appear to be shopping for daily items or stocking up? What is the shopper-merchant relationship? Is there a predominance of convenience foods or ingredients for making meals from scratch? Are most items locally made or imported? What are the staple items? Does there seem to be an emphasis on certain types of foods? Can all the groceries be obtained at a single source? If not, how does the shopper travel between stores?

By contrast, ask yourself these same questions about the market where you usually shop. What, if any, are the differences? If there are differences, to what might they be attributed?

Obviously, understanding a culture, whether our own or different, is a complex task. According to Hall:

> An important part of understanding a different culture is learning how things are organized and how one goes about learning them in *that* culture. This is not possible if one persists in using the learning models handed down in one's own culture.[11]

Each culture has its own value system. One can learn to speak, to act, even to think in another culture. What is far more difficult, if not impossible, is to *feel* in the value-attitude system of that culture. We can, however, become more sensitive to those different values by becoming more aware of our own culture and recognizing its unique peculiarities.

Becoming aware of one's own culturally determined values is the first step in overcoming ethnocentrism and in developing an appreciation for the culturally determined values of other people. The next step is an acquisition of knowledge about the normative behavior of other cultures and an understanding of the origin and the significance of that behavior within the context of that culture.

NOTES

1. Joseph Church and Alexandria Church, "Child Development Through Age Five," *Resources for Early Childhood: An Annotated Bibliography and Guide for Educators, Librarians, Health Care Professionals, and Parents*, H.N. Scheffler, ed. (New York: Garland, 1983), p. 50.
2. Ralph Linton, *The Cultural Background of Personality* (New York: Appleton-Crofts, 1945), p. 125.
3. Robert S. Cutler, "A Comparison of Japanese and U.S. High-Technology Transfer Practices," *IEEE Transactions on Engineering Management* 36 (February 1989): 17–24.
4. Horace Miner, "Body Ritual Among the Nacirema," *The American Anthropologist* 58 (1956): 503–507.
5. Beryle Banfield and Robert B. Moore, "Perspectives," *Resources for Early Childhood: An Annotated Bibliography and Guide for Educators, Librarians, Health Care Professionals, and Parents*, H.N. Scheffler, ed. (New York: Garland, 1983), p. 409.
6. William Helmreich, *The Things They Say Behind Your Back* (New York: Doubleday, 1982).
7. John A. Axelson, *Counseling and Development in a Multicultural Society* (Belmont, Calif.: Brooks/Cole, 1985), p. 373.
8. Gordon W. Allport, *The Nature of Prejudice* (New York: Anchor, 1958), Chapters 2 and 3.
9. Ervin Staub, *The Roots of Evil: The Psychological and Cultural Origin of Genocide* (Cambridge: Cambridge University Press, 1989).
10. Elizabeth Randall-David, *Strategies for Working with Culturally Diverse Communities and Clients* (Washington, D.C.: Association for the Care of Children's Health, 1989), p. 5.
11. Edward T. Hall, *Beyond Culture* (New York: Anchor Books, 1977), p. 131.

BIBLIOGRAPHY

Axelson, John A. *Counseling and Development in a Multicultural Society.* Belmont, Calif.: Brooks/Cole, 1985.

Suggests lists of questions that enable one to think back and reconstruct early family and neighborhood experiences. Examines the personal dimensions of the professional counselor (self-identity, values, and stereotypes) and how these might influence the counseling relationship.

Barnsteiner, Jane H., and Joanne Gillis-Donovan. "Being Related and Separate: A Standard for Therapeutic Relationships." *MCN, The American Journal of Maternal/Child Nursing* 15 (July/August 1990): 223–228.

Suggests behaviors for empowering oneself in a therapeutic relationship such as seeking to understand how one's own family-of-origin experiences influence reactions to patients and families, especially as they affect tendencies toward overinvolvement or underinvolvement. Article appears in the "Professionally Speaking" column of this nursing/transdisciplinary journal.

Brislin, Richard W. *Applied Cross-Cultural Psychology.* Newbury Park, Calif.: Sage, 1990.

Examines many facets of cross-cultural experiences such as "How valid are our self-perceptions in relation to other cultures?" and "How receptive are we to the viewpoints of other cultures?" Analyzes the concept of ethnicity and describes cross-cultural orientation programs. Extensive references.

Brown, Marie Scott. "Culture and Childrearing." *Culture and Childrearing.* Ann L. Clark, ed. Philadelphia: F.A. Davis, 1981, pp. 3–35.

Advocates a broad and comparative look at human behavior from a cross-cultural perspective. Defines four distinct advantages to such an approach: (1) to free ourselves from some of our ethnocentrism, (2) to gain a more accurate perspective on how our practices compare with those of the rest of our species, (3) by first discovering phenomena in other cultures, it may help us discover the same phenomena in our own culture, which have never been realized before because they had been so much a part of our way of thinking, and (4) to provide us with new solutions to universal problems that are better than those we currently employ.

Derman-Sparks, Louise, and the A.B.C. Task Force (National Association for the Education of Young Children). *Anti-Bias Curriculum: Tools for Empowering Young Children.* Washington, D.C.: National Association for the Education of Young Children, 1989.

Provides concrete, innovative ideas for teaching children to understand and interact with people of other backgrounds, such as creating an anti-bias environment and learning to resist stereotyping and discriminatory behavior.

Represents the work of a task force of early childhood educators who were dissatisfied with current curricula for helping young children learn about human diversity.

Freeman, David S. "The Family as a System: Fact or Fantasy?" *Comprehensive Psychiatry* 17 (November/December 1976): 735–747.

Addresses problems such as biases and misconceptions that interfere with our ability to understand families that differ from our own. Freeman believes that it is crucial to examine the role of various members within a family constellation. He focuses on the emotional impact, rather than the physical proximity, that family members have with one another. To get a sense of this impact, he suggests the following questions:
    (1) Who are the most important people in your life?
    (2) Who can get you upset the quickest?
    (3) Who do you turn to first for help?
    (4) Who in the family do you spend the most time talking about?
    (5) Who has had the most impact on your own development?

Guerin, Philip J., Jr., and Eileen G. Pendagast. "Evaluation of Family System and Genogram." *Family Therapy: Theory and Practice*. P.J. Guerin, Jr., ed. New York: Gardner, 1976, pp. 450–464.

Explains the mechanics, the implications, and the applications of family genograms. Takes the reader through several step-by-step examples of developing genograms and how they aid in understanding the dynamics in specific family systems.

Harris, Marvin. *Cows, Pigs, Wars, and Witches: The Riddles of Culture*. New York: Random House, 1974.

Answers perplexing questions about human behavior by demonstrating that no matter how bizarre cultural customs seem, they are the product of intelligible and adaptive processes to specific ecological and economic conditions. Suggests that by isolating and identifying those conditions, we can understand them—as well as the rationale behind our own life-styles.

Howard, A., and R. Scott. "The Study of Minority Groups in Complex Societies." *Handbook of Cross-Cultural Human Development*. R. Munroe, R. Munroe, and B. Whiting, eds. New York: Garland, 1981.

Argues that much of the early research on ethnicity was highly ethnocentric, and therefore minority perspectives were deemed unfavorable. Points out the need for researchers (who generally represent the majority culture) to recognize their ethnocentricity and to increase their understanding of other ethnic groups.

Keen, Sam. "The Stories We Live By: Personal Myths Guide Daily Life." *Psychology Today*, December 1988, pp. 43–47.

Defines myths as "the interlocking stories, rituals, rites, customs, and beliefs that give a pivotal sense of meaning and direction to a person, a family, a community, or a culture." Explains that the myths we tell become who we are and what we believe—as individuals, families, and as whole cultures. Discusses the myths of cultures and myths about families. Suggests a number of exercises (e.g., the anthropologist game) to discover one's personal myths.

Kerr, Michael E. "The Importance of the Extended Family." *Georgetown Family Symposia*. F.D. Andres and J.P. Lorio, eds. Washington, D.C.: Georgetown University Press, 1974, pp. 49–69.

Discusses the emotional relationship of the nuclear family with its extended family system. In order to understand the dynamics in a given family, it is necessary to ask specific questions (similar to the development of a family system genogram) about sibling position, occupations, education, geographical location, nodal events, and toxic issues. Article underscores the value of a three-generational genogram.

Kumabe, Kazuye T., Chikae Nishida, and Dean H. Hepworth. *Bridging Ethnocultural Diversity in Social Work and Health*. Honolulu: University of Hawaii School of Social Work, 1985.

A resource book which highlights the need to avoid "cultural myopia" and the need to understand diverse cultures. As a means to accomplishing the "bridging" of cultures, the authors suggest ways to be objective about one's own culture, such as becoming aware of one's own cultural biases. The use of case study examples and the extensive reference list enhances the value of this monograph.

Landis, D., and R. Brislin, eds. *Handbook of Intercultural Training: Area Studies in Intercultural Training*. Vol. 3. New York: Pergamon, 1983.

Describes cultural differences in social behavior in order to minimize misunderstanding among people who work and travel in foreign countries. Identifies those cultural traits that distinguish Americans, such as the tendency to be individualistic and independent.

Leninger, Madeline. "Cultural Diversities of Health and Nursing Care." *The Nursing Clinics of North America* 12 (1977): 5–18.

A general theoretical article that primarily seeks to place nursing in a multicultural perspective and provides some useful examples. Includes definitions of cultural diversity, ethnocentrism, cultural blindness, culture shock, and cultural impositions.

Lieberman, Alicia F. "Cultural Sensitive Intervention with Children and Families." *Child and Adolescent Social Work Journal* 7 (1990).

Discusses the origins of ethnocentrism and the problems in becoming culturally sensitive in clinical intervention with members of other cultures. Suggests that in order to understand others, it is helpful to try and understand our own culture as if we were outsiders to it.

McGoldrick, Monica. "Ethnicity and Family Therapy: An Overview." *Ethnicity and Family Therapy*. M. McGoldrick, J.K. Pearce, and J. Giordano, eds. New York: Guilford, 1982, pp. 3–30.

Highlights the need to come to terms with our own ethnicity and ethnic identity in order to achieve a multi-ethnic perspective open to understanding values that differ from our own. Describes how ethnicity training for clinicians who work with other cultures is conducted and the resistances to such training. Theories are well documented and referenced.

Miner, Horace. "Body Ritual Among the Nacirema." *The American Anthropologist* 58 (1956): 503–507.

This article is based on the work of Ralph Linton, who "created/discovered" the Nacirema culture as a teaching tool for anthropology students. Nacirema is actually American spelled backward. Reading about the Nacirema culture is a unique and meaningful way for us to stop and think about our own culture and how strange it might appear to others. This particular Nacirema tale focuses on the preoccupation with body concerns of this unique culture. It is a humorous lesson in the dangers of ethnocentrism.

National Coalition of Advocates for Students. *New Voices: Immigrant Students in U.S. Public Schools*. Boston, Mass.: National Coalition of Advocates for Students, 1988.

Aids in sensitizing individuals and organizations to the feelings, concerns, and perspectives of immigrant children and their families. A research and policy report which quotes extensively from those directly involved—the immigrants themselves and those designated to assist them in their new homeland.

Phinney, Jean S., and Mary Jane Rotheram, eds. *Childrens's Ethnic Socialization: Pluralism and Development.* Newbury Park, Calif.: Sage, 1987.

Presents an extensive resource of theory and research on issues of ethnocentrism, ethnic identity, stereotypes, and prejudices. Emphasis throughout is the resultant impact on children—how they feel about themselves and how they interact with other people. References are included from a variety of disciplines.

Randall-David, Elizabeth. *Strategies for Working with Culturally Diverse Communities and Clients.* Washington, D.C.: Association for the Care of Children's Health, 1989.

Provides definitions involving cross-cultural principles, presents exercises for assessing one's cultural heritage, and suggests guidelines for working with culturally diverse persons and groups.

Schweder, R., and E. Bourne. "Does the Concept of the Person Vary Cross-Culturally?" *Cultural Conceptions of Mental Health and Therapy.* A. Marsella and G. White, eds. Dordrecht, Holland: Riedel, 1982.

States that attempts to study other cultures are often impeded by the difficulties of understanding cultural conceptions which differ fundamentally from one's own. Recommends that each culture (and ethnic group) be understood in the context of its own conceptions of the world.

Zborowski, Mark. *People in Pain.* San Francisco: Jossey-Bass, 1969.

A medical anthropologist, Zborowski addresses the origin, the perpetuation, and the consequences of cultural stereotypes. This book primarily deals with cultural responses to pain and illness, yet it eloquently portrays how these attitudes and stereotypes become (unconsciously) engrained in our culture.

A FRAMEWORK FOR ASSESSING CULTURE AND ETHNICITY

Principles for assessing children—and their families—in terms of culture and ethhnicity are, in many respects, similar to a parable used in Change Theory:

> A grasshopper went to see the venerable consultant of the animal kingdom, the owl, about a personal health problem. He suffered severe pains every winter due to the cold weather. The grasshopper had tried many treatments, none of which proved effective. The owl listened patiently, then advised, "Simply turn yourself into a cricket and hibernate during the winter." The grasshopper jumped for joy, thanking the owl for his sage advice. After discovering, however, that this knowledge was not transformable to action, he returned to the owl and asked *how* he could perform this metamorphosis. The owl replied curtly, "Look, I gave you the *principle*. It's up to you to work out the *details!*"[1]

The following principles are merely general guidelines; each child and each family are unique. The reader is cautioned against relying upon cultural stereotypes and generalities whether they be positive or negative. Although *traditional characteristics* of people exist in any cultural or ethnic group, knowing that a child is of a certain cultural background does not ensure that he embodies all—or any—of those characteristics. To understand each child, a number of variables must be considered, such as the family's level of acculturation to the host country, educational level, and socioeconomic status.

This chapter provides the *principles*—a framework—for identifying the cultural characteristics of an individual or a group. The *details*—an assessment of the variables unique to each individual—will vary with each child and family. These variables are summarized in a chart at the end of the chapter.

An awareness of, or sensitivity to, cultural and situational influences helps one focus on the *how* and the *why* of any differences instead of on the differences themselves. Consideration of these guidelines also facilitates a family systems approach to assessment; it underscores the transactional nature of child, family, and environment and emphasizes the need to evaluate a child within the context of his or her unique family.

Cultural characteristics will usually reflect the situational changes that occur in a culture over time. This is another manifestation of family systems theory: a change in one part of the culture affects all other parts. Some of the traits described below are vestiges of traditions from the past and are not regularly practiced today. It is equally important to recognize which situational influences are *not* assignable to culture or ethnicity:

> Cultural variables include, for example, how people feel about, manifest and treat health, illness, and physical, mental, and emotional disabilities; the group of people in one's life who are considered to be family members and the relationships these people have to each other; childrearing techniques, and language and the different ways in which people communicate. It is important to remember that situational and environmental conditions such as poverty, homelessness, lack of formal education, and other factors that put children and families at grave risk are *not* cultural attributes. These conditions are variables which cut across *all* cultures.[2]

These variables are presented without regard to the order of their significance or to the importance of their implications. Many of these variables are considered in the context of children and families who have immigrated to the United States.

Name

A child's name—and that of his family—is highly significant. It is important to ascertain the meaning of a name (in its entirety) as this

A Framework for Assessing Culture and Ethnicity

often signifies the position of the child within the family, family expectations for this child, and the status of the family in its community.

In some cultures, children are named after their parents; in others, after loved ones or deceased relatives. A child may be named to commemorate a nodal event in the family (often involving that child), or the name may reflect cultural heritage. Some children are given names that indicate a special attribute in their appearance or behavior.

In many cultures the conferring of a name involves a ceremony that is religious or festive in nature. Some cultures, especially those with high infant mortality, delay the naming of a newborn child for several months. Still others bestow different names upon a child as he passes from one developmental stage to another.

The significance of a child's name is eloquently expressed in a recent book on children in modern-day China. Chin, born in Taiwan, has included interviews with many children in the book. Noting that she has changed their names, with great reluctance, to protect their privacy, she explains:

> In China, names give meaning to a person. He is not just an Andrew or a Samuel. He is a *jing* (tranquil) or a *jin* (resolute); he is a *yun* (cloud followed by a dragon) or *shou-ren* (one who holds on to his humanity). A person's name is what his parents and grandparents expect of him, and, later on, perhaps, what he expects of himself. Thus, to give him a new one arbitrarily as I have done, is, in a way, to take away his essence.[3]

Whether the child's name or surname has cultural significance or not, it is important to ask about the name. To do so indicates an interest in the child/family as a unique entity; it also is a sign of respect and acceptance. Asking about the name also affords an excellent opportunity to learn more about another culture.

Country of Origin

Race is not the same as culture. Racial characteristics are physical and inborn, while cultural characteristics are learned and acquired after birth. Race refers to a population having in common a combination of inherited physical characteristics that set it apart from other populations which have other combinations of physical characteristics. Examples are the Caucasian race and the Mongoloid race. A person's race tells us nothing about his religion, nationality, language, manners, or morals. It is, for example, incorrect to speak of the Japanese race or the Scandinavian race.

Nationality is a rather elusive term that is used in a variety of ways. It is often used to imply a religious or linguistic unity, or both, though neither is necessarily involved. Like religion and language, nationality is an aspect of culture that often sets people apart from one another, yet each of these is part of our social, not our biological, heritage.[4]

Country of origin is a significant factor in evaluating cultural and ethnic influence—*but only when considered in combination with other assessment factors*—such as migration history and socioeconomic status. For example, a child born in China of missionary parents and subsequently raised in the United States is apt to have little in common, culturally or otherwise, with a child born in China to a peasant family.

When asking about one's country of origin, it may prove revealing to also ask, "What is the most common misconception you find that people have about your country?" The answer is often indicative of the respondent's value system and ethnic identity, as well as a propitious opportunity to learn more about that person's cultural and ethnic background.

Migration History

Whether a family has newly emigrated from its homeland or has resided here for a generation or two, migration has had a major impact on most peoples' lives. An assessment of a family's migration history—who, when, why, how, and from where—is a vital component in understanding a family's cultural heritage.

The *who* may be indicative of economics in the country of origin at the time the person emigrated. If the family did not come together, the husband or wife may have been perceived as the most likely to secure employment. On the other hand, many immigrant families would first send the father or eldest son to secure employment and housing. The rest of the family would follow sequentially, as jobs and housing arrangements became available. If the breadwinner-to-be came alone, was it his intention to send for the rest of the family later or merely to acquire finances and ultimately return home? Immigrants who see themselves as temporary residents are not as likely to become acculturated to a new way of life. Families who migrate together face different stresses from those who are separated, but whatever these struggles are, they have a lasting impact on the children and the children's children.

The *how* of immigration is also significant. The blacks of Africa came to this country as slaves, their families cruelly separated. Immigrants who came as "boat people" in recent years had to leave everything behind, even family and material possessions. Aliens who enter this country illegally face additional problems, such as securing medical care and education for their families. The huge wave of European immigrants who came to America at the turn of the century had different experiences. They usually had done some planning, however unrealistic, before emigrating. Refugees, on the other hand, are forced abruptly from their homeland and feel totally uprooted.

Why people emigrated has also had an impact on their descendants. People who came to this country to seek a better life reacted to immigration far differently from those who came as unwilling slaves or came to avoid political persecution.

It is also important to ascertain *when* immigration occurred. The experiences and reactions of the newly immigrated are naturally quite different from those of second- and third-generation settlers. *When* also refers to the age of the immigrant. A child of elementary school age who is quickly integrated into the new culture via the school system can be expected to assimilate into the dominant culture much more rapidly and successfully than an aged parent. Teenagers are especially vulnerable to the vicissitudes of immigration. Peer conformity is very important and can be a stimulus to rapid and complete assimilation. To their families, however, this may be interpreted as rejection of their own culture and a source of conflict.

A pressing problem for any immigrant is learning to adapt to strange cultural practices and then develop life survival skills within that new culture. Such skills include finding employment, learning a new language, and gaining access to transportation. An awareness of immigration history can help in understanding the problems of children and families of different cultures. Acculturation will certainly be different for illegal aliens, for those who plan to return to their homeland, and for those whose family stability and economic status have undergone rapid and drastic changes.

Residence/Neighborhood

The neighborhood of one's youth, be it ethnic, rural, or urban, has a significant impact on development. Did the neighborhood (and neighbors) reflect the values of the family at that time? Were family members minority residents? Did they feel like "outsiders"? How does this compare to present residence? Is residence (past as well as present) by choice or otherwise? Is the family involved in the neighborhood and with their neighbors?

A crucial factor in residence is the availability of a support system, be it family, extended family, friends, or community services. In addition to a support system, are there other co-ethnics nearby? Is the family able to practice its religion and other cultural/ethnic customs? Is ethnic food available?

Living in an ethnic neighborhood is likely to increase the impact of cultural heritage on family life. It can also strengthen ethnic identity by imparting a sense of security and pride. Ethnic neighborhoods foster the retention of the language and food of a culture. In studying ethnic identity in the United States, Steinberg identified three determining institutions: (1) the family, (2) the church, and (3) the local community. He found, however, that all of them are now diminishing in tradition and influence.[5]

Place of residence, occupation, education, and socioeconomic status are often interrelated. In some countries, educational opportunities are limited to those children residing in urban areas. The availability of health care services may also be scarce in rural areas. Immigrant populations from rural areas of their homeland, representing an "underclass" of unskilled people with limited education and who practice traditional folk medicine can be expected to adapt more slowly to new situations than middle-class professionals from an urban setting.

Household Composition/Closeness of Family

There is wide variance among cultures as to what constitutes a family and how its members relate to one another. The composition and closeness of a family are highly significant because family structure is a basic mechanism by which ethnic culture and heritage are transmitted. Who actually comprises the family? What roles do various members perform? Does more than one generation live together? Is this a family by marriage or common law? Who else resides in the home? Is this a nuclear, blended, or extended family? Do household members represent more than one cultural or ethnic background? If so, does one particular heritage predominate? To whom does the family turn in time of need? What is the support network? How often does the family congregate? Are non-family members included or excluded? How often, and by what means, do family members keep in touch with those who live elsewhere? Who usually initiates such communication?

A careful consideration of these questions is helpful in assessing a family's culture and ethnicity. The purpose is not to compromise a family's privacy but to gain a sense of how that family system operates. If a home visit is appropriate, a dinnertime visit is usually very revealing. To a trained observer of family systems, much can be learned about the family dynamics (within the cultural norms) by attention to who eats together, who sits where, who serves whom and in what order, the presence or lack of ritual or formality, and the amount, content, and direction of any conversation.

Family Life Cycle Stage

Closely related to immigration history and household composition, a family's life cycle stage is a major factor to be assessed in determining its level of cultural integration or segregation. Adjustment to a new culture presents different problems for families in different stages of the family life cycle. In studying reactions to cultural change, Hinkle determined:

> Migration is so disruptive in itself that we could say it adds an entire extra stage to the life cycle for those families who must negotiate it. The readjustment to a new culture is

by no means a single event, it is a prolonged developmental process of adjustment, which will affect family members differently, depending on the life cycle phase they are in at the time of the transition.[6]

Life cycle stage is important because it often determines the people and the agencies with which a family interacts. For example, a family with young children will have occasion to become involved with child-oriented agencies and with other families having young children. Families whose children are grown and independent have different needs, concerns, and possibly different interests and involvements. They may be less flexible to change and more concerned about losing their cultural and ethnic identity than younger families.

It is especially at periods of transition from one life cycle stage to another that ethnic traditions may be in conflict with those of the dominant culture. Intergenerational struggles may result when "the old ways" are seemingly discarded as children grow up and become independent. Transitional periods are often stressful, and one's tolerance for change/difference usually diminishes under stress.

Language/Education/Communication Style

Communication style is a learned behavior, strongly influenced by culture and ethnicity. Communication is the lifeblood of relationships:

> Once a human being has arrived on this earth, communication is the largest single factor determining what kinds of relationships he makes with others and what happens to him. ... How he manages his survival, how he develops intimacy, how productive he is, how he makes sense, how he connects with his own divinity—all are largely dependent on his communication skills.[7]

It is important to know a child's educational status and language proficiency in his homeland as well as in the new culture. A person's language is closely related to his personality and situation in life. What language(s) is spoken in the home? Do the parents speak and/or understand English? What is the communication style or pattern in the home? (Remember that communication encompasses more than spoken language alone.) Does the family encourage learning the language of its new country? How does it value education? Does the family feel that the public schools undermine and devalue the culture of its heritage? What are the special problems that this child faces in learning English?

Communication between people of different cultures requires special skill and sensitivity. In Arab cultures and among some American Indians, long periods of silence are a normal part of conversation. To others, it is entirely appropriate to speak before the other person has finished talking. Certain words may have a cultural connotation that is offensive to others. Idioms, colloquialisms, and regional dialects can be very confusing to others. Immigrants need to learn the *cultural* as well as the *verbal* language: how to request, how to suggest, how to apologize, how to politely assert an opinion, how to disagree, and how to debate.

Body language varies considerably among different cultural groups. To some, touching is welcomed and appropriate; to others, (e.g., Asians), even a casual pat on the shoulder is totally inappropriate. Insensitivity to such nuances can lead to serious misunderstanding. For example, in the case of a Southeast Asian, touching the head (considered sacred) or only one shoulder is tantamount to a grave insult. In most Latino cultures, people stand very close together when speaking and their conversation is apt to be rather expressive. Most Asians, on the contrary, feel comfortable with more personal space and minimal emotional expression. Various cultural and ethnic groups respond differently to pain and grief; some are outwardly emotional while others are stoic.

A common misconception in communication between Western and Eastern cultures is the meaning/implication of saying "yes" or "no." In many Eastern cultures, a child is taught to answer "yes," so as not to be disrespectful, when he really means "no." A yes answer may mean that the child does not understand the question, or that he has no intention of complying. It is almost as if he were saying, "Yes, I will not do that." Communication style in most Asian cultures generally stresses harmonious interpersonal relationships, thereby avoiding directness, confrontation, and loss of face.

In attempting to determine the educational status of someone from a different culture, it is best to avoid direct comparisons with our school system. Rather than ask, "What grade were you in?," it is more meaningful to say, "Tell me about the school you attended." The answer thus obtained is more likely to describe the structure, standards, and curriculum of the previous school.

Religious and Political Ties

Religion, as discussed in Chapter I, strongly influences all aspects of personality development. It is therefore crucial to know the religion of a family, what that religion entails, and how devoutly family members adhere to the traditions and tenets of that religion. A child's behavior and the child-parent relationship are more understandable when viewed in the context of religion and culture.

It is critical to assess a family's religious ties on an individual basis; generalizations can be very misleading! In a complex society, many different religions (combinations and/or variations thereof) may be represented in the same culture. In Japan there is a humanistic attitude toward religion. Traditionally, most Japanese practiced a combination of Buddhism and Shinto. Most households still observe some ceremonies of both religions, such as Shinto marriages and Buddhist funerals, and have small shrines in their homes. Most Hispanic cultures are predominately Catholic, yet there may be some combination of ancient religious practices (e.g., spiritualism, sorcery, witchcraft, ancient herbal lore) along with modern religious beliefs. Knowing that a family is Jewish does not tell one whether it is Orthodox, Conservative, or Reform: there is a wide variance of religious practice, values, and family rituals among these different branches of Judaism.

With respect to religion, it is important to ask the right questions, and in the right way. It is not sufficient to merely ask, "What is your family's religion?" It is also helpful to inquire, "Are you able to practice/maintain your traditions here? Which holidays and religious observances are most important to you and your family?"

Political affiliation is also strongly influenced by ethnicity. Is this family involved in organizations that traditionally attract co-ethnics? Does it still maintain an affiliation with political organizations in its homeland? The answers *might* be indicative of strong nationalistic feelings, strong ties with relatives left behind, or just a tendency to become involved with co-ethnics and the community at large. Politics and religion are important aspects of people's lives.

Parenting Practices and Family Values

Differences in childrearing practices have evolved for a number of reasons and have generated diverse theories:

> ... differences in childrearing patterns evolved in response to environmental risks threatening the child's survival and self-maintenance ... occupational roles affect an adult's attitudes and values and thus influence his or her role as parent. A related theory is that parents rear their children so as to encourage the development of those qualities and attitudes needed for the expected adult roles, which differ from society to society. Cross-cultural differences in childrearing orientations are multi-determined, and it may be that all of the processes operate to some extent.[8]

There is a universal repertoire of potential parenting responses to children, yet caregivers may define their tasks differently or carry them out under different conditions. All parents seek to provide optimal care to their children, but they must adapt their behavior to the realities of their socioeconomic and demographic conditions and to their cultural and ethnic traditions. Child care practices, discipline, and parental decision-making differ accordingly.

Many parenting practices represent an unconscious repetition of the way in which parents themselves were raised. They also reflect the cultural norms and standards of the time, the community, family size and status, and the personalities and experiences of family members. Some cultures indulge their children; others encourage independence. The life-style in some cultures facilitates close mother-child interaction; in others, it is necessary for the mother (and possibly the child as well) to work outside the home. Differences in parenting practices and family values are seen between cultures that embody an extended family system and those that embody a nuclear family structure.

The manner in which children are socialized varies considerably among different cultural and ethnic groups. Such socialization practices are a reflection—and an indication—of a family's value structure. It is important to consider the parenting practices of each family unit regarding time orientation, discipline, children's play, and whether children are encouraged to be cooperative or competitive, dependent or independent, individualistic or collective. These issues are addressed in greater detail in the chapter "The Role of Culture and Ethnicity in Personality Development."

To determine a particular family's parenting practices and family values, it is useful to ask: Does the way you raise your child(ren) differ much from the way your parents raised you? Who takes care of the child most of the time? Who disciplines the child and how? What kind of a person do you want your child to be? What are your hopes for your child's future? Who makes the final decision on family matters? A family's attitude toward authority and power, if it can be determined, is often reflective of their parenting practices.

Another way of ascertaining a family's value system is by a visit to their home. A family's house is often most revealing of a family's "collective personality" and system of values. A trained observer (e.g., public health nurse, social worker) can see beyond the furnishings, which will vary according to the culture, economic situation, and family status. Are there books or other reading material available? Are religious symbols displayed? Family photos? Is the emotional atmosphere one of caring? Family values regarding marriage, childbearing, childrearing, and life-style are strongly affected by culture, ethnicity, and the surrounding societal norms.

Role of Women/Value of Children

In most cultures, there is a belief that children are desirable because they satisfy certain basic parental—and especially maternal—needs such as love, fulfillment of religious tradition, achievement and creativity, utilitarian necessities, and economic security. These needs are usually influenced by social and economic considerations. Women's fertility rates are also affected by their role and status in that culture. Some open-ended questions that might indicate a family's attitude toward children (and women) are: What would you say are some of the advantages or good things about having children, compared

A Framework for Assessing Culture and Ethnicity

with not having children at all? What kind of a person would you want your son or your daughter to be when he or she grows up?

In some cultures, the role and status of women depend on the quantity and sex of children she bears. In others, it is dependent upon her household management skills or the financial resources and social status she brings to the marriage. It is therefore enlightening to ascertain the legal status, educational and career opportunities for women in a particular culture, as well as the legal protection and social supports for children and their families.

Specific factors to consider are the infant mortality rates in a culture (and their implications), child labor laws, availability of maternal and child health care, availability and attitudes toward contraception, status of women's rights, rates of child abuse and wife abuse and how each is dealt with, and the cultural acceptance or non-acceptance of mothers working outside the home. There is often a correlation between the availability of child care and the cultural acceptance of mothers working outside the home

Health Care Practices and Beliefs

Basically this involves a determination of the type of health care practiced in a particular culture—is it conventional or Western-style medicine, folk medicine, spiritual or psychic healing, health care based on unity with nature, preventive health care, or some combination thereof? What is the relationship between religious beliefs and health care? Exploration of this realm devoid of ethnocentrism is important. Health care beliefs, attitudes, and practices are closely intertwined with religion and values, which are personal and sensitive issues.

Cultures vary in their attitudes and even in their definitions of health and illness. They vary in their beliefs about the cause, prevention, and treatment of illness. When religious beliefs are tied to health, illness may be viewed as a curse for sins, and people may seek a cure through good deeds and forgiveness from a spiritual source rather than through medical care. In some black communities "laying on of hands" and prayer are used as common methods of healing. In some Hispanic and Asian cultures, folk belief has it that illness occurs when the balance of elements outside or inside the body is disturbed. Other cultures, such as in the Philippines, believe that most childhood diseases are due to supernatural causes. The perception of health will also vary from culture to culture, as some cultures equate "good health" with longevity, while others place greater emphasis on the quality of life.[9]

Alternative health care beliefs can include traditional medicine (herbs, potions, and home remedies) and nonmedical healers (spiritualists, curanderos, and herbalists). It is important to recognize that these beliefs often serve deep psychological needs and rarely conflict with modern medical practices.

It is helpful to ask (when discussing a health concern): What do *you* think is the cause of this condition? In your own country, how would this condition be treated? What advice/treatment have you received from other practitioners? This subject is discussed in greater detail in the chapter "Implications for Health, Education, and Social Services."

Diet and Eating Habits

Food symbolizes nurturance and can therefore evoke strong emotions in people. Ethnic foods are one link to traditions of the past. In fact, Steinberg has written:

> People desperately wish to "feel" ethnic precisely because they have lost the prerequisite for "being" ethnic. Ethnic foods are the last bastion.[10]

Food and eating are largely habit. Cultural and ethnic food habits have evolved for a number of reasons—availability of food supply, climate, geography, health, and religious sanctions. We are all guilty of criticizing the ethnic food habits of others, while indulging in ethnic food preferences and taboos of our own. In India, cows are considered sacred and people have been known to starve rather than eat beef. In parts of Asia, dog meat is considered a delicacy. In the United States, where beef is popular and dogs are favorite pets, people have trouble understanding a prohibition on beef yet find the thought of eating dogs repugnant.

In some ethnic groups, food habits are linked to health beliefs. Some Hispanic cultures follow dietary regimes that are based on maintaining an equilibrium between "hot" and "cold" body fluids, or "humors." This practice originated from the Greek theory of disease that considers illness to be the result of humoral imbalance. Similarly, some Asian cultures believe that *Yin* and *Yang* forces influence health: *Yin* represents female, cold, and darkness, while *Yang* represents male, hot, and light. Digestion converts foods to air, which is either *Yin* or *Yang*, and excesses of one force must be balanced with foods from the opposite force.

Dietary practices are frequently related to health concerns (prevention and treatment of illness) and religious traditions. Seventh Day Adventists abstain from eating meat. They also prohibit the taking of all narcotics and stimulants (including alcohol, coffee, and tea) because they believe the body to be the temple of the Holy Spirit. Orthodox (and many Conservative and other traditional) Jews follow strict dietary rules of Kashruth, which prohibits the mixing of meat and dairy foods and specifies the avoidance of certain "unclean" foods. Most Semitic cultures prohibit the use of pork. In addition, many cultures advocate special dietary regimes for pregnant and nursing mothers as well as for infants. Many foods are considered taboo during pregnancy and lactation; breastfeeding is common in many cultures and usually continues until the child is two or three years of age.

Eating habits, much like food habits themselves, have evolved because of life-style, practicality, and accessibility of utensils. Eating with the fingers is traditional in nomadic lands, chopsticks are the norm in Asia, and Europeans hold and use their silverware in a somewhat different way from Americans. Similar differences are seen with the rituals associated with dining. According to Brown:

> There are few, if any, societies in which the partaking of food is a purely casual, unregulated affair. The culture not only determines in large measure what and when one eats, but with whom one eats, and indeed the whole ritual surrounding the giving and taking of food. Each society has its own etiquette pertaining to food and people who eat with their fingers out of a common bowl may observe a very rigid code of manners.[11]

It is therefore essential to ask people of other cultures and ethnic groups about possible dietary prohibitions that they follow. For example, "Are there any foods or combination of foods that your family does not eat?" If there are, inquiring whether this is because of religion or heritage can provide valuable information on the family's cultural and ethnic background and adherence to traditions.

Socioeconomic Status and Occupation

Socioeconomic status and occupation are closely related. They are also highly significant factors in how a family expresses its cultural and ethnic heritage. It is important to distinguish between behavior that is culturally determined and behavior that is determined by socioeconomic status. The occupational level of the family wage earner often defines the parameters of the family life-style and standard of living: these are frequently clues to the level of acculturation and upward mobility of a family. The essence of this crucial factor is captured in the following quote:

> The way a man makes a living and the kind of living he makes defines a man's worth, both to himself and to his neighbors, friends, lovers, and family . . . this is the controlling factor in their lives, distorting their values, their family relationships, and their concept of themselves.[12]

In some societies, certain occupations are restricted to specific cultural groups. This can be the result of class consciousness, racial prejudice, or economics.

Greater differences may exist between the upper and lower classes of an ethnic community than between similar socioeconomic classes of different ethnic communities. Although members of different social classes may share many cultural features, their adjustments (as immigrants) to a new country and its institutions will be influenced by other factors such as their level of education and English language skills.

The impact of socioeconomic status on child development appears to be closely related to the educational opportunities afforded by income and occupation. In the United States, one of the leading risk indicators for infants is the mother's educational level. This correlates with adequate prenatal care, proper nutrition, child safety, and developmentally appropriate child care.

A Framework for Assessing Culture and Ethnicity

Strengths and Weaknesses

In assessing a child or a family in terms of culture and ethnicity, it is essential to not only ascertain the differences in terms of weaknesses but to consider also their unique strengths. Just because some aspect(s) of another culture is starkly diverse from one's own does not mean that the trait is an inferior one; such thinking is ethnocentric.

Many traditions of other cultures have distinct advantages, not only for that culture but possibly for others as well. To understand the impact of culture and ethnicity on a child, one must contemplate the strengths *as well as* the weaknesses of that particular culture on that particular child. There is much to learn from the study of other cultures.

The extended family can provide support and security unequaled in the modern nuclear family. Certain folk medicine and religious dietary practices are often found to be based on sound medical and scientific knowledge. Childrearing that emphasizes indulgence and de-emphasizes competition can produce children who are better adjusted emotionally than those whose independence and individuality are fostered.

The unique strengths of the black family are seldom acknowledged, while its weaknesses are frequently cited. Within the black culture, the church is a monumental source of strength and meets many needs. Through the church, blacks can socialize, obtain a sense of recognition, develop leadership abilities, and release emotional tension. Their extended family and complex kinship network provide an unparalleled support system. The role of the mother as the "strength of the family" is a positive model for women. Within the family structure, the ability to interchange roles, jobs, and family functions has helped the black family persevere through adversity.

Your Own Cultural Background

Divesting one's self of one's own prejudices and cultural stereotypes is accomplished slowly; it takes a concerted effort. It is not easy to be understanding of or to work effectively with people of cultures and ethnic groups that have been historical enemies of one's own ethnic group. There are also understandable difficulties in working with people whose life-style is totally different from one's own. It is essential to be aware of our personal cultural and ethnic biases. We cannot and should not judge others by our own standards and experiences.

To work effectively with children and families of other cultures, we must be sensitive to *their* background and develop our relationships and intervention strategies (if indicated) to fit *their* cultural and social patterns of behavior. One cannot be expected to be an expert on all aspects of all cultures. One can, however, be sensitive to the knowledge that distinct cultural variations do exist and that misinterpretations *can* be avoided:

> With so many cultures and so many belief and value systems within each culture, it is impossible to be culturally sensitive as a general quality because this would demand an encyclopedic ethnographic and anthropological knowledge well beyond the reach of most of us. As a clinician, I find it less daunting to think of cultural sensitivity as a form of *interpersonal sensitivity*, an attunement to the specific idiosyncracies of another person. . . . To do this, we need a conscious temporary putting aside of our own values and preconceptions in the service of finding out about the values and preconceptions of the other.[13]

One might consider describing his own background according to the factors delineated in this chapter to see if it yields an objective assessment of one's own cultural heritage.

The factors expanded upon in this chapter are intended to provide a methodology for assessing a child and family in terms of the uniqueness of their culture and ethnicity. They should provide some direction in knowing what questions to ask and how to ask them in order to gain an understanding of a person's behavior from the perspective of cultural heritage and experiences. As in the parable of the owl and the grasshopper, these factors are the *principles*; it's up to you to work out the *details* in accordance with the unique characteristics of each child and family.

A Framework for Assessing Culture and Ethnicity

Variable	Significance	Questions to Ask
Name	May indicate family values, expectations, position in family or community selected	What does the child's family name mean? How/why was child's name selected?
Country of Origin	Significant *only* in conjunction with migration history and socioeconomic status	What is the most common misconceptions you find people have about your country?
Migration History	Effect on family (short/long term); Assimilation and acculturation	Who came first? Why? How? When? From where?
Residence/ Neighborhood	Ethnic identity; Effect on occupation, education, and socialization; In homeland and present	Is neighborhood rural? urban? ethnic? What do you like/dislike about it?
Household Composition & Structure	Nuclear/extended/blended; Inclusion/exclusion of unrelated members; Emotional closeness and and availability of of support	Who lives in the home? To whom do you turn when in need? How often does the family get together?
Family Life Cycle Stage	Determines interaction with community, needs and stresses; Related to household composition	What are the ages of family members? What are the important milestones for children/adults in your culture?

Variable	Significance	Questions to Ask
Language & Communication Style	Proficiency in native tongue and new culture; Determines body language and personal interactions	What language is spoken in the home? What special problems do you have learning the language, understanding and being understood in the new culture?
Educational Status	May be related to residence, socioeconomic status, and gender	Tell me about the school you attended
Religious Affiliation	Pervasive influence on personality development	What is your religion? Which holidays do you celebrate and how?
Parenting Practices and Family Values	Determines socialization practices: cooperative/ competitive; dependent/ independent; individual or group emphasis	Are you raising your child(ren) any differently from the way you were raised? What kind of a person do you want your child to be as an adult?
Role/Status of Women and Value of Children	Effect on educational/ career opportunities; rights; maternal/child health services; family support services	Is it better to be born a boy or a girl in your culture? Is it better for a woman to be a single/married/ mother?
Health Care	Closely intertwined with religion and values; Western style/folk medicine/spirits/a unity with nature/preventive/fatalistic; Attitude toward care of handicapped	What do *you* think is the cause of the illness? What do you think might help you? To whom do you turn for help with health/illness problems?

A Framework for Assessing Culture and Ethnicity

Variable	Significance	Questions to Ask
Dietary Practices	May have originated due to climate, geography, availability of food, or life-style; may be related to health concerns or religion	Are there any foods or combination of foods that you do not eat? Is it for health reasons? religious?
Socioeconomic Status and Occupation	May be related to residence, education, prejudice, family values or traditions	What type of work do you do? How did you happen to become a _____? What type of work did your father do?
Strengths and Weaknesses	Important to recognize positive aspects of the extended family, folk medicine, various religions, beliefs, childrearing practices on development	Is the professional considering *all* the issues?
One's Own Culture	Danger of ethnocentrism; Important to understand own culture, be sensitive and open to other cultures	Is the professional aware of own prejudices?

NOTES

1. Warren Bennis et al., *The Planning of Change*, 3rd ed. (New York: Holt, Rinehart, & Winston, 1976).
2. Penny P. Anderson and Emily Schrag Fenichel, *Serving Culturally Diverse Families of Infants and Toddlers with Disabilities* (Washington, D.C.: National Center for Clinical Infant Programs, 1989), p. 7.
3. Ann-ping Chin, *Children of China: Voices from Recent Years* (New York: Knopf, 1988), p. 9.
4. Ina Corrine Brown, *Understanding Other Cultures* (Englewood Cliffs, N.J.: Prentice-Hall, 1963), p. 8.
5. Stephen Steinberg, *The Ethnic Myth: Race, Ethnicity, and Class in America* (New York: Atheneum, 1981), p. 57.
6. L.E. Hinkle, "The Effects of Exposure to Culture Change, Social Change and Changes in Interpersonal Relationships on Health," *Stressful Life Events*, B.S. Dohrenwend and B.P. Dohrenwend, eds. (New York: Wiley, 1984).
7. Virginia Satir, *Peoplemaking* (Palo Alto, Calif.: Science and Behavior Books, 1972), p. 30.
8. Lois Wladis Hoffman, "Cross-Cultural Differences in Childrearing Goals," *Parental Behavior in Diverse Societies,* R.A. LeVine, P.M. Miller, and M.M. West, eds., New Directions for Child Development Series, no. 40 (San Francisco: Jossey-Bass, 1988), pp. 99–100.
9. United States Department of Agriculture/Department of Health and Human Services, *Cross-Cultural Counseling: A Guide for Nutrition and Health Counselors,* FNS–250 (Washington, D.C.: USDA/DHHS, 1986), pp. 3–4.
10. Steinberg, *The Ethnic Myth,* p. 63.
11. Brown, *Understanding Other Cultures,* p. 24.
12. *Tally's Corner: A Study of Negro Street Corner Men,* quoted in Stephen Steinberg, *The Ethnic Myth: Race, Ethnicity, and Class in America* (New York: Atheneum, 1981), p. 125.
13. Alicia F. Lieberman, "Culturally Sensitive Intervention with Children and Families," *Child and Adolescent Social Work Journal* 7 (1990): 5.

BIBLIOGRAPHY

Allen, James Paul, and Eugene James Turner. *We the People: An Atlas of America's Ethnic Diversity.* New York: Macmillan, 1988.

Examines the plural population and ethnic identity of Americans as a follow-up to the 1980 census, the first ever to ask about ancestry. Divides the population into nine general groups such as "People of Early North American Origin" and "People of Asian and Pacific Island Origin." Considers "People of African Origin" as a regional rather than a racial group. Includes insert maps which chronicle internal migration patterns of the various groups. Provides an overall picture of geographical residence/neighborhood and its significance.

Berg-Cross, Linda. *Basic Concepts in Family Therapy: An Introductory Text.* New York: Haworth, 1988.

Presents an overview of the theoretical viewpoints involved in understanding and assessing families. Book promotes a family systems perspective and incorporates anecdotal examples for clarification of various concepts.

"Beliefs That Can Affect Therapy." *Pediatric Nursing* (May/June 1979): 40–43.

An alphabetical outline of thirty-two religious denominations throughout the United States, with emphasis on any special beliefs and/or prohibitions concerning birth, death, health crisis, diet, and beliefs. Intended as guidelines for nursing personnel who might encounter families of these faiths as patients. In addition to the major religious groups, includes information on Black Muslims, Eastern Orthodox (Turkey, Egypt, Syria, Romania, Bulgaria, Cyprus, Albania, Poland, Czechoslovakia), Quakers, Hindu, Islamic, Mennonite, Moravian, Nazarene, Pentecostal, Russian Orthodox, and Spiritualism. A valuable cross-cultural reference for both nurses and non-nurses.

Bernardo, Stephanie. *The Ethnic Almanac.* Garden City, N.Y.: Dolphin/Doubleday, 1981.

Examines the customs and traditions of thirty-six ethnic groups. In addition to the information relevant to this chapter (especially the importance and meaning of names), this book contains a brief history of each group, cites their language, literature, famous people, games, and ethnic superstitions and beliefs. A reference book that is interesting reading.

Bowette, T.R. "Parenting: Special Needs of Low-Income Spanish-Surnamed Families." *Pediatric Annals* 6 (1977): 613–619.

Claims that very little is currently known regarding their core culture, family values, and childrearing practices. Stresses the need to avoid cultural generalizations. Individual cultural values and practices, poverty-specific concomitants influencing child care beliefs and practices, and the unique role of both mother and father in the Spanish culture must be considered. Urges the health professional to be sensitive to intervening influences of prejudice, social class, nativity, biculturation, family differences, and physical and or mental pathology when servicing this population.

Brislin, Richard W. *Applied Cross-Cultural Psychology*. Newbury Park, Calif.: Sage, 1990.

Emphasizes basic theoretical issues such as family intervention; work attitudes, leadership styles, and managerial behavior in different cultures; understanding individuals moving between cultures; and the psychological effects of acculturation. Extensive references.

Brown, Ina Corrine. *Understanding Other Cultures*. Englewood Cliffs, N.J.: Prentice-Hall, 1963.

Examines the many different ways that various societies approach and solve common problems, such as food, clothing, shelter, families, art, religion, and values. Presents a multitude of information in a manner understandable to the general reader as well as the professional anthropologist. Characterizes the four types of magical or religious phenomena worldwide as:

(1) Dynamism	—	Belief in impersonal power
(2) Animism	—	Belief in spiritual beings
(3) Polytheism	—	Belief in a hierarchy of gods
(4) Monotheism	—	Belief in one god

Includes extensive notes, references, and bibliography.

Clark, Ann L., ed. *Culture and Childrearing*. Philadelphia: F.A. Davis, 1981.

Explores the childrearing values, beliefs, and practices of the major cultures in America today. Chapters are written by nurses of various cultures: American Indian, Black, Japanese, Chinese, Filipino, Mexican, Puerto Rican, Vietnamese, and "mainstream" American.

Cormican, J.D. "Linguistic Issues in Interviewing." *Social Casework* 59 (1978): 145–151.

Discusses three linguistic problem areas that the practitioner may encounter during interviews: language differences between practitioner and client; labeling, which may lead to practitioner's or client's lack of individualization of each other; and client's inability to articulate certain kinds of problems clearly. Suggests ways to minimize linguistic problems in interviewing.

Dugan, T.F., and Robert Coles, eds. *The Child in our Times: Studies in the Development of Resiliency.* New York: Brunner/Mazel, 1989.

Reinforces the concept of the individual child as a unique moral person who is an authentic representative of his or her society and particular culture.

Fishman, Joshua. "A Journey of Hearts and Minds: The Faces Have Changed But Immigrants Today Travel Familiar Paths of Struggle and Hope." *Psychology Today,* July 1986, pp. 42–47.

Compares the immigrants of today, who generally arrive via Tijuana, Miami, or San Francisco, with those who arrived at Ellis Island at the turn of this century. Examines their skills, their demographics, and how and why they came. Explores the adjustment problems they encounter, and how this affects their family life. Describes the first year as a "high" period, when the refugees report their greatest feelings of happiness and satisfaction, the second year as the period when happiness plummets to its lowest level and distress is the greatest. During the third year, these feelings stabilize and "exile shock" passes. Article includes maps and graphs.

Flaherty, Mary Jean. "Cultural Nursing: A Point of View." *Image, The Journal of Nursing Scholarship* 14 (June 1982): 37–39.

Description of the experiences of this nursing educator and nun as a nursing consultant in a developing country in Southeast Asia. Believes that in cross-cultural communications, emotions and values are crucial because they are fundamental to behavior. Describes how "health" takes on a different context in hostile and disease-producing environments. Stresses the need to examine the values, priorities, and motivation for health care in other cultures, as well as an evaluation and discussion of one's personal values. A provocative article.

Greeley, Andrew M. *Why Can't They Be Like Us?* New York: Institute of Human Relations Press, 1969.

Argues against the myth of the United States as a "melting pot." Provides evidence that ethnic values and identification are retained for many generations after immigration, influencing family life and personal development.

Gussler, Judith. "Bridging Cultural Gaps in Health Care Delivery: The Fallacy of the Empty Vessel." *Public Health Currents* 23 (May-June 1983): 9–12.

The author, a medical anthropologist, describes cross-cultural blindness as "the fallacy of the empty vessel," which is not limited to health care professionals. To Dr. Gussler, it is the tendency to "not see" parts of cultures that differ from their own. If the distance between the two health cultures is great, the health care provider may tend to accept the fallacy of the empty vessel and overlook the significance of the beliefs held by he client. Cites many examples and suggests ways of assessing cultural differences. Emphasizes the impact of social and cultural background on infant feeding practices.

Harwood, Alan. "Guidelines for Culturally Appropriate Health Care." *Ethnicity and Medical Care*. A. Harwood, ed. Cambridge, Mass.: Harvard University Press, 1981, pp. 482–507.

Suggests that useful social and demographic characteristics can be assessed rapidly by eliciting a client's concept of disease and of their own condition. Harwood, an anthropologist, recommends determining the following characteristics in the initial discussions with clients:

- Level of education, literacy, and skills in English
- Number of generations in this country
- Household composition/family members in vicinity
- Proximity of co-ethnics
- Previous experiences with scientific medical systems
- Age at immigration, if applicable
- Contact with country of origin after immigration
- Rural or urban residence in home country

Kumabe, Kazuye T., Chikae Nishida, and Dean H. Hepworth. *Bridging Ethnocultural Diversity in Social Work and Health*. Honolulu: University of Hawaii School of Social Work, 1985.

Sensitizes professionals to the transcultural problems of immigrants and how their own cultural biases influence the worker-client relationship and the ethnic consumer's use of services. Provides examples of situations in which the norms and values of ethnic subcultures do not coincide with mainstream societal standards. Suggests ways to avoid conflict in these situations, such as balancing folk medical practices with Western concepts of appropriate medical care.

Leghorn, Lisa, and Katherine Parker. *Woman's Worth: Sexual Economics and the World of Women.* Boston: Routledge & Kegan Paul, 1981.

Explores the meaning of "women's work" from a multi-racial and multi-ethnic perspective. Authors contend that the truths about women and labor have been buried as deep as the truths of sexuality. An examination of the role of women and the impact of their economic value in different cultures.

LeVine, Robert A., and M.I. White. "Parenthood in Social Transformation." *Parenting Across the Life Span.* J. Lancaster, J. Altmann, A. Rossi, and L. Sherrod, eds. Hawthorne, N.Y.: Aldine, 1987.

Explains culture-specific influences in childrearing. Authors contend that each culture draws on its own symbolic traditions and supplies models for parental behavior. When implemented under local conditions, these models become culture-specific styles of parental commitment. It is these patterns of parental activity in local context that affect the health, welfare, and psychological development of children.

LeVine, Robert A., Patricia M. Miller, and Mary Maxwell West, eds. *Parental Behavior in Diverse Societies.* New Directions for Child Development Series, no. 40. San Francisco: Jossey-Bass, 1988.

Addresses current concerns for defining and assessing "good child care" now that more mothers are in the work force. Explores the contexts of parental behavior in other cultures to uncover universals and variables in the parental predicament and to place the current problems in a broader perspective. This volume proposes a theoretical model of parental behavior and examines its validity in case studies from three continents and in cross-cultural comparisons of mother-infant observations and parental survey data. Includes chapters on child care in the Outer Fiji Islands, in Kenya, Yucatan, Italy, suburban Boston, and Sweden. Extensive bibliographies for each chapter.

Lieberman, Alicia F. "Culturally Sensitive Intervention with Children and Families." *Child and Adolescent Social Work Journal* 7 (1990).

Urges professionals to consider the interface between an individual and one's own culture, how the individual perceives his or her own culture, and to what extent one consciously identifies with that culture and feels like a representative of that culture. Emphasizes that the degree of acculturation is an important variable, inversely related to recency of immigration. Describes the adjustment problems of recently arrived people.

McGoldrick, Monica, John K. Pearce, and Joseph Giordano, eds. *Ethnicity and Family Therapy*. New York: Guilford, 1982.

Initial chapters provide a wealth of information on both the need to assess each family as a unique entity within their ethnic group and suggestions for doing so. A theoretical rationale is presented for assessing those factors which will determine the extent to which particular families will fit into the traditional paradigms: migration experience, whether they live in an ethnic neighborhood in the United States, their upward mobility, socioeconomic status, educational achievement, rate of intermarriage, and the strength of their political and religious ties to their group. Extensive reference bibliographies included.

Maheady, Donna C. "Cultural Assessment of Children." *MCN, The American Journal of Maternal-Child Nursing* 11 (March/April 1986): 128.

A brief article, describing a challenge to nursing students who are enrolled in a course on transcultural nursing and childbearing to develop a concise guide for cultural assessment of children. The Guide for Cultural Assessment of Children, developed by the students, comprises a list of fourteen questions, divided among five major factors: religion, diet, language, healing beliefs and practices; and parenting practices and family values.

Mead, Margaret, and Martha Wolfenstein, eds. *Childhood in Contemporary Cultures*. Chicago: University of Chicago Press, 1955.

A compilation of diverse childhood behavior and parenting styles from the old Polish ghetto to Bali, Russia, Western Europe, and America. The chapters include: Cultural Approaches to the Study of Childhood, Observational Studies, Interviews with Parents and Children, and Clinical Studies. Considers the different methods and results possible from research on children's behavior.

Meleis, Afaf Ibrahim, and Leila Sorrell. "Arab American Women and Their Birth Experiences." *MCN, The American Journal of Maternal-Child Nursing* 6 (May/June 1981): 171–176.

Highlights the unique cultural outlook of Arab American women which can be a source of communication problems not only to health care professionals, but to anyone unfamiliar with the role and status of women in a culture so different from our own. Arab women have strong feelings about modesty, derive their power from careful management of household affairs, and their source of identity from bearing and rearing children, particularly sons. The extended family is traditionally very close, and the Arab male is involved in all aspects of health care for his wife and children.

National Coalition of Advocates for Students. *New Voices: Immigrant Students in U.S. Public Schools.* Boston, Mass.: National Coalition of Advocates for Students, 1988.

Identifies the problems which immigrant students and schools create for each other and offers recommendations for changes in school policy and practice. The results of a national two-year research project.

Olmstead, Patricia P., and David P. Weikart, eds. *How Nations Serve Young Children: Profiles of Child Care and Education in 14 Countries.* Ypsilanti, Mich.: High/Scope Press, 1989.

Contains national profiles of early childhood care and education in 14 diverse countries around the world. Part of an ongoing international study investigating "the nature, quality, and effects of the experiences of children prior to formal schooling."

Orque, Modesta S., B. Block, and L. Monrroy. *Ethnic Nursing Care: A Multicultural Approach.* St. Louis, Mo.: C.V. Mosby, 1983.

Identifies eight major factors to consider when making a nursing assessment of a pregnant woman, some of which are applicable to cross-cultural assessment in general. The factors identified include religion, diet, art and history, language and communication process, healing beliefs and practices, family values, intragroup and intergroup social patterns, and parenting practices.

Phinney, Jean S., and Mary Jane Rotheram, eds. *Children's Ethnic Socialization: Pluralism and Development.* Newbury Park, Calif.: Sage, 1987.

Explores the various relationships possible between ethnic groups within a culture of assimilation, acculturation, and pluralism. Assimilation is described as a situation in which the minority ethnic group gradually loses its distinctiveness and becomes part of the majority group. Acculturation (or accommodation) implies an acceptance of both one's own group and another group—through contact, conflict, and finally adaptation. Pluralism is defined as the maintenance of separate norms, customs, values, and possibly language by different groups within a culture.

Randall-David, Elizabeth. *Strategies for Working with Culturally Diverse Communities and Clients.* Washington, D.C.: Association for the Care of Children's Health, 1989.

Presents guidelines for assessing an individual's acculturation; cultural background and values; and sociological, psychological, biological/physiological status. Considers norms for different ethnic/cultural groups. Also provides guidelines for assessing a neighborhood and for using interpreters to enhance cross-cultural communication. Includes bibliography.

Santoli, Al. *An Oral History: Immigrants and Refugees in the U.S. Today.* New York: Viking, 1989.

Conveys the stories of "new Americans," how and why they immigrated to the United States, how they are remaking themselves, their aspirations for their future and that of their children. The word "education" rings out magically through all their accounts; they are fervently involved in the education of their children. Most are optimistic, determined, and have a strong sense of family. States that by the middle of the next century, Americans of European ancestry will be a minority. Most "new Americans" come from the Philippines, Korea, India, the Dominican Republic, Cuba, Jamaica, Iran, and Taiwan.

Seligman, Milton, and Rosalyn Benjamin Darling. *Ordinary Families, Special Children: A Systems Approach to Childhood Disability.* New York: Guilford, 1989.

Demonstrates how to apply a systems approach to assessment of the child as an integral part of a family. Examines the effect a disabled child has on the family throughout the life cycle and the cultural and subcultural diversity in response to childhood disability.

Selye, H. Ned. *Teaching Culture: Strategies for Intercultural Communication.* Lincolnwood, Ill.: National Textbook Co., 1985.

Stresses the need to understand behavior in terms of its cultural context. Presents examples of communication errors and misinterpretations that can result when people fail to develop an intellectual and emotional appreciation of other cultures.

Steinberg, Stephen. *The Ethnic Myth: Race, Ethnicity, and Class in America.* New York: Atheneum, 1981.

Explores the implications of education, occupation, socioeconomic status, and literacy on ethnicity and assimilation. This book is a critique of ethnic nostalgia, documenting the interplay between race, ethnicity, and class.

United States Department of Agriculture/Department of Health and Human Services. *Cross-Cultural Counseling: A Guide for Nutrition and Health*

Counselors. FNS-250. Washington, D.C.: U.S. Government Printing Office, 1986.

Developed in a collaborative effort with the Department of Health and Human Services, this booklet provides a wealth of useful information on understanding cultural values, health beliefs, and communication styles. Suggests culturally appropriate ways to improve health and nutrition practices. It includes a Quick Counseling Guide and a selected bibliography, which is organized by topic. It is a useful reference source which should not be limited to health and nutrition counselors.

Waldinger, Roger, Howard Aldrich, and Robin Ward. *Ethnic Entrepreneurs: Immigrant Business in Industrial Societies.* Newbury Park, Calif.: Sage, 1990.

Argues that the conventional wisdom—immigrants do well in business because their culture makes them entrepreneurial—is just a myth. Authors attribute the development of ethnic business to a blend of circumstances and factors: the opportunities that newcomers encounter, the ethnic group characteristics they share, and the strategies they adopt to exploit openings in the market.

Zero to Three 10 (April 1990).

This issue of the bulletin of the National Center for Clinical Infant Programs is devoted to the assessment and understanding of children and families of diverse cultures and ethnic groups. Includes articles on black children/families, Latino children/families, Central American children/families, and on ethnic differences in the transition to parenthood. Also reviews recent books on the subject.

IMPLICATIONS FOR HEALTH, EDUCATION, AND SOCIAL SERVICES

Providing services to children and families of different cultures and ethnic groups requires an understanding of ethnic values, beliefs, and traditions. This often necessitates special staff training and policy modification. Such strategic modifications can minimize misunderstandings or errors in communication, assessment, and service delivery.

This chapter will focus on the cultural and ethnic issues that are most likely to have implications for professionals in health, education, and social services. It examines disparate health beliefs and practices, learning styles, and attitudes toward social/emotional support services and suggests culturally sensitive interventions.

Children do not seek services on their own; they are referred by their parents and teachers. Following initial contact with the parent, ongoing service delivery will involve interaction with the family as a unit. Meaningful services in health care, social work, and education must be based on an understanding of the cultural context.

The provision of culturally sensitive services can facilitate progress toward cultural pluralism. An appreciation of differences can foster ethnic pride as well as improve service provision. The goal is not to facilitate assimilation into a monocultural society but rather to facilitate acculturation into a multicultural community.

Some cultural implications are relevant to health, education, and social services alike; others are more situation specific. Communication problems are likely to occur whenever an assessment or interview is indicated. The use of an interpreter may even complicate the situation. The use of a child as interpreter between parent(s) and professional should be avoided if at all possible. When the child functions in this capacity, it can be harmful to the parent-child relationship. In a family systems sense, it blurs the boundaries. The parent should remain the authority figure, in control of the situation, both to the child and to the interviewing professional. Besides, the information under discussion may not be deemed appropriate for discussion in front of the children. Professionals should allocate additional time when interviewing people of other cultures. A brief, get-acquainted interval prior to business is considered respectful in many cultures. Many Asians will be reluctant to discuss personal or family problems with non-family members for fear of shame. Furthermore, they will speak indirectly about such problems, expecting the practitioner to understand their veiled references to problems. One way to overcome resistance to uncomfortable questions is to explain why such questions are being asked. This sense of relevancy can help to de-personalize an otherwise sensitive subject area. A reassurance of confidentiality is also helpful. Gender might be another obstacle to an open exchange of information, for some people are culturally conditioned not to discuss certain matters with someone of the opposite sex.

It is important to ascertain that both parties understand each other. Frequent opportunities for feedback must be presented to avoid cultural misunderstandings or misinterpretations. For example, is the client or patient saying "yes" because he means "yes," because he is too ashamed to admit he doesn't really understand the question, or because he respects the professional even though he disagrees with the advice given? The use of open-ended questions or questions phrased in several ways is preferable to questions requiring a "yes" or "no" answer.

In addition to determining the social, demographic, and life-style characteristics of the population to be served, the professional must also determine the prevailing beliefs, attitudes, and practices toward health, mental health, and education. An extremely valuable resource to utilize is the minority community itself, if there is one nearby, and its leaders.

One pitfall to be avoided at all costs is the assumption that all Hispanics (or all Asians, etc.) are alike. There may be similarities in language or religion, but there are also distinct differences among Puerto Ricans, Colombians, Cubans, Mexicans, and Costa Ricans, just as there are distinct differences among Cambodians, Chinese, Japanese, Koreans, and Vietnamese:

> Compared to Puerto Ricans, Cubans have an almost fanatic interest in their bodies and its functioning; they have high expectations of health care and are aggressive in seeking this help; they are cooperative with medical personnel and anxious to give full historical and current

Implications for Health, Education, and Social Services

> information about their health. The expectation by white Anglo health workers that other Spanish-speaking clients will show similar behavior works a disservice on the Puerto Ricans who will need far more encouragement, explanation, and gentle questioning.[1]

Generalizations are only useful in framing *basic hypotheses* about a cultural group to be served. The professional must also understand what is normative behavior for children and parents of a subculture within a particular culture. Otherwise, one may fail to recognize a problem by attributing aberrant behavior to the child's ethnicity.

Conversely, the child's ethnicity may be the cause of a problem. For example, a teenage boy, described by the school psychologist as seriously withdrawn and passive in the classroom and disturbingly aggressive and violent on the playground, was referred for treatment. The treatment center was geared to meet the needs of ethnic minorities and recognized that the boy, a Filipino, was in fact responding normally to his parents' expectations. A cultural emphasis upon passivity and respect for elders had reached the point of obsequiousness, and the boy allowed his repressed tensions to explode outside the classroom. Rather than being psychiatrically disabled, as the school psychologist had suggested, the child was well within his cultural context.[2] Similarly, a professional may incorrectly interpret as child abuse the physical punishment that is acceptable discipline among many blacks, Greeks, Iranians, and Puerto Ricans.

Small or unique subcultures, such as the Hmong and Khmer, may pose a special challenge to professionals. Large numbers of Hmong refugees came to the United States from the mountains of Laos, the Khmer from Kampuchea (Cambodia). While they reflect certain traditions of other Southeast Asians (e.g., animistic religion; tight-knit, extended family), their differing background has resulted in unusual adjustment problems in this country, especially in the provision of health, education, and social services:

> The Hmong and Khmer are having the most problems. About 92 percent of the Hmong and 53 percent of the Khmer come from rural backgrounds. Their educational level is extremely low—averaging 1 and 1/2 years and 5 years of school, respectively—and most cannot read or write in English. Not surprisingly, these groups have the

lowest incomes, highest unemployment and highest welfare-dependency rates of all the refugee groups [Southeast Asians in San Diego] studied. . . . These refugee groups also had very different experiences surrounding their migrations. . . . These experiences have taken their toll on some refugees' mental health.[3]

Health Care

Health and culture are inextricably related. This relationship has been described by a medical sociologist in the following manner:

> . . . in all societies, health, illness, and medicine constitute a nexus of great symbolic as well as structural importance, involving and interconnecting biological, social, psychological and cultural systems of action. In every society, health, illness, and medicine are related to the physical and psychic integrity of individuals, their ability to establish and maintain solid relations with others, their capacities to perform social roles, their birth, survival, death, and to the ultimate kinds of "human condition" questions that are associated with these concerns. As such, health, illness, and medicine also involve and affect every major institution of a society, and its basic cultural grounding.[4]

An important factor in providing health care to people of other cultures is the patient's belief about the causation of illness, disease, or disability. It is especially difficult to institute preventive health measures in a culture where people believe that illness and disability are punishment from God for unacceptable behavior or are caused by evil spirits over which they have no control. Many cultures take a holistic approach to treating illness. Mind (spirit) and body are considered inseparable; psychological and physiological treatment are offered simultaneously (a variation of our use of the "placebo"?). For these reasons, the crucial questions to ask a patient of a different culture are: "What do *you* think is the cause of this condition? In your own country, how would this condition be treated? What advice/treatment have you received from other practitioners? What treatment do you wish/expect us to provide?"

Hispanics usually define health as the ability to work, resulting from good luck, good behavior, or a gift from God. On the other hand, illness (the presence of symptoms) is perceived as an imbalance of the body due to wrongdoing, bad luck, an excess of "hot" or "cold" factors, or heredity, and is accepted fatalistically. As one elderly Mexican American woman put it, "If God wants you to be ill, no special medicine, nurse, doctor, or hospital can help."[5]

Some blacks, by contrast, perceive health as related to the degree of harmony or discord in one's body, mind, and spirit. Consequently, they believe that serious illness can be avoided by prayer and religious beliefs. This relationship between health and religion stems from the traditional African belief about life and the nature of being.[6]

Many Asian cultures, however, traditionally believe that health and illness are related to spirits and fate. Illness is seen as a disharmony with nature and therefore preventable by seeking protection from the deity and/or appeasement of evil spirits.

Different beliefs as to the cause of illness/disease must be considered when dealing with a handicapped child. For example, one must understand the deep shame felt by Puerto Ricans with a retarded child, whose presence may seem to indicate a retribution from the Lord.[7]

If the patient's beliefs and practices are in conflict with those of a health care practitioner trained in Western medicine, it may be necessary to adjust the medical approach to one that is compatible with the cultural beliefs of the patient. It has been aptly stated that:

> Whenever individuals from one culture with their particular beliefs about health, illness, and the prevention and cure of disease [live] within another culture which has a vastly different medical system, emotional and social conflicts often result when illness brings members of the two systems together.[8]

Health care practitioners trained in Western or traditional medicine tend to misunderstand the role of alternative or non-traditional practitioners such as the *curanderos* (folk healers), *espiritualistas* (spiritualists), the sorcerers and *brujos/as* (witches) of Hispanics, the acupuncturists of Asian patients, or the shamans of American Indians.

When people turn to folk healers (or any health/spirit practitioners) and *which* healers they turn to are largely culturally determined.

Hispanics generally consult family members, neighbors, or folk healers for psychosomatic, supernatural, or ethnic ailments such as *empacho* (indigestion believed caused by being forced to eat against one's will), or *caida da le mollera* (sunken fontanel believed to be caused by a fall or too rapid a removal of bottle or breast). When ill, home remedies are usually tried first, often with the help of a *jerbero* (herbalist). If that treatment fails, a folk healer is then consulted. Folk healers are believed to receive their curative powers as a gift from God and are seen as religious figures: their aim is to restore the body's harmony. Cases of infectious diseases, broken bones, and serious wounds, however, are taken to a physician.

Puerto Ricans will usually visit a spiritualist for psychosomatic or psychological problems, purification, or protection from witchcraft and sorcery. Spiritualists are called upon to interpret dreams and premonitions. Sorcerers and witches do not cure but are believed to be capable of causing illness or even death.[9]

When a Taiwanese child is colicky and irritable, yet without fever, this is a *ching* (fright), caused by the child's soul having been scared away or "dispersed." The accepted treatment is a *chao hun* (ritual) by the local folk healer that calls the lost soul back to the body.

In the southwestern United States, Hispanic cultural and spiritual links to *curanderismo* are especially prevalent. Some studies suggest that as many as 50 percent of Hispanic families in the Southwest have visited *curanderos*. Most of them are first-generation immigrants who shy away from modern medicine for reasons of culture, language, and money. Traditional physicians are beginning to recognize the value of folk healers, especially when illness is psychosomatically based. Some medical schools are even beginning to instruct their students about the hold that folk medicine has on some cultures and how to deal with those beliefs. Folk practitioners are invited to demonstrate to medical students and community physicians the use of herbs and other folk-healing practices. Ethnic patients are often receptive to and benefit from a combined treatment approach.

Family plays a highly significant role in health care in most cultures. Patients may need to consult with family members before making medical decisions. The extended family, including children and godparents, is expected to be present at times of birth, death, and

Implications for Health, Education, and Social Services

serious illness. These members offer support, perform traditional rites, and prepare ritual foods. The family can be a key mediating force in all aspects of health services:

> Typically the family decides whether or not a member is ill, the meaning of an illness, and the method of coping with it. In many cultures a key member of the family, rather than a physician, is seen as the authority in health matters and decisions regarding health care are made by that person. . . . The family's influence on decision making continues during each phase of a member's illness, including the decision to seek medical care, the response to diagnosis, and whether the patient follows (or fails to follow) medical recommendations. The response of the family to a member's illness also influences how the member assumes a "sick role," how well the person is able to cooperate and use medical services, and whether the member is motivated to recover or to prolong the sick role.[10]

Illness in one family member creates an imbalance within the entire family system.

The perception and expression of pain differs from culture to culture. The meaning of pain as well as responses to pain are culturally determined and learned early in childhood:

> The role of the family is of paramount importance in shaping the child's response to pain. In each culture the child learns directly or indirectly how to react to pain from the parents, whose approval or disapproval will promote specific forms of behavior. The child also learns from directly observing the behavior of family members when in pain and by ultimately imitating that behavior.[11]

The health professional must recognize this cultural influence and avoid judging the child by his own interpretation of pain.

Medications or dietary recommendations must not conflict with cultural or ethnic beliefs of the patient, and to ensure that medication is taken even after symptoms are gone, it is prudent to advise parents specifically to finish the bottle. Dietary and medical recommendations for Hispanics should include a recognition of the "hot-cold" classification of that particular subculture; there are variations. Culture determines which foods are acceptable and which are not.

Also, many ethnic people have some degree of lactose intolerance. They will require special dietary recommendations to ensure culturally appropriate sources of calcium. It is estimated that two-thirds of the world's population experiences some degree of lactose intolerance after early childhood. The affected groups are primarily American blacks, Asians, American Indians, Hispanics, and Middle Easterners.[12]

Obviously, the health professional will encounter a variety of beliefs and customs. It may be helpful to categorize these practices as either neutral or harmful and act accordingly. Examples of neutral customs are the wearing of ritual beads or outlining the eyes with a mixture of carbon and oil to ward off the evil eye. Harmful practices include restrictive swaddling (which increases the incidence of congenital dislocation of the hip) and the consumption of pica (nonfood items) during pregnancy.

Education

Ethnic minorities are increasingly represented in school enrollments. Demographers estimate that by the year 2000 one of every three schoolchildren will be from a minority group.[13] Education is often the key to assimilation for children of immigrants and refugees. Providing educational services to children of varied cultures does, however, entail special considerations.

Cultural influences impact on both educational opportunities and learning experiences. Educators must understand cultural diversity and how it is manifested in the classroom. In the past, emphasis has been on a child's psychological characteristics rather than on the cultural characteristics. Educators now must focus on the child as an integral part of his larger environment—family, community, cultural and ethnic group—rather than just on the child within the school setting.

Cultural and ethnic values affect *how* and *what* a child learns. The values placed on cognition (intellectual function), psychomotion (motor skills function), and affect (emotional function) vary from culture to culture. A classic example of a culture that values psychomotion is Margaret Mead's description of the competence in

Implications for Health, Education, and Social Services 101

canoeing and swimming achieved by five- and six-year-old Manus children in New Guinea.[14] Cognitive skills and competition are highly prized values in middle-class America. By contrast, American Indians typically teach their children to be silently respectful. Many societies seek a balance of these three functions. The values of a culture are thus fostered in succeeding generations.

Language skills often reflect a child's family and school life. Ethnic dialects, gestures, vocabulary, bilingualism, and socialization practices are all part of communication. Children may exhibit problems in school if language patterns of the school and the home are incompatible.

A noteworthy educational experiment validating this concept occurred in the Piedmont Carolinas in the late 1960s. A group of middle-class white teachers recognized that they were not communicating well with their working-class black students. Specifically, students were ignoring teachers' questions in the classroom, although they were otherwise talkative. A close examination of the language patterns in the students' homes was conducted by a former teacher who was also an anthropologist and linguist. Language patterns in the teachers' homes were also explored. Special attention was placed on the use of questions. Teachers were found to use questions when teaching their own children to label and identify objects ("What's this called?" "What color is that?") Also, commands were often softened into questions ("Wouldn't you like to hang up your coat?"). In contrast, the students grew up with different ways of talking. Their parents did not phrase behavioral expectations as questions, nor did they use questions to draw out information. Instead, these children learned to emulate the metaphoric language of their parents ("He's a low-down polecat." "She has eyes like a hawk."). These children became fluent at storytelling and other oral tasks that involved their powers of description. What had previously been seen as the children's failure to participate or obey was then recognized as a gap in communication and was satisfactorily resolved.[15]

Cultural values and communication patterns are learned during the preschool years. Due to social changes in the United States, China, and Japan, young children are rarely cared for by full-time mothers at home. In these countries, as indeed worldwide, preschool education is rapidly becoming the format for providing care, education, and group experiences for children.

In China, for example, preschools are viewed as an antidote to the "4-2-1 syndrome" (four grandparents and two parents lavishing attention on one child.) In Japan, preschools are seen as a way to teach children to function in a large group and still become, in Japanese terms, truly human. In the United States, preschools are expected to compensate for the problems resulting from working mothers, a high divorce rate, and single-parent families. In all three cultures, the preschools are being asked to preserve traditional values in a time of change.

Each of these cultures believes that the development of language skills is a primary task of preschool education; each has different priorities. In China, the emphasis is on enunciation, diction, memorization, and self-confidence in speaking and performing. In Japan, language is divided into formal and informal systems of speech. Preschool children spend most of the day speaking loudly and unrestrainedly to each other. Teachers, on the contrary, use formal and polite speech and lead group recitations of giving thanks, blessings, and farewell. Language in Japan is viewed as a medium for expressing group solidarity rather than self-expression. In the United States, by contrast, language is seen as the key to promoting individuality, autonomy, problem solving, friendship, and cognitive development.[16]

A closer look at educational strategies in Japan reveals a great deal about its cultural value system. A key concept to educational success in Japan is the careful structuring of the beginning student's introduction to learning situations. This involves systematic training in the basic attitudes and cognitive support skills fundamental to mastering the task.

The Suzuki method, a system of teaching musical instruments to young children, provides an excellent example of this process because it exemplifies the cultural beliefs and practices used to develop proper learning skills and attitudes of early education in Japan. According to the Suzuki method, children as young as three begin music lessons on instruments that have been scaled down or modified in size. The child's mother is the primary figure in the learning process; the teacher's role is to teach the mother how to teach the child at home. Initially, the process involves the child and mother observing other children and their mothers taking lessons. Meanwhile, the child is told by all how much fun it is to play that instrument and that if he or she is very good they may be allowed to take lessons. It is only after the child's interest is aroused that the mother begins taking lessons with the child as an onlooker. By this time the child is highly motivated and is "permitted" to take lessons as well.

This period of observation is the time-honored *minarai kikan,* or period of learning though watching, that is typical of Japanese educational and social institutions. This observation period also involves long hours of standing on the sidelines and waiting to be accepted by the teacher and one's older peers. This cultural structuring of the process of group membership and activities serves to arouse and maintain individual motivation to participate in the learning process.

This same structure is applied to classroom education. Each routine basic to daily classroom life is broken down into steps and practiced until it becomes automatic. Students are carefully trained in the behavior expected of them at the beginning of their school career. For the remainder of their school career, the class calls itself to order and sits with all lesson materials prepared, ready for the teacher to begin.[17]

Still other learning styles typify other cultures. A recognition of these learning styles is the first step in the development of teaching practices that enable minority children to achieve academic success. The Kamehameha Early Education Project (KEEP) in Hawaii determined that native children were more accustomed to learning from one another and from older children than from adults. Though taught to respect their parents, they did not automatically defer to other adults, such as teachers. To native Hawaiian children the model for the nonparental adult was the soft, supportive "Aunty." Furthermore, these children were unaccustomed to the usual classroom practice of waiting one's turn and responding individually. They were used to the Hawaiian-Polynesian "talk-story" style of participation in conversation. In "talk-story" style, participants assist one another in the telling of stories. They talk in pairs, triplets, or ensembles and act as both supporters and critics of one another's contributions. When teachers changed their teaching practices and classrooms were reorganized to incorporate these cultural values, educational achievement improved dramatically.[18]

The academic performance of immigrant children is strongly influenced by family background, parents, and the circumstances that led to their emigration. Middle-class Cubans who fled Castro's Cuba were largely well educated. Their children have generally fared better academically than the children of poorly educated Mexican farm workers who crossed the river because of economic depression.

The first waves of boat people from Vietnam, along with immigrants from Hong Kong and Taiwan, became known as "model minorities." They were generally middle-class families with a passion for education. More recent immigrants from rural areas of China and refugees from Southeast Asia are often poorly educated.

It is time to stop characterizing all Asian-Americans as "model minorities" and to recognize that many of these immigrant students are disadvantaged and require special services. Some have had little or no formal education. Both parents usually work long hours, and the students are frequently left on their own. The parents want them to do well in school, but since many of them don't speak English, they can't be much help with language problems. In addition to academic deficits, these children face other cultural adjustments. They have been taught not to challenge authority, and their teachers may misinterpret their silence as comprehension. Coming from a culture that discourages outward displays of emotion, these students frequently have trouble adapting to a culture where one is supposed to deal with problems in terms of emotion.

Attention to this "socialization climate," along with learning style, is necessary; it can be a major factor in a child's adjustment between cultures. The "socialization climate" of the family can differ from the "socialization climate" of the school; contrasting styles can also occur between different cultures on a broader scale. Consider, for example, the socialization style of the Soviet school system:

> One of the most important goals of the educational system is the teaching of collectivism. Students learn that a collectivist works to improve society, not to further his or her own well-being. . . . Games also emphasize the group rather than the individual. Children are taught to help fellow students who are slow learners. . . . Children get their first taste of the *kollektiv* when they enter kindergarten at the age of three or younger. In kindergarten, collective behavior is imposed through strict discipline. . . . They take a nap for one and one-half hours every day. During this time, it is *Nyelzya!* (Forbidden!) to get up, even to go to the bathroom. . . . All children are required to play the same games, follow the same schedule, and behave the same

way.... The concept of uniformity dominates almost all of their lessons.[19]

Clearly, culture has a tremendous impact on education. Teachers of children from other cultures must learn what that culture entails—its values, customs, and its learning style. Teaching strategies will have to be modified to facilitate positive learning experiences for minority children. This involves much more than just providing bilingual classes. The cultural effects on learning should be taught at the pre-service level in teacher-training courses.

Social Services

Professionals from several disciplines provide social services to ethnic minorities. The social service provider may be a social worker for a hospital, a school, or a community social service agency. The provider may be a nurse, a psychologist, or a mental health professional. It is their function, rather than their specific job title, that is significant.

The social worker or counselor often functions as liaison with families of other cultures. He is often expected to coordinate services, be the child or family advocate, and perhaps even the interpreter. To understand the individual, the social service professional must first understand the individual's culture.

The social service professional is often the professional that spends the most time with families of other cultures. He must make a conscious effort to avoid an ethnocentric reaction to any disparities between their cultures and his own. Their relationship is a crucial one; it is also vulnerable to conflict caused by impatience, misunderstanding, and generalizations.

In addition to service coordination, the social service provider is increasingly expected to function as: (1) an information broker, (2) an opinion maker, and (3) a definer of issues. The role of broker involves translating the problems of clients into functional strategies. Such strategies are likely to involve modifications in practice or policy. The function of opinion maker involves interpreting the philosophies, perspectives, and technologies of agencies to each other. The third function, the definer of issues, involves the ability to redefine the problems of a system and the possible approaches to them.[20]

Regardless of which function the social service professional serves, it is critical that this person *first* think of the child in terms of normal developmental needs (e.g., he is a four-year-old who happens to be Korean, etc.). Regardless of the cultural or ethnic background, children are more alike than different! Similarly, meeting the needs of the ethnic child must be considered within a family context. It has been noted that:

> [m]ost social services, social work, therapeutic activity and even most education still takes place within the family unit. Increasingly, we hear from directors of social institutions that they cannot undo what the family has done, nor can they do what the family has left undone.[21]

The culturally skilled counselor will be aware of the need to vary intervention strategies in accordance with the client's beliefs and value systems. For example, the concept of counseling is antithetical to Asian philosophy, where, traditionally, problems can only be solved within the group—the family. Similarly, taking the initiative for decision making in a relationship with authority figures is an alien concept to many Puerto Rican clients.

Social service professionals have a crucial role in the provision of services to minority children. They must be skilled in personal interaction, only more so, because they are the individuals most likely to have an ongoing relationship with the family. They must be knowledgeable in child development theory, only more so, because they must often advocate for the child with agencies unaccustomed to pediatric concerns. They must be cognizant of family systems theory, only more so, because they must often intervene between the child and his family. They must be aware of their own culture, only more so, because they must avoid a conflict of cultures in their relationships. They must be sensitive to the uniqueness of different cultures, only more so, because they are most likely to be the liaison between that client and others less well informed.

NOTES

1. E. Bestman et al., "Culturally Appropriate Interventions: Paradigms and Pitfalls," Paper presented at the 53rd annual meeting of the American Orthopsychiatric Association, Atlanta, 1976, p. 29.
2. Richard Baron, "Mental Health Services for Ethnic Minorities," *Currents* 3 (Winter 1978): 5.
3. Joshua Fischman, "A Journey of Hearts and Minds," *Psychology Today*, July 1986, p. 44.
4. Renee Fox, "The Medicalization and Demedicalization of American Society," *Daedalus*, Winter 1977, pp. 13–14.
5. Gabriele C. da Silva, "Awareness of Hispanic Cultural Issues in the Health Care Setting," *Children's Health Care, Journal of the Association for the Care of Children's Health* 13 (Summer 1984): 4–9.
6. Betty Greathouse and Velvet G. Miller, "The Black American," *Culture and Childrearing*, A.L. Clark, ed. (Philadelphia: F.A. Davis, 1981), p. 90.
7. Baron, "Mental Health Services for Ethnic Minorities," p. 4.
8. Margaret Clark, *Health in the Mexican-American Culture: A Community Study* (Cambridge, Mass.: Riverside Press, 1959), p. 21.
9. da Silva, "Awareness of Hispanic Cultural Issues in the Health Care Setting," *Children's Health Care*, pp. 4–10.
10. Kazuye T. Kumabe, Chikae Nishida, and Dean H. Hepworth, *Bridging Ethnocultural Diversity in Social Work and Health* (Honolulu: University of Hawaii School of Social Work, 1985), pp. 132–133.
11. Huda Abu-Saad, "Cultural Components of Pain: The Asian-American Child," *Children's Health Care, Journal of the Association for the Care of Children's Health* 13 (Summer 1984): 11–14.
12. United States Department of Agriculture, *Cross-Cultural Counseling: A Guide for Nutrition and Health Counselors* (United States Department of Health and Human Services, September 1986), p. 9.
13. *Harvard Education Letter* 4 (March 1988): 1.
14. Margaret Mead, *Growing Up in New Guinea* (New York: William Morrow, 1975).
15. *Harvard Education Letter* 4 (March 1988): 1–3.
16. Joseph J. Tobin, David Y.H. Wu, and Dana H. Davidson, "How Three Key Countries Shape Their Children," *World Monitor*, April 1989, pp. 36–45.
17. Lois Peak, "Training Learning Skills and Attitudes in Japanese Early Educational Settings," *Early Experience and the Development of Competence*, New Directions for Child Development Series, no. 32 (San Francisco: Jossey-Bass, 1986), pp. 111–123.

18. *Harvard Education Letter* 4 (March 1988): 1–3.
19. Nancy Traver, *Kife: The Lives and Dreams of Soviet Youth* (New York: St. Martin's Press, 1989), p. 8.
20. Paul A. Wilson, "Expanding the Role of Social Workers in Coordination of Health Services," *Health and Social Work* 6 (1981): 57–64.
21. Andrew M. Greeley, *Ethnicity in the United States: A Preliminary Reconnaissance* (New York: Wiley, 1974), p. 174.

BIBLIOGRAPHY

Abu-Saad, Huda. "Cultural Components of Pain: The Asian-American Child." *Children's Health Care* 13 (Summer 1984): 11–14.

Describes research on pain perception with Asian-American children, ages nine to twelve. These children were interviewed regarding causative factors and word descriptors of pain, feelings, and coping strategies. Results were in accordance with known cultural indicators. Article includes an overview of Asian attitudes toward health and illness. Study findings indicate that pain has meanings that are individual and personal as well as culturally derived. Author cautions the health care professional to look at the child as an individual within a cultural group yet to avoid group generalizations.

Anderson, Penny P., and Emily Schrag Fenichel. *Serving Culturally Diverse Families of Infants and Toddlers with Disabilities.* Washington, D.C.: National Center for Clinical Infant Programs, 1989.

Addresses the issue of how best to provide effective, culturally sensitive, and comprehensive early intervention programs to *all* infants and toddlers with disabilities and their families in an equitable way. Designed to assist policymakers and practitioners in developing programs which are sensitive to a family's cultural heritage and life-style.

Axelson, John A. *Counseling and Development in a Multicultural Society.* Belmont, Calif.: Brooks/Cole, 1985.

Offers a comprehensive approach to counseling in a culturally diverse society. Organized around three basic themes—people, issues, and counseling practices. Includes chapter summaries, suggested experiental activities, and interdisciplinary references.

Baron, Richard. "Mental Health Services for Ethnic Minorities." *Currents* 3 (Winter 1978): 1–10.

Highlights the need for mental health for ethnic minorities. Defines "ethnic community" as those neighborhoods set apart from the American mainstream by the race, cultural background, or national origin of their inhabitants. Identifies and discusses key problem areas as concern, structure, research, training, and therapy.

Bransford, Louis A., Leonard Baca, and Karen Lane, eds. *Cultural Diversity and the Exceptional Child.* Reston, Va.: Council for Exceptional Children, 1974.

Proceedings of a CEC (Council for Exceptional Children) Institute and Conference Program held in Las Vegas in August 1973. Attempts to develop multicultural awareness, more effective communication skills, and insights into making teaching strategies and curricula more relevant to the special needs of culturally and linguistically different children. Provides specific suggestions for working with Asian, black, Native American Indian, Mexican, and Puerto Rican children.

Brembeck, Cole S., and Walker H. Hill, eds. *Cultural Challenges to Education: The Influence of Cultural Factors in School Learning.* Lexington, Mass.: Lexington Books, 1973.

Identifies cultural characteristics and differences such as communication patterns and competitiveness versus noncompetition. Suggests ways to appreciate and respect those differences and presents strategies for using them constructively in educational planning and learning experiences. Assumes that cultural characteristics (1) are as much a part of a child's endowment as psychological characteristics; (2) are influential in learning; (3) are persistent and continuous; (4) diminish selectively and may actually elaborate over time; and (5) are just as available for use in the improvement of teaching as are psychological characteristics.

Clark, Ann L., ed. *Culture and Childrearing.* Philadelphia: F.A. Davis, 1981.

Describes the traditional attitudes regarding health and education among American Indians, blacks, Japanese, Filipinos, Chicanos, and Vietnamese. Relates how these beliefs have been modified as these groups have assimilated into the mainstream American culture.

Cole, M., et al. *The Cultural Context of Learning and Thinking: An Explanation in Experimental Anthropology.* New York: Basic Books, 1971.

Specifies the conditions under which various cognitive processes are manifested and suggests techniques for seeing that these conditions occur in the appropriate educational setting.

Combrinck-Graham, Lee, ed. *Children in Family Contexts: Perspectives on Treatment.* Foreword by Salvadore Minuchin. New York: Guilford, 1989.

Utilizes a family systems approach in exploring contemporary issues such as changing family structure, handicapping conditions, interaction with the education and legal systems, and changes in community life due to poverty, ethnicity, and immigration.

Comer, James. *School Power: Implications of an Intervention Project.* New York: Free Press, 1980.

Reports on the process developed to improve opportunities for academic success for poor, inner city, minority children. Comer, a professor of child psychiatry at Yale, bases his School Development Program on the axiom that students in troubled schools learn better when families and educators work together. The program has been successful in the New Haven schools for over twenty years.

Cormican, J.D. "Linguistic Issues in Interviewing." *Social Casework* 59 (1978): 145–151.

Discusses three problems that practitioners may encounter when interviewing clients of other cultures: (1) language differences between practitioner and client, (2) labeling, which may lead to inaccurate generalizations, and (3) the inability of the client to clearly articulate certain kinds of problems. Suggests actions that practitioners can take to minimize these linguistic problems.

"Cultural Differences in the Classroom." *The Harvard Education Letter* 4 (March 1988): 1–3.

Explores the debate about whether or not schools should attune instruction to students' cultural backgrounds. Based on two research projects described, offers the following guidelines: (1) Interaction is a key to learning; language is a key to interaction; (2) Academic standards and teacher expectations should not and need not be lowered; (3) Local colleges, parents, and other community members can help schools acquire a better understanding of home cultures; and (4) In attending to students' cultures, teachers expand their repertoire of teaching practices—to the benefit of all students.

da Silva, Gabriele C. "Awareness of Hispanic Cultural Issues in the Health Care Setting." *Children's Health Care* 13 (Summer 1984): 4–10.

Deals with some of the health-related traditions, values, and beliefs held by various groups of Hispanic extraction in this country. A number of culture-specific disease entities and treatment modes are discussed, with special reference to patient behaviors and attitudes. Outlines implications for health care delivery to Hispanic individuals and families and offers suggestions for service providers.

Delgado, M. "Puerto Rican Spiritualism and the Social Work Profession." *Social Casework* 58 (1977): 451–458.

Characterizes the psychotherapeutic benefits of spiritualism as a needed therapeutic discharge for unresolved aggression or frustration. Discusses the similarity of intervention techniques between social work practitioners and spiritualists.

Derman-Sparks, Louise, and the A.B.C. Task Force. *Anti-Bias Curriculum: Tools for Empowering Young Children.* Washington, D.C.: National Association for the Education of Young Children, 1989.

Addresses issues such as creating an anti-bias environment; learning about racial and cultural differences and similarities; learning about disabilities and gender identity; learning to resist stereotyping and discriminatory behavior; and working with parents.

Ferrari, Michael, and Marvin B. Sussman, eds. *Childhood Disability and Family Systems.* New York: Haworth, 1987.

Deals with the contemporary context of disability, ethical issues, family effects, and care systems. Integrates empirical knowledge of the families and the contemporary context of disability. Examines current changes in attitudes and services.

Flaherty, Mary Jean. "Cultural Nursing: A Point of View." *Image: The Journal of Nursing Scholarship* 14 (June 1982): 37–39.

States that nursing practice should develop to fit the culture; nurses should not try to shape the nursing of another culture according to their own standards. Article is based on the author's experience as a consultant in developing countries. Contends that nursing must be based on cultural and social patterns of behavior as well as the health needs of the people in order to be accepted and produce change.

Gartner, Alan, Dorothy Kerzner Lipsky, and Ann P. Turnbull. *Supporting Families with a Child with a Disability: An International Outlook.* Baltimore: Paul H. Brookes, 1990.

Provides a cross-cultural perspective of how different countries view disability, culture, and the family. Explores the underlying myths, realities, and cultural perceptions behind society's views of disability. Chapters address issues such as social services, education, emotional support, and collaboration among service providers.

Gibbs, Jewelle Taylor, Larke Nahme Huang, and Associates. *Children of Color: Psychological Intervention with Minority Youth.* San Francisco: Jossey-Bass, 1989.

Provides guidelines for understanding and dealing with the psychological and behavioral problems of minority children and adolescents. Offers critical insights into the religious beliefs, cultural heritage, sexual attitudes, family structure, and educational goals of children from Asian, black, and Hispanic cultures.

Ginsburg, Sol W. *A Psychiatrist's Views on Social Issues.* New York: Columbia University Press, 1963.

A collection of essays intended to help social scientists, psychologists, social workers, educators and theologians become aware of the relevance of the social environment for the prevention and treatment of emotional disorders. Chapter 7, "Cultural Factors in Social Work," provides an overview of culture and its influence on human development. Provides examples of how an understanding of cultural anthropology enhances the effectiveness of social service providers.

Giordano, Joseph. "Health and Culture." *Families*, July/August 1981, pp. 68–70.

Explains why one's ethnic background determines the way one takes care of his health. This is a person's "health culture," a cluster of ideas and perceptions about disease and its treatment, which strongly influences everything from our perception of pain to how we make use of health-care services. Stresses the need for health professionals to ascertain a patient's cultural background in order to make an accurate medical evaluation.

Hall, William S., Elsa Bartlett, and Alva T. Hughes. "Patterns of Information Requests." *Black Children and Poverty: A Developmental Perspective.*

D.T. Slaughter, ed. New Directions for Child Development Series, no. 42. San Francisco: Jossey-Bass, 1988.

Reviews literature on the requestive language patterns of middle- and working-class black and white kindergarten children. Research documents that ethnicity and social class decidedly affect this language function. Extensive bibliography.

Hoang, G.N., and R.V. Erickson. "Cultural Barriers to Effective Medical Care Among Indochinese Patients." *Annual Review of Medicine* 36 (1985): 229–239.

States that many of the recent Indochinese refugees need medical treatment for significant personal and health problems yet rarely utilize existing health care services because of major cultural barriers between patient and provider.

Huff, C. Ronald, ed. *Gangs in America: Diffusion, Diversity, and Public Policy*. Newbury Park, Calif.: Sage, 1990.

Focuses on the historical and cultural perspective of gangs. Compares and contrasts the components of gang membership for various ethnic groups.

Hunt, J. McVicker. "The Effect of Variations in Quality and Type of Early Child Care on Development." *Early Experience and the Development of Competence*. W. Fowler, ed. New Directions for Child Development Series, no. 32. San Francisco: Jossey-Bass, 1986.

Reviews literature on the quality and type of infant care in different cultures and social classes and its effect on cognitive development. Attention to language appears to be particularly important for facilitating development. Results show minimal difference across cultures. Cites studies which show that children of poorly educated, poverty-stricken parents (regardless of race) suffer from a basic semantic deficiency in the symbolic processing of information. This deficit hampers their subsequent success in school. Describes how early remedial programs, such as Head Start, can make a positive difference. Extensive references.

Jelliffe, D.B., ed. *Diseases of Children in the Subtropics and Tropics*. 2d ed. London: Edward Arnold, 1970.

Explores the relationship between cultural patterning on health and behavior. Suggests that the customs associated with pregnancy and lactation are as important as those of infancy and childhood. Advocates the adoption of a curative and preventive health-care system that is based on beneficial local customs. States that home visiting is the key to providing preventive services to at-risk children.

Kleinman, Arthur. *Patients and Healers in the Context of Culture: An Exploration of the Borderland Between Anthropology, Medicine, and Psychiatry.* Berkeley: University of California Press, 1980.

Describes health care in Taiwan from the perspective of a psychiatrist who is trained in anthropology. Promotes the study of culture as a prerequisite to understanding a health-care system different from our own. Presents a theoretical framework for studying the relationship between medicine, psychology, and culture. Includes photographs, charts, and graphs in addition to a glossary and extensive bibliography.

Kleinman, Arthur, Leon Eisenberg, and Byron Good. "Culture, Illness, and Care: Clinical Lessons from Anthropologic and Cross-Cultural Research." *Annals of Internal Medicine* 88 (February 1978): 251–258.

States that how we communicate about our health problems, the manner in which we present our symptoms, when and to whom we go for care, how long we remain in care, and how we evaluate that care are all affected by cultural beliefs. Discusses the difference between disease and illness and urges that both be treated simultaneously. Proposes that social science be developed as a clinical discipline in medical schools, with input from anthropology and sociology. Presents several case studies to illustrate his hypotheses. Extensive reference list.

Kumabe, Kazuye T., and Yvonne Bickerton. *Ethnocultural Factors in Social Work and Health Care: A Selected Annotated Bibliography.* Honolulu: University of Hawaii School of Social Work, 1982.

An annotated bibliography of reference books, journals, and monographs intended for students and practitioners serving ethnic-minority groups. Selections include a few classic works along with recent publications. Emphasis is on the client-practitioner relationship. Includes references from the fields of public health, medicine, nursing, education, sociology, anthropology, and psychology. The ethnic groups included are blacks, Chinese, Filipinos, Hawaiians/Part-Hawaiians, Japanese, Koreans, Mexicans, Puerto Ricans, Samoans, Southeast Asians, and whites.

Kumabe, Kazuye T., Chikae Nishida, and Dean H. Hepworth. *Bridging Ethnocultural Diversity in Social Work and Health.* Honolulu: University of Hawaii School of Social Work, 1985.

A monograph that stresses sensitivity and understanding of varying ethnic values, beliefs, and traditions for students, educators, practitioners, and volunteers in the human services. The use of case studies emphasizes the need for a cross-cultural and pluralistic perspective.

Lawson, Lauren Valk. "Culturally Sensitive Support for Grieving Parents." *MCN, The American Journal of Maternal/Child Nursing* 15 (March/April 1990): 76–79.

Highlights the need for health care and social service professionals to provide care within a cultural context. Describes culturally distinctive characteristics of Native Americans, Mexican Americans, and Southeast Asians. Includes an annotated bibliography in addition to references.

Lieberman, Alicia F. "Culturally Sensitive Intervention with Children and Families." *Child and Adolescent Social Work Journal* 7 (1990).

Presents guidelines based on research and clinical experience for effective intervention with children and families of other cultures.

McGoldrick, Monica, John K. Pearce, and Joseph Giordano, eds. *Ethnicity and Family Therapy*. New York: Guilford, 1982.

Focuses on the cultural differences in clients and therapists which affect the provision and utilization of services. Provides general guidelines as well as culture specific information on the influence of ethnicity on behavior. Presents a focus on family behavior within the context of culture.

Meleis, Afaf Ibrahim, and Leila Sorrell. "Arab American Women and Their Birth Experiences." *MCN, The American Journal of Maternal/Child Nursing* 6 (May/June 1982): 171–176.

Explains the health care traditions of Arab Americans and the cultural origins of those beliefs. Practices such as a present time orientation, the strong need for affiliation, belief in the "evil eye," and extreme modesty can create misunderstanding and communication problems. Discusses the perception of and reaction to pain, attitudes toward contraception, and problems with verbal and written agreements in hospitals. Suggests nursing care strategies which incorporate respect for these beliefs. References and bibliography included.

Miller, C. Arden. *Maternal Health and Infant Survival: An Analysis of Medical and Social Services to Pregnant Women, Newborns and Their Families in Ten European Countries, with Implications for Policy and Practice in the*

United States. Washington, D.C.: National Center for Clinical Infant Programs, 1987.

Evaluates the provision of maternal and child health care services in Belgium, Denmark, France, the Federal Republic of Germany, Ireland, the Netherlands, Norway, Spain, Switzerland, and the United Kingdom. Characteristics cited provide an insight into traditional values and priorities in a variety of countries. Home visiting is cited as a feature of nearly every country's maternity care. This analysis acknowledges the influence of cultural traditions on service delivery patterns.

Miller, Jean R., and Ellen H. Janosik. *Family-Focused Care*. New York: McGraw-Hill, 1980.

Combines family theory with concepts related to physical and mental health. The chapter "Variation in Ethnic Families" is especially relevant. Cautions professionals that ethnic membership is not to be equated with minority status. A text for health and mental health practitioners which incorporates clinical examples and includes chapter summaries and references.

Morris, Lee, ed. *Extracting Learning Styles from Social/Cultural Diversity: Studies of Five American Minorities*. Norman, Okla.: University of Oklahoma, 1986.

Suggests that educators can improve their relationships with minority students and influence the process of learning and the cognitive and affective outcomes of instruction by being culturally sensitive. Discusses cultural influences on cognitive, affective, and psychomotor learning. Explores the learning styles of Afro-American, Chicano, Native American, poor white, and Chinese-American students.

National Coalition of Advocates for Students. *New Voices: Immigrant Students in the U.S. Public Schools*. Boston: National Coalition of Advocates for Students, 1988.

A national research and policy report. Presents the viewpoints of immigrant leaders, educators, advocates, and immigrant students on a variety of subjects. Suggests extensive policy recommendations, including actions for local boards of education.

Olmstead, Patricia P., and David P. Weikart, eds. *How Nations Serve Young Children: Profiles of Child Care and Education in 14 Countries*. Ypsilanti, Mich.: High/Scope Press, 1989.

Contains national profiles of early childhood care and education prepared by research teams in Belgium, Germany, Finland, Hong Kong, Hungary, Italy, Kenya, Nigeria, China, the Philippines, Portugal, Spain, Thailand, and the United States. Volume is part of an ongoing international study and addresses cross-cultural differences and similarities.

Payer, Lynn. *Medicine and Culture: Varieties of Treatment in the United States, England, West Germany, and France.* New York: Holt, 1988.

Examines four different (though common) cultures, how each views the human condition, their concepts of health and disease, and approaches to medical practice. Suggests that medical diagnosis is strongly influenced by culture: what the doctor learned in medical school, what he knows other doctors say, and what he knows will reassure the patient. Caricatures French doctors as courtesans; German doctors as authoritarian-romantic; English doctors as kindly but paternalistic; and American doctors as aggressive.

Peak, Lois. "Training Learning Skills and Attitudes in Japanese Early Educational Settings." *Early Experience and the Development of Competence.* W. Fowler, ed. New Directions for Child Development Series, no. 32. San Francisco: Jossey-Bass, 1986.

Explores how Japanese children are introduced to learning situations in structured ways that develop early control of their learning behavior. This philosophy of education reflects and reinforces traditional Japanese values. This methodology is based on motivation, repeated practice, and self-monitoring. Cross-cultural references.

Phinney Jean S., and Mary Jane Rotheram, eds. *Children's Ethnic Socialization: Pluralism and Development.* Newbury Park, Calif.: Sage, 1987.

Reviews current knowledge and research on the influence of culture and ethnicity on educational practices and language development. Authors advocate for increased multicultural education programs geared to the needs and perspectives of minority children. Suggests strategies for modifying educational practices, for training professionals, and for designing research to promote multicultural education.

Ramsey, Patricia G., Edwina Battle Vold, and Leslie R. Williams. *Multicultural Education: A Source Book.* New York: Garland, 1989.

Provides theoretical, research, and practical information related to the implementation of a multicultural perspective in early childhood and elementary school classrooms. Chapter II, "Ethnic Diversity and Children's Learning," which addresses behavioral dimensions and educational implications, is especially relevant. Extensive references and annotated bibliography accompany each chapter.

Randall-David, Elizabeth. *Strategies for Working with Culturally Diverse Communities and Clients.* Washington, D.C.: Association for the Care of Children's Health, 1989.

Suggests guidelines for working with culturally diverse persons and groups. Focuses on Amish, Asian American, African American, Haitian, and Hispanic populations. In addition to bibliography, offers "Guidelines for Analysis of Sociocultural Factors in Health" and a list of organizations serving culturally diverse communities.

Rautenberg, Ellen L. *Ethnicity and Health Care.* New York: Institute on Pluralism and Group Identity of The American Jewish Committee, 1983.

Discusses cultural differences in health behavior, health culture and compliance, access barriers, and problems with service delivery. Provides case examples which emphasize each point. Recommends training in the behavior and social sciences for physicians and other health care personnel. Offers specific guidelines for culturally sensitive health services.

Sagan, Leonard A. *The Health of Nations: True Causes of Sickness and Well-Being.* New York: Basic Books, 1987.

Reviews historical, epidemiological, and sociological studies on human behavior and life expectancy. States that matters of cultural decision making are what really account for health in modern nations. Questions conventional ideas that sanitation, nutrition, and medical technology account for low Western-world mortality rates and argues instead that social class, "life skills," cohesiveness of family, community feelings, and education all determine life expectancy.

Santoli, Al. *An Oral History: Immigrants and Refugees in the U.S. Today.* New York: Viking, 1989.

Examines the background, experiences, and dream of "the new Americans." Many, like Cambodians interviewed, have encountered harrowing obstacles to immigration. Others, like Guatemalans and Hmong, have come ill prepared "directly from prehistory" into "electric America." All exhibit intense pride and a faith in the future. They are determined to make a better life for their children. The word "education" rings out magically through all their accounts. All have a strong sense of family and are passionately involved in the education of their children.

Stiffman, Arlene Rubin, and Larry E. Davis, eds. *Ethnic Issues in Adolescent Mental Health*. Newbury Park, Calif.: Sage, 1990.

Focuses on the effects of ethnicity on adolescent mental health. Discusses the necessity for understanding ethnic values and attitudes in developing culturally sensitive intervention strategies.

Sue, Derald W. *Counseling the Culturally Different: Theory and Practice*. New York: Wiley, 1980.

Analyzes the practitioner-client relationship in counseling Asian-Americans, blacks, Hispanics, and American Indians. Discusses generalizations, stereotypes, and barriers to practitioner-client relationships. Describes characteristics of the culturally skilled counselor.

Tobin, Joseph J., David Y.H. Wu, and Dana H. Davidson. "How Three Countries Shape Their Children." *World Monitor*, April 1989.

Compares and analyzes a typical day for four-year-olds attending preschools in China, Japan, and the United States. Authors view preschools as agents more of cultural conservation than of change. Their findings indicate that preschools both reflect and moderate social change in these three cultures. Article is adapted from their book, *Preschool in Three Cultures*, published in 1989 by Yale University Press.

Traver, Nancy. *Kife: The Lives and Dreams of Soviet Youth*. New York: St. Martin's Press, 1989.

Provides first-hand observations of Soviet youth in the *Glasnost* era. Traver, a former Moscow correspondent for *Time*, found young Soviets preoccupied by *kife*, a word for things both desirable and unobtainable, such as the material goods, rock music, and democratic ideals of the West. Provides illuminating perspectives on education and indoctrination; sex, courtship, and marriage; diet and health care; religion and atheism; and culture in modern Soviet society.

United States Department of Agriculture/Department of Health and Human Services. *Cross-Cultural Counseling: A Guide for Nutrition and Health*

Counselors. FNS–250. Washington, D.C.: U.S. Government Printing Office, 1986.

Highlights the need for cross-cultural counseling, and suggests specific guidelines for understanding cultural values, health beliefs, and dietary concerns. Describes the causes and remedies for verbal and nonverbal communication problems. Includes a Quick Counseling Guide, references, and a selected bibliography arranged by subject matter. The Appendix supplies a brief overview of four cultural minority groups—Asian and Pacific Americans; black Americans; Hispanic Americans, and Native Americans.

Wagner, Daniel A. "Indigenous Education and Literacy in the Third World." *Child Development and International Development: Research-Policy Interfaces.* D.A. Wagner, ed. New Directions for Child Development Series, no. 20. San Francisco: Jossey-Bass, 1983.

Presents a rare look at the wide variety and purposes of indigenous schools around the world and their role in child development. Some experts believe that education and functional literacy are essential for labor productivity and economic development; others promote the nonformal, more cost effective indigenous programs for Third World countries. Describes the African bush schools in Liberia and the Quranic Islamic schools in Indonesia, Yemen, Senegal, Morocco, and Egypt. In each country, education is influenced by cultural constraints.

Zborowski, Mark. *People in Pain.* San Francisco: Jossey-Bass, 1969.

A classic study which analyzes attitudes and reaction to pain among Jewish, Italian, Irish and "Old American" patients. Study reveals characteristic ethnic group differences in health behavior. Zborowski contends that there are definite ethnic patterns to how pain is tolerated and perceived.

ASIAN CULTURES

The Asian cultures addressed in this chapter will be limited to those of East Asia and Southeast Asia. The majority of Asian immigrants who have, both recently and in the past, come to this country are from those regions.[1] An essential purpose of this book is to promote an understanding of the unique characteristics of *each* cultural and ethnic group; to view all Asians as one homogeneous culture is totally incorrect. This overview of East Asian cultures will therefore examine the cultures of China, Taiwan, Hong Kong, Japan, and Korea as well as the Southeast Asian cultures of Singapore, Thailand, the Philippines, and Vietnam, Cambodia, and Laos.

Cultural traits which are traditionally shared by East Asian and Southeast Asian nations alike are presented here first; they provide a general frame of reference for understanding Asian children and their families. Similarities which exist between the two regions are mainly philosophical, based on Confucianism and Buddhism. But there are also distinct differences in heritage, life-style, language and childrearing practices. Following the generalizations, a "profile" of each country is given, focusing on the distinctly unique features of each.

The reader is cautioned that both the generalized and the more specific similarities and differences are merely guidelines for understanding behavior within a cultural context. To discern the uniqueness of a specific child and his family, it is essential to consider these cultural traits in conjunction with the assessment guidelines set forth in Chapter IV.

Traditional Characteristics of Asian Families

Asian families generally do not stress independence and autonomy; rather, the individual is seen as secondary in importance to the family and to the group. Roles, relationships, and behavior are specified by tradition. Important among the guiding principles and values of these families are the following:

Harmony: Emphasis upon harmony in Asian cultures is rooted in Confucianism. Maintaining harmony and good relations in the home and with others is very important. To prevent offending or hurting someone's feelings, Asians will usually avoid direct confrontation, avoid saying "no," and avoid expressing anger or displeasure.

"Saving Face": Embarrassing oneself or shaming the family is intolerable. The actions of one member can bring shame upon the entire family; family concepts of loyalty and mutualism extend to the group, the community, and the nation. The stigma of "losing face" is frequently used to control deviant behavior.[2]

Obligation: This is of two kinds, *ascribed obligation*, incurred through the roles in family relationships or in status (e.g., parent to child), and *reciprocal obligation*, incurred through actions requiring a return for kindness or helpfulness.[3]

Filial Piety: Filial piety refers to the devotion of children to their parents. It is extended to include not only one's parents and home but one's attitude toward others and one's conduct in society. The father-son relationship is especially important. Parents demand strict obedience; their word is absolute.

Proper Form: Traditional observance, decorum, and proper form are very important and usually strictly adhered to in social practices and customs. Love and affection, for example, are openly expressed only with infants; after that, they are expressed by actions which are culturally prescribed, such as providing for one's family.

Communication Style: Communication is often indirect; one talks around a point, relying on the other person's sensitivity to pick up the crux of the conversation. Communication style is generally reserved and formal. Outward displays of emotion are discouraged. Directness, which may lead to disagreement, confrontation, and loss of face, is avoided.[4] Laughter may indicate embarrassment or distress rather than amusement.

Touching: The head is considered sacred since it is believed to be the site where one's soul resides. It is offensive to touch Asians on the head or only on one shoulder. Touching of strangers is considered inappropriate.[5]

Family Structure and Gender Roles

Elders are highly regarded in Asian cultures. They are not to be questioned but to be obeyed and are considered correct or justified in their judgment and behavior. Family structure is usually paternal in lineage, with wives joining the families of their husbands. Marriage is viewed as the union of families rather than of individuals. All household members, even married sons, are expected to obey the father as head of the household. Traditionally, men are expected to earn the family money, women to manage it. Women have a strong influence on family decisions, even though they are raised to be submissive and passive. They have the primary responsibility for raising the children, running the household, and caring for the elderly.[6] In rural areas, they may also be expected to contribute to the work force.

Childrearing Practices

Children are highly valued. Having children fulfills a biological and social obligation. Historically, large families have been desired; males are highly regarded and are preferred. The present emphasis on population control (especially in China) places an increased value on the one or two children permitted. Childrearing practices during infancy and early childhood are highly indulgent. A close mother-infant bond is maintained and a strong sense of acceptance and security is fostered. The paternal grandmother is often directly involved in childrearing.[7] Formal discipline and limit setting usually do not begin until about age four or five. Educational achievement and excellence are stressed. Older children are disciplined by social controls and by psychological punishment, such as inducing guilt or shame.

Religion

Religion is more a guiding philosophy than a set of dogmas or ritual observances and church attendance. Traditional religions in Asia and Southeast Asia include Confucianism, Buddhism, Taoism, Shintoism, and Animism. They coexist without conflict or contradiction.

Confucianism is not a religion in the sense in which Westerners commonly understand that word; it does not include a belief in God nor does it incorporate specific rituals. It is, rather, a code of ethics and morals which emphasizes relationships among men and harmony with nature; it is a way of life. It teaches respect for elders and education, loyalty to the family, justice, and formality of behavior. Confucianism is a humanistic system devoted to man's relationship to man, not to God. It stresses obligation rather than right and group spirit rather than individualism. The purest forms of Confucianism are found in South Korea, Japan, and Taiwan.

Buddhism has many sects and is basically a philosophy, although it does incorporate rituals associated with births and funerals; it teaches self-negation, modesty, humility, and reincarnation. Taoism stresses that harmony with nature requires an equilibrium between *yin* (negative) and *yang* (positive) elements. It also emphasizes charity, patience, and the avoidance of confrontation. Shintoism (primarily in Japan) is not so much a religion as a set of traditional rituals and customs involving pilgrimages to shrines and the celebration of festivals; it teaches reverence for ancestors, ceremonial purity, and body cleanliness. Shamanism (primarily in Korea) is "the practice of contacting and controlling the supernatural through ritual, in which drumming and trance are essential religious techniques."[8] Animism is based on the belief that within every object there dwells an individual spirit or force that governs its existence; it teaches that all life exists because there is a spirit energy and that removal of this energy results in illness, famine, or death.

Buddhism has a pervasive influence on life in Asia and Southeast Asia. Mahayana Buddhism is practiced in China, Korea, and Japan, and parts of Vietnam. Theravada Buddhism, coexisting with animism, prevails in most of Southeast Asia:

> One reason for its favor with the people is the ease with which animistic ideas can be amalgamated with Buddhist cause and effect. Animism shows how bad action can arouse the ire of spirits and condemn the individual to a miserable life. So in the Theravada karma we have a direct parallel: "One is always accountable for one's actions." Thus people have free choice; they can influence their times, expressed in good ways or bad; there is always a consequence. It is therefore normal to find a Buddhist

> temple in a Southeast Asian village and an animistic shrine—without a basic contradiction between them.[9]

The meaning of animism in Southeast Asia is also clarified:

> But in Southeast Asia all life exists, all things function because there is a spirit energy, however it is called. . . . Clearly the Southeast Asian's animism not only classifies the world by function but it structures it also. For there are obviously planes of existence: the world of animals, of spirits, of gods, of evil, and of human beings. . . . Human existence, then, is influenced by supernatural forces, which must be controlled by ritual, rite, amulet, prayer, and sacrifice.[10]

Attitude Toward Work and Education

The Asian commitment to hard work and to education is almost legendary. Both the school calendar and the work week are longer than in the United States. Asian students frequently excel in science, mathematics, and language-learning skills. The ability to learn languages may be a survival skill developed over centuries of war and occupation. Skill in mathematics may be the result of the use of the abacus, which aids in understanding abstract concepts.[11] Rote learning is common and individual creative abilities are not usually fostered. Model behavior, in educational and work settings alike, is by collective action. Students and workers are encouraged to work hard, stay out of trouble, tend to business, succeed within the established system. There is a high commitment to task orientation, details, precision, and orderliness. There is a preoccupation with protocol, procedures, and tasks.[12]

In reviewing traditional characteristics of a culture (or grouping of cultures) it is essential to consider the environment in which the tradition originally evolved, societal modifications that have occurred over time, and how these traditions are affected by acculturation and assimilation with other cultures. Three general categories of Asian Americans are identified in a guide on cross-cultural counseling:

(1) Those who maintain traditional Asian values and behavior (new immigrants)
(2) Those who practice both traditional Asian and Western values and behaviors (immigrants who have been acculturated to some extent or U.S.-born children of immigrants who have been exposed to both cultures
(3) Those who have fully adopted Western values and behavior (U.S.-born Asian Americans whose parents or grandparents may also be U.S.-born)[13]

However, these distinctions are appropriately accompanied by the reminder that "it is important to stress that these characteristics vary in degree according to individuals and groups, and only some of these may be present in any one culture."[14]

Traditional Asian Characteristics Most Likely to Have Implications for Health, Education, and Social Services

- A communication style that is reserved and indirect.
- A reticence to discuss matters of a personal or sexual nature.
- Stoicism in the presence of pain.
- A method of calculating a child's age that considers a child one-year-old at birth; another year is added each Tet (New Year). Conceivably, a child born in January could be considered two years old the following month.[15]
- The expectation that the entire family unit will be involved in any health care decisions and treatment.
- A traditional belief that health and illness are related to spirits and fate; that ill health (disharmony with nature) is preventable; and that parents may be to blame for handicapping conditions in their children.[16]
- A reliance on herbs and acupuncture and the use of Western medicine as a supplement to traditional therapies.
- Stress upon the importance of diet in the prevention and treatment of illness. Basic diet consists of rice and fish. The consumption of vegetables, fruits, poultry, meats, and eggs varies with availability and wealth. Milk products are rarely

available or consumed. Because the diet often lacks adequate calcium intake and because sweets are frequently used as rewards, dental problems are prevalent, especially among refugee children.

Brief Profile of Japan

Family Structure: Japanese society is based on a strong family structure, bound together by obligation and duty. The Japanese family, in accordance with Confucian tradition, is patriarchal and patrilineal. Age and tradition are honored. Many older parents reside with their married children, although large, multigenerational families are no longer common. There are usually one or two children per family. The absence of prolonged verbal exchange is characteristic of family interaction.[17] The typical life cycle of the Japanese has been described as a great shallow U-curve, with maximum freedom and indulgence allowed to babies and the elderly.[18] Group unity, as personified by the Japanese family, is reflected in many aspects of their life-style. The current changes in family structure are usually reflections of contemporary economics, necessities of urban life-style, and increasing intercultural contact. Increasingly, Japanese women are pursuing careers.

The term *Issei* refers to the first generation born to Japanese who immigrated to the mainland United States and Hawaii, *Nisei* are the second generation, and *Sansei*, the third. This terminology, by generation, may be indicative of traditional values and practices.

Childrearing Practices: Children, especially sons, are highly valued. In the past, a Japanese infant was named at seven days of age; the name, selected by the grandparents, was intended to help mold the child's character. Today, an infant is often given an English first name and a Japanese middle name, still selected by the grandparents, and still significant. There are numerous celebrations which honor each child and children in general. Children are greatly indulged during the preschool years, but they are raised to be docile and obedient. Male children are encouraged to develop manliness, determination, and the will to overcome all obstacles in the path of success; for females, emphasis is placed on poise and grace. Orderliness and conformity are highly stressed. Role behavior is defined by sex, age, and birth order.

The mother-child relationship is intense; a child's successes and failures at any age reflect on the mother.[19] Japanese children are socialized to be dependent on the family and the group; this concept of obligation is called *amae*.[20] These are the traditional childrearing practices of the past; many of these traditions are undergoing modifications along with changes in family structure and other socioeconomic factors.

Religion: There is a humanistic attitude toward religion; religious celebrations are now largely social traditions. Families generally follow a combination of beliefs from Buddhism, Confucianism, and Shintoism. Many Japanese homes contain a *kamidana* (spirit shelf) of Shinto shrines. A description of Shintoism explains that:

> The term Shinto means the "Way of the Spirit, or Kami." Kami can be conceived of as a benign and elevated spirit in a world of spirits. It is at once personality within things and a quality counter to the destructive, or bad luck, elements of life. Although the Japanese are conscious of a dualism in nature, it is never as sharp as the Yin-Yang in Chinese Taoism. . . . Shinto offers a means of interrelating with the elevated qualities of life.[21]

Christianity is practiced by less than 1 percent of the population. There appears to be an emphasis on the work ethic, on meditation, ancestor worship, ritual cleansing, and a respect for nature's beauty rather than on actual religious practices.

Values: The Japanese value education, achievement, ethnicity, preservation of the family name, obligation, humility, modesty, self-restraint, responsibility, and loyalty to the group and to one's superiors.[22] In contemporary Japan, group loyalty is often manifested by a strong sense of corporate affiliation. Membership is by situation rather than by qualification (e.g., "I work for Sony," rather than "I am an engineer").[23] Most large corporations expect complete dedication from their employees and, in turn, offer many benefits (e.g., housing, lifetime security) in return. No nation—whether Asian or other—has as formal and prescribed a manner of social behavior as the Japanese; much of this prescribed social interaction is non-verbal (e.g., bowing). Conformity and dependency are valued over spontaneity and independence.

Traditional characteristics, however, *have* changed and *are* changing in Japan:

> With Westernization, the class divisions and with them the strict behavioral patterns broke down. Up to World War II, however, both the Confucian family ethic and formality of behavior still had a significant place. Today, with more women in the work force, with most Japanese in cities, with nuclear family life in apartment houses, and with the overall effect of American-style mass media, the whole social system has undergone great change. . . . Even with change, the Japanese sense of social position remains and respect is still displayed to the elderly, to the people in authority. It is clear that the Japanese ultimately respect one another.[24]

Language: As a spoken language, Japanese is not closely related to Chinese. The written language, however, is directly related to Chinese ideographs from ancient times. There are two phonetic alphabets (*hiragana* and *katakana*) simplified from these ideographs. English is taught in all secondary schools, and is used increasingly in business.

Health: Preventive health care is stressed. Ethnic foods such as tofu are part of a well-balanced diet. Parents take pride in their child's physical health. When a child is ill, parents will usually seek out proper medical assistance regardless of cost; minor illnesses will often be treated with home remedies. The Japanese have one of the highest life expectancies in the world.

Education: Education is valued greatly; it is the basis of success in Japan. The school system is highly structured and fosters group behavior. Education is free and compulsory up to age fifteen. Entrance exams to the leading universities are rigorous and highly competitive. The literacy rate in Japan is 99 percent.

Other Significant Data: Japan is a densely populated, mostly urban country. The population is 99 percent homogeneous, with only a small number of Koreans, Chinese, and native Ainu. The standard of living is high; unemployment is quite low; and the crime rate is one of the lowest in the world.

Brief Profile of the People's Republic of China (Mainland China)

Family Structure: Traditionally, the Chinese have been considered the most family-oriented people in the world. The characteristic Chinese family—extended, patriarchal, and patrilineal—was the basis of Chinese culture and way of living for many centuries. The family is still the major unit of society, even though under communism, there seems to be an attempt to shift the people's loyalty away from the family and toward the state. Parental respect and ancestor worship are essential ingredients of family relationships. There is a historic emphasis on filial piety; the parent-child relationship is emphasized over that of husband and wife. A wife is allocated a subordinate position until she produces a son or becomes a mother-in-law. Extended families often live together because living space is scarce.[25] Present law limits couples to only one child. The role of women has changed since the "cultural revolution"; now, women are increasingly working outside the home.

Childrearing Practices: Childhood in China is marked by simplicity, schooling, and a sense of security.[26] Infancy is a warm and nurturing period. The mother-infant relationship is an intimate attachment; babies are often called *Bao Bei* (valuable and precious thing).[27] The devotion of Chinese parents is attributed to "their belief in the continuity of their biological and moral lives via their children and grandchildren."[28] According to tradition, the mother is responsible for an infant's prematurity or defect. This is considered to be her punishment for wrongdoing during the pregnancy, such as looking at an ugly animal.[29] Attention is lavished on young children by the extended family. As they grow older, children are taught to bring honor to themselves and their families. Children are given a great deal of responsibility at a comparatively early age. Desired behaviors in children are obedience, sharing, non-competitiveness, and achievement. In many ways, they are expected to behave as little adults: obedient, unspoiled, unemotional, and polite.[30]

The father is responsible for discipline and is apt to be strict. Physical punishment is used only as a last resort and is forbidden at school. There is an old Chinese proverb that states, "Rearing without instruction is the fault of the father while instruction without strictness is the laziness of the teacher."[31]

A baby's name carries special significance: the Chinese character name reflects individuality, conveys a positive meaning, is suitable for his social status, and does not duplicate the names of relatives. Traditionally, Chinese names consist of a one syllable family name followed by a one-or-two-syllable given name.

Games involving physical activity are less prized than those which challenge the mind. Playing with dolls may be avoided because of their traditional Chinese association with magical powers; in Chinese, the word "doll" comes from the same root as "idol" or "fetish."[32]

Religion: Religion does not play a meaningful role in the present society, especially among intellectuals. Traditional religions, such as Buddhism, Taoism and folk religions, as well as Christianity, are not widely practiced. Religious expression is carried out in the context of ancestor worship, practiced in the home and in ancestral temples. Religious freedom is guaranteed, but religious activity is discouraged by the government; atheism is encouraged.

Values: Moral purity is highly valued in mainland China. Customs stressing moral purity are reflected in all aspects of dating, marriage, and social relationships. Filial piety is more than a fulfillment of duty to one's parents; it is a moral act. Other esteemed values are patience, self-control, self-sacrifice, good manners, hospitality, and reserve. Strong family influence is reflected in the emphasis placed on collective responsibility and group shame.[33]

Language: Standard Chinese, based on the Mandarin dialect, is the national language and is spoken by a large majority of the people. Most Chinese are bilingual, speaking a native dialect as well as the national language. Shanghainese, Szechuanese, and Cantonese are also spoken. In the Chinese language, there are no gender pronouns, tenses, plural endings, or verb conjugations. Word distinction is achieved via the addition of words, not modification. Conversational Chinese differs from written Chinese. Chinese writing is ideographic, (i.e., each sign stands for a word). To write Chinese means "to conceive of meaning and to select the right characters for that meaning, not on the basis of their sound values, but for semantic reasons."[34]

Health: The standard of medical care is high. The use of "barefoot doctors" to deliver health care in rural areas has been effective. A balance of *yin* and *yang* is considered essential for health maintenance. Folk medicine is based on *yang* factors of warmth, light, and heat to the body and *yin* elements of cold, dark, and cooling to the body. The use of acupuncture is highly regarded. *Yin* and *yang* distinctions are also applied to food:

> According to Chinese philosophy adapted by the macrobiotic practitioners, yin represents the passive and feminine forces in nature and includes most vegetables; yang represents active and masculine forces, and includes most animal foods and most cereals.... Central to the diet is the concept of balance. When food from the sea is served, it is supposed to be combined with food from the land. Or when a yang food like grain is served, it should be combined with a yin food like vegetables.[35]

Food has a special significance not merely for existence but also as an art and a source of enjoyment. The diet is healthy, high in vegetables and low in fat and sweets. Rice symbolizes life and fertility; eggs symbolize good luck, happiness, and fertility.

Education: Six years of education are mandated, although some rural children receive none. The literacy rate is approximately 75 percent. Memory skills are emphasized and children tend to excel in spatial, nonverbal reasoning tasks. The abacus is utilized to teach math concepts. A high value is placed on education, educational achievement, and scholarly industriousness.

Other Significant Data: China is the world's oldest living civilization. It is also the most populous country in the world. The economy is based on both agriculture and industry. Over 10 percent of the population lives in urban areas; even the major agricultural areas are densely populated. Ninety-four percent of the population is ethnic Han Chinese. There are 54 other ethnic minorities. The Chinese lunar calendar celebrates many holidays; fireworks are a traditional part of many celebrations. In China, red is the color of prosperity, happiness, and celebration of happy occasions; white, while symbolic of purity, is also the color of mourning.

Brief Profile of Taiwan (Republic of China)

Family Structure: A strong, extended family, as in mainland China, is the basic social structure. Families in Taiwan are generally quite large and multigenerational. Family unity and obligation are strong. Proper social and family relationships are crucial. Affection is not openly displayed.

Childrearing: Childrearing follows traditional Chinese customs and traditions. Family size is not restricted.

Religion: Predominant religions are Buddhism, Confucianism, and Taoism, usually in combination with other beliefs. Approximately 7.5 percent of the population is Christian and less than 1 percent is Muslim.[36]

Values: Values reflect those of traditional Chinese culture. High moral standards, refinement, moderation, loyalty, respect, punctuality, and a strong work ethic are stressed. Acceptable standards of behavior reflect the Confucian ethic of proper social and family relationships.

Language: The Mandarin dialect of Chinese is the official language. A majority of the people also speak Taiwanese. The Hakka dialect is also spoken. Many of the older population speak Japanese.

Health: Health care standards and practices are high. There is an extensive program of maternal and child services. Health education teams are assigned to villages for community organization and health teaching, home visiting for better housing and environmental sanitation, training of community leaders, production and distribution of educational materials, and mass education.[37] The diet includes a variety of soups, seafood, pork, chicken, vegetables, and fruit. Many foods are fried. Rice and tea are always served with meals.

Education: Education is highly valued and compulsory until age fifteen. Attendance at colleges and universities is highly competitive. The literacy rate is over 90 percent.

Other Significant Data: Taiwan is a densely populated island with a strong diversified economy and a high standard of living. The population is approximately 84 percent Taiwanese, 14 percent mainland Chinese, and 2 percent aborigine. Over 60 percent of the people live in rural areas. Men are required to serve 2–3 years in the army.

Brief Profile of Hong Kong

Family Structure: The family unit in Hong Kong is traditionally Chinese, large and multigenerational. A strong sense of family loyalty, obedience, and respect prevails.

Childrearing: Modifications in childrearing (from traditional Chinese practices) reflect the cultural and socioeconomic environment of Hong Kong, the Western influence, and the lack of restrictive family size. Chinese childrearing and socialization consist of two distinct phases. The early phase, *Yang Yu*, from birth until the child begins to understand adults' demands, is one of love and affection: it is characterized by leniency and satisfaction of physical and affectional needs; attention is centered on the infant's health. The later phase, *Jiao Yang*, begins when the child can understand the expressions and demands of adults, and is characterized by strictness and harsh discipline. It is during this period that parents concentrate on the development of the child's character. This training phase constitutes an essential role in personality development and seems to represent an effort to fit the child into a demanding adult world.[38]

Hong Kong Chinese tend to be very lenient with children as long as they are healthy. They generally think that a handicapped person has done something bad in his previous life and is being punished.[39]

Religion: Religion in Hong Kong reflects the Chinese heritage of diversity in moral philosophy and formal religion. There is a blending of Taoism, Confucianism, and Buddhism along with folk religion and ancestor worship. There are also many Christian denominations, representing about 10 percent of the population.

Values: Traditional Chinese values are maintained in Hong Kong. The Confucian ethic of proper social and family relationships is the basis of society.

Language: There are two official languages in Hong Kong—Chinese and English. All street signs, phone directories, and official documents are written in both languages. Cantonese is the dominant Chinese dialect, although many dialects are spoken.

Health: A high standard of health care is available. In spite of overcrowded conditions and areas of poverty and poor sanitation, life expectancy (76 years) is the highest in the world, and the death rate one of the lowest.

Education: Nine years of education are free and compulsory. Most students study English. Educational achievement is valued highly and higher education is very competitive. The literacy rate is approximately 90 percent.

Other Significant Data: Hong Kong (meaning "Fragrant Harbor") is referred to as the "Pearl of the Orient." It is primarily a manufacturing and trading center. There is a wide range of diversity in the socioeconomic level of the population. The country is densely populated, with more than half of the people residing in the city. Hong Kong is an ethnically homogeneous country, 98 percent Chinese. Its residents are presently British subjects, but Britain is scheduled to return Hong Kong to China in 1997.

Brief Profile of Korea

Family Structure: Traditionally, the family is the foundation of society in Korea, bound together by a strong sense of duty and obligation. "Family" is not differentiated from the "clan" (those with the same family name tracing their ancestors to the same family seat). The extended family and clan system seem to be diminishing in North Korea as the government stresses loyalty to the state over loyalty to one's lineage. Koreans attach a special significance to *chip* (family), a father-to-son sequence of inheritance. Failure to beget a son can mean the extinction of a family. This is the basis for treating sons preferentially and for holding the father-son relationship in higher regard than the husband-wife relationship. A family exists on the basis of father and son, not husband and wife. The status of women in Korea has traditionally been low. In the past, women were denied an education and were raised to be subservient to the male and his family; a woman's major role was to produce a male heir. Korean women were taught not to make direct eye contact with outsiders, smile at them, or touch their hands. The role of women has improved dramatically in the postwar era. Co-education is now common, and women are allowed and even encouraged to work.

The traditional sense of family has undergone rapid changes in recent years:

> The Western principle of family life has come to exert many influences on the daily life of the Korean people. The

change in family life took place largely in two directions. One was the modernization of the Korean economic structure in the wake of the introduction of Western culture. The other was the modernization of families as a direct consequence of the introduction of modern Western currents of thought.[40]

Childrearing Practices: Korean tradition regarded the unmarried as children, regardless of age. Childhood roles and activities are divided according to sex. Korean children do not really become members of society until 100 days after birth at which time a celebration is held. Names have a special significance. Koreans have three names: the family name is first; the name to identify the generation is second; and the given name third. Male children only are given (in addition to their childhood name) a lifelong name, a marriage name, and a career name. Koreans sometimes change their given names (which indicate status within the family) but never their family names. Korean women keep their original family name even after marriage.[41] In North Korea, large families are encouraged by the government and day-care is provided so that both parents may work.

Religion: Religion and culture in Korea were traditionally and fundamentally based on Confucian thought and Shamanistic worship. Today only 13 percent of the people follow basic Confucianism. About a quarter of the population, predominately in rural areas, are Shamanists who practice native folk religions. Approximately 35 percent of the population are now Christian (primarily Protestant), while about 18 percent are Buddhists. *Ch'ondogyo* (or *Tonghak*), a unique blend of Buddhism, Confucianism, and Christianity, is practiced in parts of North Korea.

Values: Korea has managed to maintain a unique value system even though it has been occupied by both China and Japan at various times in the past. The Korean way of life has traditionally been based on an authority-subordinate role, a hierarchy of persons, and inequality. One was taught to control one's emotions and passions; self-control and social obligations were paramount. Today, these characteristics of Korean culture are diminishing. Many of these changes in tradition are the result of increasing contact with Western cultures. Filial piety and status, based upon authority, are still valued by a majority of the people. A lowered occupational status, resulting from immigration and/or economic changes, can create problems in the Korean family structure. The class system in Korea is not as strong as in other Asian countries, but the drop from white to blue collar (in immigrants to America) affects the entire family's self-esteem.[42] Modesty and proper decorum in social relationships remain important. Group identity is very strong and takes precedence over individual relationships; men act as members of a family, not as independent individuals. Koreans believe in living harmoniously with nature and with each other. Traditionally, time orientation is to the present rather than to the future.

Language: The Korean language is spoken in both North and South Korea. The written language is based upon the phonetic alphabet *Hangul*. In South Korea, Hangul is interspersed with a mixture of Chinese script; North Korean publications use only Hangul. In North Korea, Russian, Chinese, and English are taught as second languages. English is widely taught at the high school level in South Korea. Many older people still speak Japanese.

Health: Health care (by Western standards) is rather poor. Over half of the modern health services are located in urban centers (where slightly less than half of the population resides); Shamans (folk healers) provide much of the health care in rural communities. Most medications, including antibiotics and narcotics, are available "over the counter." The present-time orientation is reflected in health care by the expectation of quick cures and the reluctance to take long-term medications. Herbal treatment and acupuncture are widely used.[43] Health care has always been considered a traditional role for women in Korea: even today it offers the best opportunities for women, since almost half of all Korean health professionals are women.[44] Diet in Korea consists largely of rice and other grains, *kimchi* (spicy pickled cabbage and peppers), fish, and soups. Meat is consumed according to income. The Koreans are not tea drinkers.

Education: Education is highly valued in Korean culture and is considered essential to wealth and success. Education is free and compulsory for eleven years in North Korea, where literacy is almost 100 percent. In South Korea, education is free and compulsory from ages 6–12 and literacy is 90 percent.

Other Significant Data: Today there are two Koreas: North Korea (Democratic People's Republic of Korea) and South Korea (Republic of Korea). There is strong nationalistic pride in both North and South Korea. Korea (especially South Korea) is the most ethnically homogeneous country in the world. Korea is presently undergoing a rapid change in industrialization. The standard of living is increasing in both Koreas but is still not high by Western standards. Most immigration to the United States has occurred since 1965; this is one reason why Americans probably know less about the Koreans than they do about any other Asian Americans.[45]

Brief Profile of Singapore

Family Structure: Limited space and resources have necessitated restricting family size to two children. The extended family unit remains large and cohesive; it stresses respect for elders.

Childrearing: Childrearing practices generally reflect the cultural diversity of the country (Chinese, Malay, and Indian), the scarcity of space and resources, and the high standard of living.

Religion: Taoism and Buddhism predominate. There are also Muslims, Christians, Hindus, and other religious groups.[46]

Values: Traditional Chinese values are prominent, especially the strong work ethic and family loyalty. Cleanliness is highly valued; Singapore is often referred to as the cleanest city in Asia.

Language: Four official languages (English, Mandarin Chinese, Malay, and Tamil) reflect the wide racial diversity of Singapore. Even though Malay is designated as the national language, all Singaporeans are expected to learn English. Government business as well as many other businesses are conducted in English. Mandarin Chinese is the required second language for most citizens yet it is not the native dialect of many Chinese. Most Singaporeans are at least bilingual, while many speak 3–5 languages.

Health: Health standards and practices are of high quality. Varied cultural health practices exist. Rice is the staple ingredient in the Singaporean diet, with fish providing the main protein source. Highly spiced food, typical of warm, humid regions, is common in Singapore. Life expectancy is high.

Education: Education is highly valued and available to all children from ages six to fourteen. English is the language of instruction in over 80 percent of the primary schools, and bilingualism is often emphasized. The literacy rate is over 85 percent.

Other Significant Data: Singapore is small, culturally diverse and wholly urban. There is a noticeable British influence. The average personal income is one of the highest in Southeast Asia. Industry is diversified; Singapore is a major center for trade and commerce. Over three-quarters of the population is Chinese, 15 percent of Malay descent, 7 percent Indian (including Sri Lankan).[47]

Brief Profile of Thailand

Family Structure: Thai families are large, extended, and multigenerational. Family life generally reflects an agricultural based existence, with the entire family working on the farm together.

Childrearing Practices: Children are valued and grow up in a warm, nurturing, structured environment. There is a strong sense of loyalty to the family.

Religion: The influence of Buddhism is pervasive; the people are over 95 percent Buddhist. There are many *wats* (Buddhist temples) and Buddhist monks have a revered status in Thai life. In the past, young men were expected to spend several months as Buddhist monks. There is a small, non-Buddhist population of Muslims, Confucianists, and Christians.

Values: The king and queen are highly respected and honored. Wealth and education are measures of success, whereas, in the past, religious and nationalistic attitudes were so considered. Virtue and unselfishness are important values. The Thai people are reserved but cheerful and content. A favorite Thai expression is *mai pen rai* (it doesn't matter). This expression typifies their outlook that life should be enjoyed: they have regard for a sense of humor, laughter, and a pleasant, smiling attitude. There is strong respect for law and order. The traditional Thai greeting is the *wai* (hands together in praying position at the chest with a slight bow). Shoes are removed before entering a Thai home or Buddhist temple.

Language: The Thai language has evolved from Indo-Chinese with an alphabet of Sanskrit origin. There are many regional dialects. Chinese and Malay are also spoken. English is the second language of the well educated.

Health: Modern health services are mostly limited to the urban centers although the availability is improving. The diet is well balanced and usually spicy. Rice is a staple food, with fish, fruits and vegetables, eggs, beef, chicken, and pork widely available. Forks, held in the left hand, and spoons, in the right, are used for eating; the fork is used to push food onto the spoon. Fingers, rather than utensils, are used in some areas to eat a steamed, sticky rice. Many people chew betel nuts, which blacken the teeth and color the lips red.

Education: Kindergarten (one–three years) and six years of elementary school are compulsory. Secondary education is available at private expense. The literacy rate is approximately 84 percent.

Other Significant Data: The official name for Thailand is *Muang Thai* (Land of the Free); Thais take great pride in the fact that theirs is the only country in Southeast Asia that has never been ruled by a European country. The population is over 85 percent rural and agricultural. About 75 percent of the people are ethnically Thai, originally descended from the Mongols of China.

Brief Profile of the Philippines

Family Structure: Filipino families are generally large, extended, patriarchal, and strongly bound by loyalty and tradition. Close family ties influence many aspects of Filipino life. Rules of descent, inheritance, and residence are bilateral and generational. The oldest child, regardless of sex, has special rank; decreasing status is accorded the next sibling, etc. While the father is the acknowledged head and primary provider, the mother (in addition to childrearing and household management) is the family spokesperson, family treasurer, and a full partner in the relationship. The status of equality of Filipino women is unparalleled in the Far East. For many families, life revolves around the small rural, agricultural communities known as *barrios*.[48]

Childrearing Practices: Children are considered a sign of God's blessing, the basis for a mystical feeling of continuity between generations, and a source of security in old age. Infants are raised in an atmosphere of great indulgence and affection by the family, relatives, and neighbors. Parents receive much support in childrearing responsibilities; the extended family often functions as surrogate parents. The Hispanic *compadre* (godparent) system exists in many Roman Catholic families. Childrearing is generally permissive and gentle. Discipline varies according to socioeconomic status; the desire to conform and to avoid shame or disgrace is a guiding principle. Obedience and dependency are fostered. Childrearing is one of the most important functions of the Filipino family and a variety of practices prevails:

> Filipino parents do not have any scientific methods in rearing children; much is left to chance, common sense, and the influences of customs, traditions, education, beliefs, myths, legends, folklore, and prevailing practices. Sometimes childrearing is done haphazardly, but whatever method is used abounds in love, politeness, and respect.[49]

Religion: The population is 85 percent Roman Catholic, a reflection of its Spanish heritage. It is the only Christian nation in Asia. The remaining population is Protestant, Muslim, or belongs to the Philippine Independent (Aglipayan) Church. Traditional folk beliefs and ancestor worship are practiced in rural and remote regions.

Values: Customs and values reflect the influence of a blend of Chinese, Malayan, Moslem, Spanish, and American cultures. Filipinos follow the Asian pattern of nonconfrontation and indirect communication in social interactions. Business transactions begin socially, respect and proper modes of address are necessary, and harmony is stressed over being right. As in Hispanic cultures, it is important to maintain one's *amor propio* (self-esteem) and to avoid *hiya* (feelings of shame). Other valued character traits are personal and family honor, sensitivity, loyalty, obligation, and interdependence. Innovation, change, and competition are resisted. A fatalistic attitude is common.

Language: There are many dialects (87) and languages spoken. Ilocano (in northern Luzon), Tagalog (in central and southern Luzon), and Cebuano (on the southern islands) are the major dialects. English is the primary language of education and of the educated, although Tagalog is often considered to be the national language. Many still speak Spanish. English is spoken by about 35 percent of the population, Tagalog by 23 percent. Tagalog is the basis of Pilipino, a linguistic amalgam which incorporates many Spanish and English words. There have been efforts to make Pilipino the national language.

Health: There is a good level of health care services in Manila and other urban centers, but folk medicine practices and lower standards of sanitation prevail in many outlying districts. Folk beliefs (e.g., that supernatural powers cause disease) are still prevalent; a child's disability may even be blamed on the parents' illicit sexual behavior. According to folk belief, "illness occurs when the balance of elements inside or outside the body is disturbed."[50] Protective rituals, prayers, and protective devices are common. Diet consists mainly of rice, fish, vegetables, and fruit.

Education: Education is highly valued in the Philippines and considered a key to upward mobility.[51] Elementary school education is free and compulsory; secondary education requires a small tuition fee. There are many private and parochial schools. The literacy rate is about 88 percent.

Other Significant Data: The Philippines are a nation of 7,107 islands. The economy is basically agricultural, yet almost half the population is now employed in industry. The culture is unique to its region, primarily due to its Spanish and Christian heritage.

Brief Profile of Vietnam

Family Structure: The family is one of three major Vietnamese institutions—the other two are the village and the state.[52] Families are large and cohesive, usually consisting of three or four generations. According to past tradition, a woman in Vietnam was taught to submit to her father as a girl, to her husband as a wife, and to her eldest son as a widow. As in most countries, the role of women has improved. Many changes in family structure are attributable to socioeconomic and political changes.

Childrearing Practices: Children are considered wealth—the more children in the family, the better the parents will be taken care of in old age. A Vietnamese usually has three names: the family name is first, the name indicating sex is second (*Van* for males, *Thi* for females), and the given name last. Nicknames are commonly used "to confuse the spirits."[53] Infants are usually indulged by the extended family; discipline begins at about three years of age. Obedience, socialization, and school readiness skills are instilled by the family. Vietnamese children are taught to control their emotions and to respect their elders. They are taught to be responsible for their own actions. Regardless of age, dependency on parents and dependency on other authority figures are stressed. Socialization and school readiness skills are considered important and are encouraged by parents.[54]

Religion: Vietnamese culture is influenced by Buddhism, Confucianism, and Taoism. Over half of the population practices Buddhism. Vietnam has the second largest population of Catholics in Southeast Asia outside of the Philippines; it is approximately 10 percent. About 12 percent practice Taoism and some ethnic minorities remain animists. Ancestor worship is prevalent; most homes have an altar for ancestor worship.

Values: The Vietnamese consider status to be more important than money. The manner of addressing people is very formal; titles are widely used. Children do not address adults by name without a title; they are therefore likely to call many unrelated people Aunt or Uncle. Vietnamese customs emphasize humility, modesty, and restraint.

Language: Because of the French heritage, the Vietnamese language is written in the Latin alphabet. As a result, Vietnamese can usually learn English faster than other Asians. Vietnamese is the official language; it is a tonal language and is spoken with distinct regional accents. English and French are also spoken, especially among the well educated.

Health: Health care is a family concern. Ill health, believed to be the result of disharmony with the universe, is considered preventable. The use of rituals, deity worship, sorcery, herbs, and folk medicine practices are common. Hospitalization (Western medicine) is shunned and, if unavoidable, a family member (usually the grandmother) is expected to accompany the patient to prepare traditional Vietnamese foods.[55] Diet plays a crucial role in health maintenance. Many Vietnamese mothers believe that illness can be cured by rubbing a coin repeatedly against the skin of the afflicted body part until lesions occur. This common folklore practice of *Cao Gio* has been observed in refugee families and has been misdiagnosed as child abuse.[56] Rice is the staple food of Vietnam. *Nuoc mam* (a fermented fish sauce) is the main seasoning used. Seafood, vegetables, and meat are widely available.

Education: Education has always been prized in Vietnam. Success in education is believed to bring honor to one's family. Education is free and begins at age five. University education, also free, is highly competitive. Over three-fourths of the population is literate.

Other Significant Data: Vietnam is primarily a rural, agricultural country; rice farming predominates. Almost 90 percent of the population is ethnic Vietnamese, a mixture of Mongolian and

Indonesian peoples. There are also Montagnards (mountain people), Chinese, Chams, Indians, Khmers, Malays, and Pakistanis. Many of these minority groups maintain their own language and culture.

Brief Profile of Cambodia

Family Structure: Family structure is extended and multigenerational. Respect for elders is stressed; ancestors are revered. Roles are defined according to sex: the father is the unquestioned head of the family and the wage earner; women are responsible for managing the home and raising the children. Families are generally large and will adopt or raise other children in need. A close parent-child relationship is fostered, even into adulthood. Most families live in small villages and work on family-owned rice paddies near the villages. Social stratification still persists; there is a small educated elite, a nominal middle class, and a large, uneducated, peasant population.[57]

The Pol Pot regime in the 1970s changed the family structure of many Cambodians: large numbers of men were killed; many women were widowed; many children were subsequently raised in single parent families. Those who came to the United States as "boat people" underwent additional changes in family structure; women with school-age children joined the work force, and single-earner households became multiple-job households.[58]

Childrearing Practices: Children are treated with great affection but are not indulged. Early self-sufficiency is encouraged. Socialization is taught by example and is largely within the extended family. Childrearing practices reinforce traditional roles and expectations according to gender, socioeconomic level, and educational status. Children are raised to be restrained in their gestures and quiet in their speech. Strict discipline is rare.

Religion: Most Cambodians are Theravada Buddhists. A small Cham minority practices Islam. The Angkor *Wat* (temple), built eight centuries ago, is the largest religious building in the world and is the national symbol. Other places of worship are called *pagodas*.

Values: The family is of paramount value. Saving face is a crucial concept in interpersonal relations. Many cultural values are expressed through nonverbal communication: It is considered inappropriate to touch strangers; to make eye contact with strangers; to wave or point; to express emotion openly (e.g., anger, affection); to be argumentative or rude; or for women to shake hands. Like many other Asians, Cambodians consider the head to be sacred (it is disrespectful to touch another's head, especially that of a child), feel shame for needing help, and are reluctant to discuss personal problems outside the family.[59] It is proper to remove one's shoes before entering a Cambodian home or place of worship. Many rules of social interaction derive from Indian and Buddhist traditions. Individual privacy and rights are considered secondary to the good of the community. Shyness and discretion are valued. *Báng* (the privileged position of a senior over a junior), is a basic tenet of social dealings.

Language: The Cambodian (Khmer) language has its own alphabet which is derived from *paali* (a successor to Indian Sanskrit). There are similarities to Thai and Laotian. The use of French and English is limited to urban areas.

Health: Sanitation is poor. The availability of health care is improving. The infant mortality rate is high and life expectancy is less than fifty years. Rice is the staple food; soup and rice are basic dishes; fruits, vegetables, and fish are also widely used. Spoons and chopsticks are used; some foods are eaten with the fingers. Khmer food is less spicy than other cuisines of Southeast Asia.

Education: The educational system, destroyed under Pol Pot, is currently being rebuilt. Literacy is under 50 percent and is largely concentrated in the capital region. Many schools are run by Buddhist monks.

Other Significant Data: The name Kampuchea (as Cambodians call their country) is derived from the Kingdom of Kambuja, an ancient empire of Indian settlers. The region has been, at varying times in history, under the control of the French, the Japanese, the Khmer Rouge, and Vietnam. The economy is primarily based on agriculture. The population is approximately 70 percent ethnic Khmer, 10 percent Sino-Khmer (mixed Chinese and Khmer), 5 percent Chams (descendants of the Champa Kingdom), along with some Chinese and Vietnamese.

Brief Profile of Laos

Family Structure: Laotian families are large, close-knit, and extended, with several generations living together. The eldest male is the family patriarch. Age is revered and children have great respect for parents and other elders. Laotian family structure is similar to that of neighboring Cambodia.

The Hmong are a subculture of Laotians who live in small, scattered villages in the northern mountains. They are a fiercely independent people with a unique culture of their own (see pp. 95–96). They are believed to have lived originally in China. There are also Hmong villages in China and other Southeast Asian countries. A number of Hmong refugees (more than 50,000) emigrated from Laos to the United States. The Hmong believe that the larger the family, the better and more secure it is. The typical Hmong family is an extended family. Home and family are the basis of Hmong life-style. Polygamy had been dying out but increased following the recent war because of a shortage of men. The male is the family head; females join the household and clan of the husband when married.[60]

Childrearing Practices: Childrearing practices are similar to those in Cambodia. Traditional folk beliefs and practices are followed by those families who practice animism. Children are raised to be dependent, nonaggressive, and to honor their elders. Hmong children are named at a birthday celebration at three days of age.

Religion: Most Laotians are Hinayana Buddhists and the *wat* is the center of village activities. Animism, which emphasizes a reverence for all living things, is practiced to varying degrees by the Hmong.

Values: Buddhist principles and family loyalty are highly valued. Courtesy, respect, and saving face are important values. The expression *bo pen nyang* (never mind) is characteristic of the Laotian attitude towards life. Laotians and Hmong are generally optimistic people.

Language: The official language is Lao, which is similar to the Thai language. Some French and English is spoken. The Hmong speak Hmong, not Lao.

Education: Education is provided free for eleven years, although rural children are less likely to remain in school till age seventeen, the official age for ending school. Almost all Laotian youth are literate, but adult literacy is approximately 85 percent. Literacy among the Hmong is quite low as theirs is not a written language.

Health: Health facilities are limited and standards are generally poor according to Western ideas. Traditional folk medicine prevails. Infectious diseases, malnutrition, and caries are common. Infant mortality is high and life expectancy is about 50 years. The diet is primarily based on rice. Fish, eggs, chicken, and pork are also widely used.

Other Significant Data: The economy is based on agriculture. Many of the country's resources are undeveloped. Laos is one of the poorest countries in the world; unemployment and inflation are both high. It is one of the most ethnically diverse countries in Asia.

The reader is reminded that the overview of Asian cultures presented in this chapter is based on *traditional* traits and practices. Not only are these traditions subject to modification by immigration, education, and societal changes, but they exist in varying degrees and combinations. They are not presented to foster stereotypes but rather to alert the reader to characteristics they might *possibly* encounter and, if encountered, to provide a rationale for their existence.

The "general characteristics" of Asian cultures presented should assist the reader in understanding more of the *how* and *why* of the cultural variances in appreciating the nuances of the Asian philosophy of life. The "brief profiles" represent a composite of interdisciplinary literature on the unique heritage and present environment of each country. Emphasis is on family structure, childrearing practices, and societal values.

A family systems perspective is helpful in viewing Asian cultures: the interaction between family and community is intense and has a profound effect upon the developing child. The impact of Asian religion/philosophy is pervasive; it is an overriding factor in the prevailing mores. Loyalty to family, the priority of group welfare over individual need, dependency over independence, and harmony with nature are predominant themes. These are basic tenets of Asian cultures. Inter- and intragroup variability continue to evolve. The reasons are multifold: differences in geography and history; socioeconomic factors; political climate; increased interaction with other cultures; and other changes in life-style over generations. Clearly, to understand a child from an Asian culture, one has to first understand Asian cultures in general, the child's particular cultural heritage, and the child's unique family as a part of that culture.

NOTES

1. U.S. Census Bureau, 1980.
2. Jean E. Carlin, "The Catastrophically Uprooted Child: Southeast Asian Refugee Children," *Basic Handbook of Child Psychiatry*, J.P. Noshpitz and I.N. Berlin, eds., Vol. I: *Normal Development*. (New York: Basic Books, 1979), p. 294.
3. Steven P. Shon and Davis Y. Ja, "Asian Families," *Ethnicity and Family Therapy*, M. McGoldrick, J.K. Pearce, and J. Giordano, eds. (New York: Guilford, 1982), pp. 213–215.
4. Ibid., pp. 216–217, 226.
5. Elizabeth Randall-David, *Strategies for Working with Culturally Diverse Communities and Clients* (Washington, D.C.: Association for the Care of Children's Health, 1989), p. 42.
6. Shon and Ja, "Asian Families," *Ethnicity and Family Therapy*, pp. 212–213.
7. Randall-David, *Strategies for Working with Culturally Diverse Communities and Clients*, p. 45.
8. Walter A. Fairservis, Jr., *Asia: Traditions and Treasures* (New York: Harry N. Abrams, 1981), p. 207.
9. Ibid., p. 238.
10. Ibid., pp. 235–236.
11. Carlin, "Southeast Asian Refugee Children," *Basic Handbook of Child Psychiatry*, p. 293.
12. M. Cole, J. Gay, J. Glick, and D. Sharp, *The Cultural Context of Learning and Thinking: An Explanation in Experimental Anthropology* (New York: Basic Books, 1971).
13. United States Department of Agriculture/Department of Health and Human Services, *Cross-Cultural Counseling: A Guide for Nutrition and Health Counselors*, FNS–240 (Washington, D.C.: U.S. Government Printing Office, 1986), p. 27.
14. Ibid.
15. Carlin, "Southeast Asian Refugee Children," *Basic Handbook of Child Psychiatry*, p. 292.
16. Penny P. Anderson and Emily Schrag Fenichel, *Serving Culturally Diverse Families of Infants and Toddlers with Disabilities* (Washington, D.C.: National Center for Clinical Infant Programs, 1989), p. 11.
17. Aimee Emiko Sodetani-Shibata, "The Japanese American," *Culture and Childrearing*, A.L. Clark, ed. (Philadelphia: F.A. Davis, 1981), pp. 112–116.
18. Ruth Benedict, *The Chrysanthemum and the Sword: Patterns of Japanese Culture* (Boston: Houghton Mifflin, 1946).

19. Sodetani-Shibata, "The Japanese American," *Culture and Childrearing,* pp. 116–130.

20. Takeo L. Doi, *The Anatomy of Dependence* (New York: Harper and Row, 1973).

21. Fairservis, *Asia: Traditions and Treasures,* pp. 202–203.

22. Sodetani-Shibata, "The Japanese American," *Culture and Childrearing,* pp. 103–107.

23. Chie Nakane, *Japanese Society* (Berkeley, Calif.: McCutchan, 1970).

24. Fairservis, *Asia: Traditions and Treasures,* p., 206.

25. Evelyn L. Char, "The Chinese American," *Culture and Childrearing,* A.L. Clark, ed. (Philadelphia: F.A. Davis, 1981), pp. 144–147.

26. Ann-ping Chin, *Children of China: Voices from Recent Years* (New York: Knopf, 1988), p. 288.

27. Noboru Kobayashi and T. Berry Brazelton, eds. *The Growing Child in Family and Society: An Interdisciplinary Study in Parent-Infant Bonding* (Tokyo: University of Tokyo Press, 1984), p. 116.

28. Chin, *Children of China: Voices from Recent Years,* p. 304.

29. Char, "The Chinese American," *Culture and Childrearing,* p. 160.

30. Ibid., pp. 152–155.

31. Kobayashi and Brazelton, *The Growing Child in Family and Society: An Interdisciplinary Study in Parent-Infant Bonding,* p. 118.

32. Char, "The Chinese American," *Culture and Childrearing,* p. 155.

33. Evelyn Lee, "A Social Systems Approach to Assessment and Treatment for Chinese American Families," *Ethnicity and Family Therapy,* M. McGoldrick, J.K. Pearce, and J. Giordano, eds. (New York: Guilford, 1982), pp. 527–551.

34. Fairservis, *Asia: Traditions and Treasures,* p. 153.

35. Lima Ohsawa, *Macrobiotic Cuisine* (Tokyo: Japan Publications, 1984).

36. *Britannica World Data: Book of the Year 1986,* s.v. "Taiwan," p. 789.

37. Mei-Yuan (Wang) Lin, "Overview of Health and Services in Taiwan, ROC," *Image: The Journal of Nursing Scholarship* 16 (Fall 1984): 101–104.

38. Sung-hsing Wang, "Child Rearing and Training in Hong Kong Chinese Society," *The Growing Child in Family and Society,* N. Kobayashi and T.B. Brazelton, eds. (Tokyo: University of Tokyo Press, 1984), pp. 113–122.

39. Ibid., p. 119.

40. *A Handbook of Korea,* 3rd ed. (Seoul: Korean Overseas Information Service Ministry of Culture and Information, 1979), p. 335.

41. Stephanie Bernardo, *The Ethnic Almanac* (Garden City, N.Y.: Dolphin, 1981), p. 249.

42. Marian McNeil, "Korean Culture and Its Impact on Health Care," (Graduate thesis, University of North Carolina, 1984), p. 3.

43. Ibid., p. 3.

44. Susie Kim, "The Role of Women in Health Care in Korea's Social Transition," *Image: The Journal of Nursing Scholarship* 16 (Fall 1984): 99–101.

45. John A. Axelson, *Counseling and Development in a Multicultural Society* (Monterey, Calif.: Brooks/Cole, 1985), p. 105.

46. *Britannica World Data: Book of the Year 1986*, s.v. "Singapore."

47. Ibid.

48. Consuelo J. Aquino, "The Filipino in America," *Culture and Childrearing*, A.L. Clark, ed. (Philadelphia: F.A. Davis, 1981), pp. 171–180.

49. Ibid., p. 173.

50. Ibid., p. 181.

51. Ibid., p. 181.

52. Lorraine Stringfellow, Nguyen Dang Liem, and Linda Diep Liem, "The Vietnamese in America," *Culture and Childrearing*, A.L. Clark, ed. (Philadelphia: F.A. Davis, 1981), p. 233.

53. Ibid., p. 234.

54. Ibid., p. 236.

55. Ibid., p. 234.

56. G.W. Yeatman et al., "Pseudobattering in Vietnamese Children," *Pediatrics* 58 (1976): 616–618.

57. Rita Bayer Leyn, "The Challenge of Caring for Child Refugees from Southeast Asia," *MCN, The American Journal of Maternal/Child Nursing* 3 (May/June 1978): 178–182.

58. Nathan Caplan, *The Boat People and Achievement in America* (Ann Arbor, Mich.: University of Michigan Press, 1989).

59. Randall-David, *Strategies for Working with Culturally Diverse Communities and Clients*, pp. 42–43.

60. Elizabeth Bjorkman La Du, "Childbirth Care for Hmong Families," *MCN, The American Journal of Maternal/Child Nursing* 10 (November/December 1985): 382–385.

BIBLIOGRAPHY

Anderson, Penny P., and Emily Schrag Fenichel. *Serving Culturally Diverse Families of Infants and Toddlers with Disabilities.* Washington, D.C.: National Center for Clinical Infant Programs, 1989.

Presents examples of family and childrearing tendencies, illness and disability beliefs and practices, and examples of communication styles of Asian American families. Lists references, recommended readings, and resource programs.

Aquino, Consuelo J. "The Filipino in America." *Culture and Childrearing.* A.L. Clark, ed. Philadelphia: F.A. Davis, 1981, pp. 166–190.

Describes the island nation, its people, life in the *barrios* (small communities), and the structure of the Filipino family. Explores the customs and traditions of childrearing, developmental stages in family life, the educational system, and superstitious beliefs in health and disease.

Axelson, John A. *Counseling and Development in a Multicultural Society.* Monterey, Calif.: Brooks/Cole, 1985.

Profiles Asian Americans in terms of immigration history and patterns, diversity in ancestry, language, customs, religious beliefs, and life-styles. Provides a chart depicting key points of the major Eastern religions. Differentiates among the religions, languages, and class structures of South Asia, Southeast Asia, and East Asia. Explores the family processes and socialization patterns of Chinese Americans, Japanese Americans, Korean Americans, Filipino Americans, and Indochinese Americans.

Brigham Young University David M. Kennedy Center for International Studies. *CULTURGRAMS.* Provo, Utah: Brigham Young University Publication Services, 1990.

A series of brief pamphlets, updated yearly, which succinctly present information on "Customs and Courtesies," "The People," "Lifestyle," and "The Nation" of over 100 countries. *CULTURGRAMS* are available for North and South Korea, Taiwan, China, the Philippines, Hong Kong, Japan, Singapore, Thailand, Cambodia, Laos, and Vietnam.

Bransford, Louis A., Leonard Baca, and Karen Lane, eds. *Cultural Diversity and the Exceptional Child.* Reston, Va.: Council for Exceptional Children, 1974.

Presents the highlights of an institute on the language and culture of Asian, Black, Indian, and Spanish-speaking children. Discusses the diversity of language, family interaction, and value systems of these cultures and how these factors affect learning. Authors stress the need to understand a language as a prerequisite to understanding a culture.

Caplan, Nathan. *The Boat People and Achievement in America*. Ann Arbor: University of Michigan Press, 1989.

Chronicles the exodus of refugees from Indochina and their resettlement to life in other countries. Focuses on their adjustment to a new culture, the employment patterns of the adults, and the academic progress of their children.

Carlin, Jean E. "The Catastrophically Uprooted Child: Southeast Asian Refugee Children." *Basic Handbook of Child Psychiatry*. J.P. Noshpitz and I.N. Berlin, eds. Vol. I: *Normal Development*. New York: Basic Books, 1979, pp. 290–300.

Details the unique adjustment problems of refugee children from Vietnam, Cambodia, and Laos. Explores their health problems, misleading age calculation (and ramifications), language problems, aptitude in math and languages, and differences in cultural values. Suggests needed social structures to aid in the adjustments faced by these children and their families. Two case histories are presented to illustrate the characteristics of these children. References included.

Char, Evelyn L. "The Chinese American." *Culture and Childrearing*. A.L. Clark, ed. Philadelphia: F.A. Davis, 1981, pp. 140–164.

Reviews the history of the Chinese in America, explains the Chinese concept of familism, characteristics of traditional Chinese families, childrearing practices, cultural beliefs and practices, and health care. Extensive bibliography.

Chin, Ann-ping. *Children of China: Voices from Recent Years*. New York: Knopf, 1988.

Provides a rich understanding of childhood experiences in contemporary China based on interviews with hundreds of Chinese children ages six to sixteen. The author is an educator who was born in Taiwan to mainland Chinese parents. Presents the traditions and themes of social philosophy in China with sensitivity and understanding. Provides a detailed examination of the Chinese life style and educational system.

Chin, Jean Lau. "Diagnostic Considerations in Working with Asian-Americans." *American Journal of Orthopsychiatry* 53 (January 1983): 100–109.

Discusses Asian American cultural views and values. Provides specific examples of traditional Asian learning styles, educational practices, linguistic structure, and childrearing goals that need to be considered in the assessment of intellectual and personality functioning. Extensive references.

Cole, M., et al. *The Cultural Context of Learning and Thinking: An Explanation in Experimental Anthropology.* New York: Basic Books, 1971.

Authors contend that educators must determine the conditions under which various cognitive processes are manifested and develop techniques for seeing that these conditions occur in the appropriate educational setting. The learning styles of Asian cultures are characterized as formalistic, unspontaneous, and relatively uncommunicative.

Doi, L. Takeo. *The Anatomy of Dependence.* New York: Harper and Row, 1973.

Explains the concept of *amae*, which is important in understanding the basic dependency of the Japanese. Amae means the need to be loved and cherished, the manner of asking for love, and seeking recognition and acceptance. Doi states that *amae* can have serious behavioral consequences such as *ko da wa ru* (to be inwardly disturbed over one's personal relationship) or *sumanai* (to feel guilty or obligated).

Dung, Trinh Ngoc. "Understanding Asian Families: A Vietnamese Perspective." *Children Today* 13 (March-April 1984): 10–12.

Offers insights into the value systems of Vietnamese families, family relations, and childrearing practices. Discusses the cultural differences to be bridged in integrating Vietnamese children into mainstream American society. Author is a program specialist with the Office of Refugee Resettlement, Social Security Administration, U.S. Department of Health and Human Services.

Fairservis, Walter A., Jr. *Asia: Traditions and Treasures.* New York: Harry N. Abrams, 1981.

Describes the art, the history, and the traditions of the Asian continent. Published in collaboration with the American Museum of Natural History, this book is richly illustrated. Each aspect of Asian history and culture is explained in detail.

Fersh, Seymour, ed. *Learning About Peoples and Cultures.* Evanston, Ill.: McDougal, Littell, 1974.

Offers suggestions for learning about peoples and cultures, such as discerning the inter-relationships between language and culture. Discusses the importance of names and formalities in East Asian cultures. Examples are included which clearly illustrate traditional Asian communication style.

Gardner, Howard. *To Open Minds: Chinese Clues to the Dilemma of Contemporary Education.* New York: Basic Books, 1989.

Compares observations of Chinese and American education protocols with inferences concerning the differential abilities and characteristics of children in these cultures. Also draws upon his family's own experiences living in China, showing how differently Americans and Chinese treat a child trying to solve a problem such as placing a key in a lock.

Gibbs, Jewelle Taylor, Larke Nahme Huang, and Associates. *Children of Color: Psychological Intervention with Minority Youth.* San Francisco: Jossey-Bass, 1989.

Provides guidelines for understanding, recognizing, and successfully treating the psychological and behavioral problems of minority children and adolescents. Provides insight into the impact on children of Asian heritage of such cultural issues as the emphasis on education and family obligation, and high family expectations.

Grosso, Camille, et al. "The Vietnamese American Family . . . And Grandma Makes Three." *MCN, The American Journal of Maternal/Child Nursing* 6 (May/June 1981): 177–180.

Describes the modifications made by one hospital to accommodate the cultural and health care needs of a Vietnamese family. Explains the Vietnamese tradition of health and illness being a concern to the total family unit, the customs of Vietnamese child care, and the importance of traditional foods to the healing process.

A Handbook of Korea. 3rd ed. Seoul: Korean Overseas Information Service Ministry of Culture and Information, 1979.

The chapter on "Customs and Folkways" presents a comprehensive overview of the traditions in the Korean life cycle such as marriage, childbirth and childhood, family life, holidays, and death.

Haring, Douglas G. *Personal Character and Cultural Milieu.* 3rd rev. ed. Syracuse, N.Y.: Syracuse University Press, 1956.

Discusses the cultural characteristics of the Japanese personality such as family obligation, conformity, and formality. Relates how these characteristics are developed during childhood and how they influence relationships in Japan and abroad.

Hoang, G.N., and R.V. Erickson. "Cultural Barriers to Effective Medical Care Among Indochinese Patients." *Annual Review of Medicine* 36 (1985): 229–239.

Reviews the history of recent Indochinese immigration, cultural traits, religious beliefs, and health care practices. Advocates an understanding of the Indochinese culture as a means to remove cultural barriers between patient and provider.

Huff, C. Ronald. *Gangs in America: Diffusion, Diversity, and Public Policy.* Newbury Park, Calif.: Sage, 1990.

Addresses the issue of youth gangs among Vietnamese and Chinese communities—causes, characteristics, cultural and historical perspectives, connection with drugs and violence, and strategies for controlling the problem.

Khoa, L.X., et al. "Southeast Asian Social and Cultural Customs: Similarities and Differences." *Journal of Refugee Resettlement* 1 (1981): 27–47.

Presents a comparative chart providing differences in beliefs, practices, and experiences of the Vietnamese, Cambodians, Hmong, and Laotians. Focuses on topics such as the individual, the family and group, and neighborhoods.

Kim, Susie. "The Role of Women in Health Care in Korea's Social Transition." *Image, The Journal of Nursing Scholarship* 16 (Fall 1984): 99–101.

Article briefly describes the status and role of women in the traditional Korean society as a way to help understand the cultural backgrounds from which today's Korean women have emerged. It also discusses the role of women in health care today. Author is a Korean nurse educator.

Kobayashi, Noboru, and T. Berry Brazelton, eds. *The Growing Child in Family and Society: An Interdisciplinary Study in Parent-Infant Bonding.* Tokyo: University of Tokyo Press, 1984.

This book is based on a 1982 workshop that drew upon expertise in the ethology, anthropology, sociology, and pediatrics of childrearing. Discusses such cultural variations as nuclear versus extended families, dependency versus independence, socialization, discipline, and disease theories (medical versus spirits/magic). Discusses childrearing philosophies and practices in the Philippines, in Hong Kong, in China, and in Japan. Extensive reference list.

Kumabe, Kazuye, Chikae Nishida, and Dean H. Hepworth. *Bridging Ethnocultural Diversity in Social Work and Health.* Honolulu: University of Hawaii School of Social Work, 1985.

Presents a case study of a Filipino family in Chapter Seven that highlights traditional and changing attitudes about illness and disability, childrearing practices, and the family unit.

La Du, Elizabeth Bjorkman. "Childbirth Care for Hmong Families." *MCN, The American Journal of Maternal/Child Nursing* 10 (November/December 1985): 382–385.

Provides an overview of the traditional life-style and health care practices and beliefs of this Laotian subculture. Suggests ways to deliver health care services to clients from other cultures, based on an understanding of their unique beliefs and practices.

Lawson, Lauren Valk. "Culturally Sensitive Support for Grieving Parents." *MCN, The American Journal of Maternal/Child Nursing* 15 (March/April 1990): 76–79.

Describes the traditional practices of Southeast Asians regarding family life, religion and healing, and death and grief. Cautions that the term "Southeast Asian" includes people of many nations, ethnic groups, and religions, each speaking any of about 20 languages.

Lee, Evelyn. "A Social Systems Approach to Assessment and Treatment for Chinese American Families." *Ethnicity and Family Therapy.* M. McGoldrick, J.K. Pearce, and J. Giordano, eds. New York: Guilford, 1982.

Presents practical guidelines for assessing and intervening with Chinese American families. Lee states that working with Chinese families requires an integration of social, psychological, physical, and cultural phenomena into a holistic view of health, well-being, and life satisfaction. Stresses the need to understand the psychological significance and centrality of the Chinese family.

Lee, Shu-Ching. "China's Traditional Family, Its Characteristics and Disintegration." *American Sociological Review* 18 (June 1953): 272–280.

Explains how religious life in China is woven into the fabric of family organization. States that religion in China is essentially animistic and does not lend itself to church or sect organization. Contends that religious expression is carried out in the context of ancestor worship, practiced in the home and in ancestral temples.

Leyn, Rita Bayer. "The Challenge of Caring for Child Refugees from Southeast Asia." *MCN, The American Journal of Maternal/Child Nursing* 3 (May/June 1978): 178–182.

Describes various Laotian and Cambodian customs, such as religious and folk beliefs, diet, family relationships, and health care practices. Suggests ways of facilitating communication and understanding through the use of gestures, drawings, and, above all, respect for cultural traditions.

McLeod, Beverly. "The Oriental Express." *Psychology Today,* July 1986, pp. 48–52.

Examines the perception of Asian American immigrants as a "model minority on a fast track to success." States that some Asian Americans—both immigrants and native-born—are occupationally restricted, overqualified, underpaid, and underpromoted. Believes that the "model minority" stereotype tends to obscure the fact that there are many poor, uneducated, and unsuccessful Asian immigrants.

Mindel, Charles H., and Habenstein, Robert W., eds. *Ethnic Families in America: Patterns and Variations.* New York: Elsevier Scientific, 1976.

Examines the structure and function of families of Chinese and Japanese origin who have immigrated to the United States. Describes the unusual problems faced by the Japanese because of their color, their culture, and the fact that they came from "an enemy nation." Explains the Chinese ideal of familism, their lack of public display of affection, and their educational aspirations.

Morris, Lee, ed. *Extracting Learning Styles from Social/Cultural Diversity: Studies of Five American Minorities.* Norman: University of Oklahoma Press, 1986.

Explores the social and cultural heritage of Chinese Americans and how this affects their cognitive, affective, and psychomotor learning.

Nakame, Chie. *Japanese Society*. Berkeley, Calif.: McCutchan, 1970.

Describes the personality characteristics that are traditional to Japanese society. Explains how these characteristics vary among the Issei, the Nisei, and the Sansei generations.

National Coalition of Advocates for Students. *New Voices: Immigrant Students in U.S. Public Schools*. Boston: National Coalition of Advocates for Students, 1988.

Provides firsthand comments from immigrant children and their parents regarding adjustment to a new culture and its educational system. Poignantly highlights cultural differences in learning styles, childrearing practices, communication styles, and educational expectations. Addresses the unique problems of children from Cambodia, Laos, and Vietnam.

National Institute of Mental Health. *An Annotated Bibliography on Refugee Mental Health*. DHHS Publication No. (ADM) 87–1517. Washington, D.C.: U.S. Government Printing Office, 1987.

An extensive collection of reference literature on understanding refugees, specific mental health issues, and concerns of selected subgroups (e.g., children, families). Includes a list of the sources utilized in a computer search of the literature, other bibliographies, a refugee/ethnic group index, and an author and a subject index.

National Institute of Mental Health. *Handbook of Asian American/Pacific Islander Mental Health*. Vol. 1, DHHS Publication No. (ADM) 80–754. Washington, D.C.: U.S. Government Printing Office, 1980.

An annotated bibliography of mental health issues relevant to the populations profiled in this chapter. Includes topics such as Academic Performance and Education, Assimilation, Family Structure, and Generational Differences. References are indexed by subject and author.

Olmstead, Patricia P., and David P. Weikart, eds. *How Nations Serve Young Children: Profiles of Child Care and Education in 14 Countries*. Ypsilanti, Mich.: High/Scope Press, 1989.

Contains national profiles of early childhood care and education in Hong Kong, the People's Republic of China, the Philippines, and Thailand.

Queen, Stuart, and Robert W. Habenstein. *The Family in Various Cultures*. 4th ed. Philadelphia: Lippincott, 1974.

Reviews various types of family structures throughout history. Describes the classic Chinese family system as "familism," based on filial piety, obedience, and ancestor worship. States that these traditions minimize juvenile delinquency in China.

Randall-David, Elizabeth. *Strategies for Working with Culturally Diverse Communities and Clients.* Washington, D.C.: Association for the Care of Children's Health, 1989.

Outlines the cultural values and behaviors represented by the many variations of Americans of Asian heritage. Describes three modes of adaption to American society: old-line, assimilative, and bicultural. Offers suggestions for clinical application of information. Appendices contain many resources.

Shon, Stephen P., and Davis Y. Ja. "Asian Families." *Ethnicity and Family Therapy.* M. McGoldrick, J.K. Pierce, and J. Giordano, eds. New York: Guilford, 1982, pp. 208–228.

Explores the unique cultural distinctiveness of the peoples of East Asia: the Chinese, Japanese, and Koreans. Discusses the philosophical approaches to life dictated by Confucianism and Buddhism and the traditional Asian family structure and relationships. Also examines the language, historic, social, and economic distinctions between each group. Stresses that social class, geographical origin, birthplace, and generation in the United States must be considered in assessing each family's cultural identity.

Sodetani-Shibata, Aimee Emiko. "The Japanese American." *Culture and Childrearing.* A.L. Clark, ed. Philadelphia: F.A. Davis, 1981, pp. 96–138.

Identifies some of the childrearing practices among Japanese Americans. Includes a historical review of Japanese culture, traditional behavior, family life, and changes over time.

Stern, Phyllis Noerager. "Solving Problems of Cross-Cultural Health Teaching: The Filipino Childbearing Family." *Image, The Journal of Nursing Scholarship* 13 (June 1981): 47–50.

Provides a comprehensive background for understanding Filipino health care beliefs. Examines Filipino history, general cultural beliefs and customs, and communication style. Highlights the need to consider the origin and significance of cultural traditions when delivering health care to people of other cultures.

Stringfellow, Lorraine, Nguyen Dang Liem, and Linda Diep Liem, "The Vietnamese in America." *Culture and Childrearing.* A.L. Clark, ed. Philadelphia: F.A. Davis, 1981, pp. 228–241.

Provides a brief description of the history and traditional life of the Vietnamese in order to understand the special needs of Vietnamese refugees in adjusting to life in the United States. Describes childrearing practices and proposes guidelines for health care professionals providing services to Vietnamese patients.

Sue, Derald W. *Counseling the Culturally Different: Theory and Practice.* New York: Wiley, 1980.

Focuses on the values, customs, and belief systems of Asian Americans.

Takaki, Ronald. *Strangers from a Different Shore: A History of Asian Americans.* Boston: Little, Brown, 1989.

Examines the diversity and social history of Asians who have immigrated to the United States: Japanese, Chinese, Koreans, Filipinos, Indians, Vietnamese, Cambodians, and Laotians. Includes many photographs.

Thomasma, E.R., and L. Lee. *Cultural Backgrounds of the Indochinese People.* Knoxville, Tenn.: University of Tennessee Mental Health Center, 1980.

Provides an overview of Cambodian, Hmong, Laotian, and Vietnamese cultures. Highlights the diversity among the various Indochinese subgroups. Reviews each ethnic group's historical background, religion, family, social structure, economy, and character traits.

Tobin, Joseph J., David Y. H. Wu, and Dana H. Davidson. "How Three Countries Shape Their Children." *World Monitor*, April 1989, pp. 36–45.

Compares the societal structure and cultural expectations for preschool education in China, Japan, and the United States. This article is adapted from a forthcoming book, *Preschool in Three Cultures*, published by Yale University Press.

Tong, Benjamin R. "Warriors and Victims: Chinese American Sensibility and Learning Styles." *Extracting Learning Styles from Social/Cultural Diversity,* L. Morris, ed. Norman: University of Oklahoma Press, 1986, pp. 70–93.

Suggests a three-dimensional view for better understanding the Chinese American mind. Examines how Chinese values have been transformed because of immigration to the United States. Distinguishes two learning styles that have emerged—heterodox (warrior) and orthodox (victim).

Tsui, Ming. "Changes in Chinese Urban Family Structure." *Journal of Marriage and the Family* 51 (August 1989): 737–747.

Examines changes in family structure in contemporary China. Suggests that although changes in value and consumption patterns will eventually make the nuclear family the dominant pattern, a rapid decrease in the "stem" family is not likely because of traditional, social, political, and economic factors. A "stem" family consists of parents, unmarried children, and one married child with a spouse and child; it is between a nuclear and extended family in structure.

United States Department of Agriculture/Department of Health and Human Services. *Cross-Cultural Counseling: A Guide for Nutrition and Health Counselors.* FNS–250. Washington, D.C.: U.S. Government Printing Office, 1986.

Reviews relevant sociocultural issues concerning Asian and Pacific Americans such as distinctions between subgroups, family relationships, medical beliefs and practices, and dietary practices.

HISPANIC AMERICAN CULTURES

The term "Hispanic" is a word of English origin; an adjective to describe that which is Spanish or Latin American. When used as a generic title, Hispanic includes all people of Spanish origin and descent. Hispanic ancestry traces back to the sixteenth century when the Spanish *conquistadores* brought their language, values, and religious traditions to Mexico, Florida, and to the region that is now the southwestern United States. They intermarried with the Native Americans in Mexico, creating a new culture of mixed European Indians (or Spanish Indian). Their offspring became known as *mestizos*, representing a blend of European Spanish and New World Indians in the Americas. The Spaniards and *mestizos* who settled in northern New Mexico, isolated from Mexico and Spain, became known as *Hispanos* or Spanish Americans. In the ensuing centuries, additional blending of the culture occurred in Puerto Rico and Cuba with slaves from West Africa. The Spanish culture further blended with the native culture of Central America, South America, and the Philippines.[1]

Today the term Hispanic has become a catch-all label for anyone from Mexico, Central and South America, with a Spanish surname, or whose native tongue is Spanish. The term "Latino" is of Spanish origin and is often preferred by members of Hispanic subcultures. The various Hispanic American cultures are not homogeneous; they share a partial heritage and language while maintaining their own unique cultural identity. The nature and characteristics of the various Hispanic American subgroups are largely determined by the *balance* between the European Spanish traditions and values and those of the native cultures.[2] An important difference between Puerto Ricans and Mexicans, for example, can be traced to such a balance:

> In Puerto Rico, the indigenous Indians were virtually eradicated by the Spaniards, who replaced them with Negro slaves. In Mexico, Indian populations fared somewhat better; they had achieved a high degree of civilization and

were subjugated by the Spaniards, but not altogether eliminated. Thus the Mexican-American carries with him an ethnic and cultural background which is at once a blend of the Indian and the Spaniard.[3]

Currently, Hispanic American groups constitute 19.4 million, or 8.1 percent of the population in the United States. Of this number, 62.3 percent are Mexican; 12.7 percent Puerto Rican; 11.5 percent Central and South American; 5.3 percent Cuban; and 8.1 percent "Other." These figures include estimates of illegal aliens.[4] This chapter will examine the cultures of Mexico, Puerto Rico, Cuba, Central and South America. Traditional traits which are shared by these cultures are presented first; they provide a general frame of reference for understanding Hispanic American children and their families. Following the generalizations, a "profile" of each country or region is given, focusing on the distinctly unique features of that particular subgroup and its homeland.

The reader is cautioned that both the generalized and the more specific similarities and differences are merely guidelines for understanding behavior within a cultural context. To discern the uniqueness of a specific child and his family, it is essential to consider these cultural traits in conjunction with the assessment guidelines set forth in Chapter IV. Traditional characteristics are rapidly diminishing or changing, especially as a result of migration. Many of these traditions exist today only among the poor and the uneducated. Still, it is important to consider their origin and to be aware of their lingering influence.

In comparison to the Asian cultures examined in the previous chapter, there appear to be more similarities between the Hispanic American cultures than between the Asian cultures. This similitude can be traced to their common Iberian heritage and influence of the Roman Catholic religion. The diversity originates from the indigenous culture in each country, the geography, the social experiences, the political history, and the resulting economy.

Characteristics Generally Found in Hispanic American Families

The extended family concept is the foundation of the Hispanic family. The primacy of family—and of relationships in general—is reflected in the following values:

Mutualism: Sharing and cooperation, rather than competition, are stressed. A sense of shared responsibility within the group, especially the extended family, is fostered.

Interpersonal Relationships: There is a significant emphasis on dignity, trust, respect, and individual pride. A man's honor—and that of his family—is paramount. Great care is taken to avoid offending others. The privacy of others (especially non-family) is respected. Sincerity is very important.

Modesty: Modesty is important for both sexes: they prefer to be examined by a physician of their own sex and even then to be properly draped. They are reluctant to discuss personal or sexual problems.[5]

Time Orientation: Time orientation is to the present. This is often misinterpreted as laziness. It more accurately reflects a relaxed concept of time in which people are considered more important than schedules and there is total absorption in the task at hand. To many Hispanics, present time is important and should be enjoyed; tomorrow will be important—tomorrow! Time and clocks have different meanings in different cultures: In French time, the clock "marches"; in German time, the clock "functions"; in Anglo time, the clock "runs"; and in Hispanic *tiempo*, the clock "walks."[6]

Fatalism: A fatalistic attitude toward life is apparent in Hispanic time orientation and folk beliefs. The prevailing disposition is that one's destiny is beyond one's own control; there is a tendency to explain whatever happens as God's will.

Body Language: Physical proximity and warmth in relationships are common. Hispanics are generally gregarious and outgoing, animated in speech, gestures, and actions. This outgoing attitude is further evidenced by the exuberance of the many *fiestas*, the lively music, use of bright colors, flowers, clothing, and the high noise tolerance. A person of Hispanic origin will tend to utilize his "full range of psychological senses to experience things about him . . . to touch, taste, smell, feel, or be close to an object or person on which his attention is focused."[7]

Machismo: Hispanic cultures reflect the traditional Spanish role expectation that men be virile, aggressive, protective of, and dominant over their women. In Hispanic American families *machismo* usually refers more to the male's responsibility for his family than to the negative connotations.[8]

Family Structure

As the basic unit of Hispanic society, the family is the source of emotional, physical, and psychological support. Family unity, welfare, and honor are crucial; family loyalty supersedes individual interests. Family relationships are intense; behavior of the individual members reflects on the status and respect of the entire family. This respect for the traditional family is called "familism." In addition to the father, mother, and children, the extended family unit is comprised of grandparents, aunts, uncles, cousins, *compadres* (godparents), and occasionally, close friends or neighbors. The role of *compadrazgos* is unique in commitment and serves as a vital link in the family structure: *compadres* and *comadres* (literally, co-fathers and co-mothers) function as parents and *padrinos* (godparents) to the children.

It is not unusual for several generations to live together; adult children, even when married, often live at home. Children without parents are absorbed through an informal adoption system. Nuclear families are becoming more common as Hispanic American families modify their life-style to meet socioeconomic changes.

Family structure is patriarchal; the father is the authoritarian figure, decision-maker, provider, and disciplinarian. The male has few other responsibilities for childrearing; it is the female who nurtures the children. The mother's role is generally limited to childrearing and housekeeping, but it is a role that is revered. The mother often acts as mediator between an authoritarian father and the children. Marriages are often consensual; a common-law marriage is perfectly respectful in many Hispanic cultures. Elders are treated with honor; their role is that of teacher and transmitter of knowledge to the young. Grandparents, especially on the paternal side, often maintain a decision-making role in the family unit.

Childrearing Practices

Children are highly valued in all Hispanic cultures: they are seen as a gift from God. Children occupy a central position in the family; they accompany the parents wherever they go. Child care is primarily a female responsibility; the extended family provides much assistance and support. Childhood is a warm and nurturing period, and children receive much attention and affection. Childrearing practices reinforce dependence rather than independence. There is a relaxed attitude toward the achievement of developmental milestones, such as toilet training and weaning. Parents are generally more concerned with a child's physical well-being and behavior than with his cognitive skills. Discipline and good manners are very important. Children are taught to be submissive and obedient to their fathers and to other male relatives. Many parents feel that they have a legal and a moral right to physically punish their children. Eldest children are expected to assume child care and household responsibilities by the time they are pre-teens. Children are taught to be obedient and respectful of their elders by avoiding eye contact and by listening with bowed heads. Older children are expected to follow in their parents' footsteps and consult them for advice on important issues. Sex roles for male and female children are clearly defined and traditionally adhered to: girls are given less freedom and are carefully supervised. In the past, a family's honor was linked to a daughter's virtue and safeguarded by the system of chaperonage. At the same time, males were free to have extramarital affairs as a way of proving their virility.

Religion

Most Hispanics are, by heritage and tradition, Roman Catholic, although there is often some remnant of former religious practices (sorcery, witchcraft, and ancient herbal lore) combined with modern beliefs. The last few decades have seen a cultural transformation as growing numbers of Hispanic Americans in the United States (approximately one-fifth) have left the Roman Catholic Church for evangelical Protestant denominations. This shift of allegiance has been attributed to the simplicity and emotional power of the evangelical Protestant churches. Catholicism in the United States is not perceived as responsive to the more emotional and mystical religious feelings common among Hispanics. Latin American Catholicism differs from Catholicism in the United States: congregations are smaller, there is direct contact with the clergy, and traditional beliefs, such as miraculous healing, are accommodated. A similar shift (of religious allegiance) is occurring in Latin America as well but on a smaller scale.[9]

Attitude Toward Health

Good health is considered to be the result of good luck, good behavior, or a gift from God; it is generally equated with the ability to work. Similarly, illness is equated with the presence of symptoms and is seen as an imbalance of the body due to fate, heredity, wrongdoing, bad luck, some outside influence, or an excess of "hot" or "cold" factors.[10] This perception of health and illness has evolved from the Hispanic attitude toward religion and fatalism; since illness is often interpreted as a punishment from God, it is accepted fatalistically.[11] Illness is a family affair, involving the extended family, godparents, and neighbors.[12]

Traditionally, health care is for disease and injury, rather than for prevention. Hispanic folk medicine is holistic: mind and body are considered inseparable. Both psychological and physiological means of healing are used; *Estar sano* (to be healthy) implies both emotional and physical states. Many Hispanics practice self-care methods, passed down from one generation to another and by word of mouth in the neighborhood. Self-care is most likely to be used for minor illnesses such as colds, burns, and headaches. If the proprietary treatment fails, it would be interpreted as an incorrect diagnosis, not as an ineffective cure. Most folk medicine practices are based on a combination of ideas: about oneself, the environment, and about one's relationship with nature and with the supernatural.[13]

Many Hispanics believe in the Hippocratic theory of "hot/cold" which defines health as a balance of the four bodily humors and illness as an imbalance of these humors: Blood (hot and wet); Phlegm (cold and wet); black bile (cold and dry), and yellow bile (hot and dry). This Hippocratic doctrine was the basis of medical practice in Spain during the sixteenth century. These notions of *caliente* (hot) and *frio* (cold) as applied to food and medicine concern their effect on the body; they have nothing to do with temperature or spiciness. There is no general agreement as to which foods are hot and which are cold; it differs among cultures and among families within those cultures. In addition to the Hippocratic hot/cold theory, hot and cold temperatures also play an important role in health care beliefs. Cold is usually associated with threatening conditions and invisible factors such as pain and immobility; warmth is associated with reassurance; hot with irritating conditions such as rashes or diarrhea. Warm or hot foods are believed easier to digest than cold foods.[14]

Culture-specific ailments seen among Hispanics include *empacho* (indigestion), *caida de la mollera* ("sunken fontanel"), *mal aire* or *pasmo* ("bad air"), *mal ojo* ("evil eye"), *brujeria* or *embrujo* ("witchcraft" or "sorcery"), and *susto* ("fright"). These culture-specific ailments are treated with herbal home remedies, diet, or folk medicine practices. Folk healers (*curanderos/as* or *santeros/as*), spiritualists (*espiritistas* or *espiritualistas*), sorcerers, witches, chiropractors, and/or herbalists may be consulted.[15]

The diet in most Hispanic cultures is based on beans and rice; there are variations, however, according to income and geographical region. The diet is generally adequate in protein while low in Vitamin A, iron, and calcium. Obesity and anemia are common nutritional problems.[16]

Attitude Toward Work and Education

Education and educated persons are respected; professionals are highly regarded and their advice is often accepted without question. Education *is* valued, yet other values are accorded priority status. To lower-income Hispanics who are present-time oriented and fatalistic, education (for themselves and for their children) has a limited value; work tends to be seen as something necessary for survival, not as a value in itself.[17] In a society where children are raised to be dependent, obedient, and non-competitive, the schools serve to reinforce traditional principles rather than to introduce creative ideas and thoughts. Many Hispanic parents feel that the schools should be authoritarian and should teach respect. There is an emphasis on nonverbal skills rather than cognitive skills. Parental participation in educational matters is limited; teachers are considered to be well-trained authorities and their decisions are not questioned.

Traditional Hispanic Characteristics Most Likely to Have Implications for Health, Education, and Social Services

- A time orientation to the present.
- An attitude of fatalism.
- A fostering of dependency in children.
- The sense of shame felt by those parents of handicapped children who attribute the handicap (especially retardation) to retribution from God.
- The custom of having children show respect to adults by avoiding eye contact.
- The maintenance of rigid sex roles, especially the *machismo* ethic.
- The combination of folk beliefs with traditional religious practices.
- The involvement of the extended family, godparents, and neighbors in the treatment of an individual's illness.
- A holistic attitude toward health and illness.
- The belief in "hot/cold" theory; variability in the practice of this belief.
- The high incidence of ailments that are exclusively Hispanic-specific.
- A belief in folk medicine, folk healers, spiritualists, and herbalists.
- The strength and support of the extended family, especially that of godparents.
- The strength of religious ties and the involvement of the church in the community.

There is an additional factor to consider in understanding Hispanic Americans in the United States. Many recent immigrants from Mexico and Central America are undocumented immigrants (illegal aliens); this status creates further stresses on the family system and the community. There are also populations of migrant and seasonal farm workers with special needs. While some socio-demographic data can present information which over-categorizes, generalizes, and stereotypes, there are definite areas of need:

> ... it is accepted that Hispanics exist in more stress-producing situations, have higher morbidity and mortality rates, attend substandard schools, have higher school dropout rates, underemployment, poor housing, poor nutrition, a high incidence of poverty, and a shortage of relevant and accessible health care services.[18]

Brief Profile of Mexico

Family Structure: Mexican society is based on an extended family network ("familism") which is intergenerational and includes relatives, godparents, and close friends (referred to as "aunt/uncle" by the children). Relationships between cousins are often close, particularly between *primos hermanos* (first cousins); they resemble sibling relationships.[19]

Roles are clearly defined in spite of this high degree of emotional proximity and interdependency; they are determined by age and sex.[20] The father plays a dominant role in the family but is usually not actively involved with the children. He is expected to be the family protector; his authoritarianism becomes more marked as the children grow up. The role of the mother, while submissive to that of the father, is one of intense dedication to home and children. *El amor de madre* (motherly love) is sometimes considered more important than marital love.[21] The home is the central focus of socialization; all life cycle events are celebrated by the family as an affirmation of unity. Family values are reflected in religious practices and folk beliefs; these often vary according to economic level.

Childrearing Practices: Family size is large by choice; children are believed to validate and cement a marriage. The birth of a child, especially the first-born male, is an occasion for celebration. The privileged position of the oldest son has been traced by anthropologists to Mayan tradition.[22] A child is often named after the saint whose day coincides with the child's birthday. Childrearing is indulgently affectionate, and children are nurtured to develop a sense of trust and dependency. Sibling rivalry is seldom a problem. Discipline is usually maintained by means of shame, belittlement, and threats—although harsh punishment is not uncommon. According to Spanish tradition, a special celebration at age fifteen, the *quinceañera*, marks a Mexican girl's entrance to womanhood.

Religion: The majority (over 92 percent)[23] of Mexicans belong to the Catholic Church, which is an integral part of Mexican history and culture. The church plays a significant role in defining societal mores. To Mexicans, the Catholic church is often perceived as an external voice indicating what is right and wrong. In contrast to the Irish Catholic concepts of conscience and guilt, the Mexican Catholic believes that guilt can be easily disposed of by confession and penance. This belief is manifested by peasants walking on their knees (on prickly cactus leaves) to religious sanctuaries, punishing themselves physically in order to be forgiven.[24]

Membership in Jehovah's Witnesses, Pentecostal, and other Evangelical faiths is increasing. The advice and/or approval of one's priest or religious leader is frequently sought and is highly regarded.

Values: Family responsibility and unity are primary values. There is strong family pride and a resistance to help from "outsiders." Warm, close personal relationships are highly valued. Honesty and the preservation of one's *dignitad* (dignity) is a fundamental value. Individuals pride themselves on being *pobre pero honesto* (poor but honest).[25] The culture emphasizes compliance, loyalty, and dependency rather than encouraging autonomous behavior.[26] These traditional values, reflected in Mexican Americans, are commonly misunderstood:

> There is one area in which the Anglo and the Mexican American are likely to be markedly disparate. This is the area of manners, courtesy, inter-personal relations—call it what you will. The Anglo is taught to value openness, frankness, and directness. He is much more likely to express himself simply, briefly, and frequently bluntly. The traditional Latin approach requires the use of much diplomacy and tactfulness when communicating with another individual. Concern and respect for another's feelings dictate that a screen always be provided behind which a man may preserve his dignity. . . . The Mexican American often finds himself in difficulty if he disagrees with an Anglo's point of view. To him, direct argument or contradiction appears rude and disrespectful. . . . The

concept of courtesy, therefore, causes misunderstandings between Anglo and Latin.[27]

Language: In Mexico, Spanish is the official language, but many of the Indians speak only their indigenous tongues.[28]

Health: Prevention is not a priority with the population which believes in folk medicine and superstition and as a result does not feel any sense of control over personal destiny. Health is considered to have been attained when the body is sturdy, there is an absence of pain, and the individual has the ability to maintain normal physical activity. If one has no symptoms, one is not ill.[29]

To many, illness is equated with the presence of physical discomfort and is thought to be caused by exposure to the forces of nature (e.g., wind or air), supernatural causes, emotions, dislocations of internal organs, or God's displeasure with one's behavior. Some Mexican Americans believe in *mal aigre* (folk belief in cold or "bad" air); some believe in *brujeria* (witchcraft) or *mal ojo* (evil eye). The cause of an illness may be attributed to *seya por dios* (it is God's will).[30]

Any kind of blood loss is believed to cause weakness and to impair sexual strength.[31] Blood, like emotions, is believed to be closely linked to health and disease. Infants are believed to be particularly vulnerable to the cold. Extreme care is taken in handling a baby's head and in keeping the head covered.[32]

Mexican Americans are apt to consult chiropractors, naturopaths, herbalists, and practitioners in folk medicine. They charge less than physicians, usually relate better to patients and family, and utilize familiar treatments. *Curanderos* (folk healers) are popular in the rural Southwest, especially among low socioeconomic groups. Other specialty folk practitioners are the *partera* (midwife) and the *sabadora* (specialist in handling fractures and bone disorders).

Education: In Mexico, education is free and compulsory through age fifteen. As a growing middle class emerges, there is a greater emphasis on education, especially at the college level. The literacy rate is over 84 percent.[33]

Other Significant Data: Mexico is a densely populated country, and Mexico City is one of the most populated cities in the world. Young men must serve a year in the army. A vast economic disparity exists between the wealthy and the poor.

To Mexican Americans, the term *Chicano* evokes mixed reactions. To some, it represents a pride in their unique Mexican heritage; to others, it is a political and militant term; and to still others, it is slang for a socially subordinate ethnic group.

It is important to recognize the wide diversity of Mexican Americans in the United States: there are Americans of Spanish descent who have lived in the southwestern United States for several hundred years; there are native-born descendants of Mexicans who settled in this country early in this century; and there are Mexican citizens and recent immigrants.

Brief Profile of Puerto Rico

Family Structure: The family is the basic unit of Puerto Rican society. Although today nuclear and extended families may not live together as they did in the past, they remain close to each other, providing socialization and support. There is a great deal of affection and body contact between family members. Children are expected to care for their aging parents. The society is patriarchal, with the wife's role subordinate to that of her husband; the *machismo* concept is strong. Consensual marriages are common; the respectability of marriage is dependent on conduct, not on a religious or legal service. Consensual marriages do not indicate a lack of respect for religious marriage but rather a reluctance to make a permanent commitment until the couple is certain the marriage will work.[34]

When families (without job skills) migrate to the United States, the female usually finds it easier to obtain employment than the Puerto Rican male. This causes a disruption in the traditional family system and can lead to marital conflict and diminution of the male authority role. Another problem in contemporary Puerto Rican family structure is the pattern of circular migration between the island and the United States. This practice can disrupt family life and children's education, and can result in loss of income and employment, school dropout, a lack of consistent training and work experience, and subsequent poverty. Such frequent relocation to Puerto Rico, however, does preserve cultural ties and can facilitate support from the extended family who remain on the island. Cultural values vary greatly from class to class and from island to mainland. While a large percentage of

Hispanic American Cultures

the people of Puerto Rico who migrate to the United States represent the poorest and least educated inhabitants of the island, there are also professionals, artists, and a well-educated working class.[35]

Even though Puerto Ricans are U.S. citizens, migration to the mainland often involves a struggle for identity:

> Every Puerto Rican who exchanged his birthplace for any of the metropolitan centers of New York, . . . or California has to learn to adapt his body, mind, and soul to the realities of a new environment. He also remains attached to his homeland in many ways. His language continues to be Spanish. His preference for native food is evident in the existence of many stores catering to his tastes, where one can buy tropical produce such as *plátanos*, . . . and many other common items in the daily diet of the island of Puerto Rico. The ties of migrants to the towns where their ancestors were born and raised are extremely strong and emotional.[36]

Fitzpatrick has classified four family structures of Puerto Rican families living on the mainland:[37]

(1) The *extended family* includes natural kin and ritual kin (intimate friends from the social network): grandparents, parents, children, compadres, and comadres.
(2) The *nuclear family*, consisting of father, mother, and children, is increasingly seen in the growing middle class.
(3) The *mixed family* includes the father, mother, their children, and children of (an)other union(s) of husband or wife.
(4) The *single-parent* family, usually mother-based, with children of one or more men but with no man permanently residing in the home.

Other differences among Puerto Rican families reflect the historical blending of various ethnic and racial groups:

> Puerto Rican culture has been influenced by several different races and ethnic groups, and a present-day Puerto Rican family may consist of a mother who is White, a father who is Black, and children who are various shades of color. Their cultural ancestry may be a mixture of African,

Taino, Corsican, and Spanish, though their ethnic identification will be Puerto Rican.[38]

Childrearing Practices: Traditionally, family size was large and children were considered "the poor man's wealth." Recent demographic data, however, indicate a fertility rate of 2.0.[39] Motherhood is revered. Childrearing practices during the first three years of life are indulgent and permissive. Older children are disciplined by corporal punishment. Children are raised to be dependent, obedient, and respectful.[40] Socialization of children is almost exclusively intrafamilial; there is little time, interest, or need for play groups or day care. In the traditional Puerto Rican home, girls are taught to be passive, feminine, and home-oriented; boys are encouraged to be aggressive, fearless, and virile. Self-control is not stressed; early childhood behavior is not considered relevant to success in later life. Toys are usually selected for their visual appeal or popularity rather than for any educational value.[41]

Religion: The majority (over 85 percent)[42] of Puerto Ricans are nominally Roman Catholic. People participate in the Catholic religious sacraments not as members of the organized Church but rather as members of a *pueblo* (community) that is Catholic; it is a socioreligious affiliation.[43] Puerto Rican Catholicism differs from Catholicism in the United States:

> Most Puerto Ricans have some distrust of organized religion, the Church, and the priest, and believe they can make contact with God and the supernatural without the clergy. They tend to personalize their relationship with God by creating a favorable ambience through special relationships with the saints, who become their personal emissaries to God. Promises are made, prayers said, and candles lit, all in attempts to show gratitude and faith. They will call on the Church primarily for weddings, christenings, and funerals.[44]

A growing number of Puerto Ricans are Protestant or belong to austere Pentecostal or Evangelical sects. Spiritism, the supernatural, and folk beliefs are common. This exposure to experiences which involve danger, magical thinking, and extrasensory perception has an impact on the personality development of children.[45] *Botanicas* sell herbs, oils, and candles to influence the spirits; many people believe that it is possible to communicate with the dead. This belief in external forces controlling individuals' lives is an expression of fatalism. Botanicas also cater to the followers of *santaría*, a religion that combines Roman Catholicism with worship of West African deities and is practiced by many Hispanic immigrants from the Caribbean.[46] In describing the eclectic nature of Puerto Rican religious beliefs, Padilla states:

> Religion or ideas about the supernatural . . . are not circumscribed within the boundaries of any particular church. . . . They transgress into a variety of ideologies, which are not seen as conflicting with each other, but, rather, are connected under the premise that all religions are good and that religion plays an important part in the training of a good child, and (in) understanding the nature of forces that are beyond the control of individual man.[47]

Ideas about religion are closely related to health care beliefs. Charms such as a black hand (representing an appeal to the saints for protections) are often worn to ward off illness or death caused by the "evil eye."[48]

Values: *Respeto* (respect) is a value that is vital and basic to one's social worthiness. Respect—whether for the dignity of an individual or for authority—is important. A man's self-worth is defined in terms of those inner qualities that give self-respect and earn the respect of others (e.g., providing for one's family, respectful behavior). Family welfare, honor, and unity are salient values. There is more emphasis on the group than on the individual. Spiritual and human values take precedence over materialistic values, especially among the lower classes.[49] The island's cultural patterns and historical destiny are reflected in this characterization of ethnic pride:

> For the people of Puerto Rico at all social levels—the poor and the wealthy, the illiterate and the intellectual, the peasant and the town and city dweller—the concept of *mi casa, mi patria, mi tierra* (my home, my land, my soil) is an inseparable trilogy.[50]

Art (especially the visual arts) and music are valued and often reflect the blended heritage of Spanish, Indian, and African roots. Fashionable clothes are highly regarded. Physical attractiveness is valued; the selection of a beauty queen is an important part of many activities.

Puerto Ricans are emotional and demonstrative. There is a cultural concern about the control of aggression, the fear of losing control, and the expression of violence.[51] Culturally approved outlets for men are drinking, verbal threats, and angry discussions. Stressful situations for women often result in *ataques de nervios* (nervous attacks). These *ataques* have been referred to as "The Puerto Rican Syndrome."[52] Emotional problems are often manifested as somatic complaints.

Language: Spanish and English are both official languages, and English is a required subject in school.

Health: The Puerto Rican culture is health-oriented. This orientation may not always involve Western health-care practices but is expressed in the form of folklore, folk remedies, and religion. Religion has a major influence on the Puerto Rican's attitude toward health and disease.[53] In addition to the hot/cold theory often followed in Hispanic cultures, Puerto Ricans have a category of "warm." "Fresh" and "cool" are descriptive of health and well-being. The diet is generally wholesome and well balanced. The basic diet of rice and beans is liberally supplemented with poultry, seafood, fruits, and vegetables and reflects a blend of Spanish, Indian, and African backgrounds.

Education: Education (elementary and higher education) is highly valued, and there have been notable improvements in the educational system in Puerto Rico in recent decades. Teachers are trusted and respected. Many parents see the major role of the schools to be that of teaching respect and obedience rather than an emphasis on teaching cognitive skills. Concurrently, many preschool children are not raised to be either task-oriented or time-oriented, nor are they exposed to preschools or school-related activity toys such as scissors, crayons, and books.[54]

Other Significant Data: Racially, the population of Puerto Rico represents a blend of native Indians, black slaves, and Spanish conquerors. The largest Puerto Rican community is in New York City. Many of the cultural traditions that have sustained Puerto Ricans in their native land (e.g., large families, fatalism, machismo) create problems in adaptation to life on the mainland.

Brief Overview of Cuba

Cuba is the largest island in the Caribbean and is historically significant because of its strategic geographical location. Cubans represent a blend of Spanish and African cultural patterns. The Spanish conquerors destroyed much of the indigenous culture and population. While there are similarities to other Hispanics in language, religion, and family life-style, there are differences due to class, greater European and African influence, and close ties to the United States, Spain, and Russia.[55] Cuban immmigrants to the United States have primarily settled in the Miami area. Those who came at the beginning of the Castro regime were predominantly white, middle or upper class, and well educated. Those who followed in the "Freedom Flights" from Havana to Miami included more middle- and lower-middle-class Cubans, such as small businessmen and skilled laborers.[56] Those immigrants who arrived as part of the 1980 "freedom-flotilla" (commonly known as "Marielitos") included many semiskilled and skilled workers along with some "social misfits."[57] Catholicism is the primary religion while folk-healing traditions often combine Spanish Catholic medical and religious practices with African and other belief systems. *Santaría* and *espiritismo* are followed by some Cubans.

While it would be a disservice to characterize "the typical Cuban American," there are some traits that are considered characteristically Cuban: *personalismo*, an orientation toward people and persons over concepts and ideas; *choteo*, Cuban humor that ridicules people, situations, and/or things, and often involves exaggeration; *tuteo*, the use of the informal *tu* rather than *usted* (you) in familiar conversation (note the European influence, similar to the German *du*, described on page 16); and a sense of "specialness" that many Cubans have about themselves and their culture and often expressed in music, art, and literature.[58]

Brief Overview of Central and South America

Immigrants from the numerous countries of Central and South America share many traditional Hispanic characteristics. Their differences are attributable to the political climate, the geography, and the economic situation in their country of origin as well as their socioeconomic level, educational status, family life-style, and their ethnic heritage. These unique characteristics, whether personal or national, must be explored and understood in their proper context.

In all of these countries, the Hispanic tradition of large, close-knit, extended families prevails, although upper- and middle-class families tend to have fewer children. Children still occupy a central position in the family and often have the surnames of both parents. In many middle- and upper-class families, especially in Brazil and Colombia, household maids are common and are considered an integral part of the family structure. The role of women varies: Uruguayan women often work outside the home and in professions; in Ecuador, family control is the wife's prerogative; in Honduras and Guatemala, their role is mostly restricted to the home. The mother is usually influential in family matters.

There are population differences in each country. In addition to the *mestizos* there are indigenous Indians, blacks, West Indian blacks, mulattos (mixed black and white), Europeans, and Asians. Many of the ethnic variances in each country reflect the customs of the Indians indigenous to that country. Spanish is the official language in all but Brazil; the Portuguese language there is a reminder of Brazil's discovery and colonization by Portugal. There are also many Indian dialects.

Religion is predominately (about 90 percent) Roman Catholic, but Catholicism is not always actively practiced. Protestant faiths are gaining in popularity, and tribal religions exist in some regions of Brazil and Chile. Religious freedom is available to all and is highly cherished. Uruguay is the most secular country in the region, while Brazil has more Roman Catholics than any other country. Nicaraguans are among the most devoutly religious; Venezuelans are among the least religious.

Education also varies. The quality and accessibility of education are excellent in some countries while in others the rural population remains largely illiterate. There are wide disparities in national policies regarding school attendance and funding. Literacy ranges from 94 percent in Uruguay to 50 percent in Guatemala.

Health care varies considerably. The training of health care providers, sanitation measures, adequate facilities, and accessibility are generally improving. In many countries, particularly in urban centers, the quality is quite good. Problems persist, however, especially in poor, rural areas, largely due to superstition (and consequent reluctance to utilize modern medical facilities), reliance on home remedies, and folk medicine. Diet reflects ethnic traditions, geography, and economic status.

There are many stereotypes and misconceptions about Hispanic Americans and their cultural subgroups; some are the result of ethnocentrism while others are attributable to misinformation or insufficient understanding. A common misconception is that except for a few wealthy families, poverty is pervasive. In actuality, there is a vibrant middle class in just about every country. It is important to appreciate the strengths of the Hispanic American families—such as the support of the extended family, nurturance in childrearing, and the health themes of balance and holism.

Clearly, there are many Hispanic cultures in the Americas. There are more similarities than differences among them. Hispanic Americans share many similarities in language, religion, values, and family structure. There are, however, group differences in geographic distribution, ethnic origins (Castilian Spanish, Caribbean black, and Spanish-Indian mestizo), reasons for immigrating (economic versus political), along with individual differences. Each Hispanic American child and family is unique, each with distinctive traditions.

It is also important to recognize that with immigration and acculturation, intermarriage and assimilation, many of these traditions are dying out, as people confront a cultural conflict between the traditional values of their parents and contemporary values in their new culture. There are many tensions and stresses that threaten the traditional Hispanic/Latino family in the United States; one of these is a lack of understanding and appreciation by the Anglo population.

Notes

1. John A. Axelson, *Counseling and Development in a Multicultural Society* (Monterey, Calif.: Brooks/Cole, 1985), p. 78.

2. R.A. Ruiz and A.M. Padilla, "Counseling Latinos," *Personnel and Guidance Journal* 55 (1977): 401–408, quoted by John A. Axelson, *Counseling and Development in a Multicultural Society* (Monterey, Calif.: Brooks/Cole, 1985), p. 78.

3. *Latino Mental Health: A Review of the Literature,* DHEW Publication No. (HSM) 73–9143, cited by Alberto C. Serrano and Fortunato G.

Castillo, "The Chicano Child and His Family," *Basic Handbook of Child Psychiatry*, J.P. Noshpitz and I.N. Berlin, eds. (New York: Basic Books, 1979), p. 257.

4. U.S. Census Bureau, March 1988.

5. Gabriele C. da Silva, "Awareness of Hispanic Cultural Issues in the Health Care Setting," *Children's Health Care, Journal of the Association for the Care of Children's Health* 13 (Summer 1984): 5.

6. Louis A. Bransford, Leonard Baca, and Karen Lane, eds., *Cultural Diversity and the Exceptional Child* (Reston, Va.: Council for Exceptional Children, 1974), Chapter IV.

7. Stewart A. Queen and Robert W. Habenstein, *The Family in Various Cultures*, 4th ed. (Philadelphia: J.B. Lippincott, 1974), p. 426.

8. Penny P. Anderson and Emily Schrag Fenichel, *Serving Culturally Diverse Families of Infants and Toddlers with Disabilities* (Washington, D.C.: National Center for Clinical Infant Programs, 1989), p. 10.

9. Roberto Suro, "Hispanic Shift of Allegiance Changes Face of U.S. Religion," *New York Times*, 14 May 1989, p. A1.

10. da Silva, "Awareness of Hispanic Cultural Issues in the Health Care Setting," *Children's Health Care*, pp. 5–6.

11. Gloria Lacay, "The Puerto Rican in Mainland America," *Culture and Childrearing*, A.L. Clark, ed. (Philadelphia: F.A. Davis, 1981), p. 226.

12. *Delivering Preventive Health Care to Hispanics: A Manual for Providers* (Washington, D.C.: National Coalition of Hispanic Health and Human Service Organizations, 1988).

13. da Silva, "Awareness of Hispanic Cultural Issues in the Health Care Setting," *Children's Health Care*, pp. 4–10.

14. Alan Harwood, "The Hot-Cold Theory of Disease: Implications for Treatment of Puerto Rican Patients," *Journal of the American Medical Association* 216 (1971): 1154–1155; and U.S. Department of Agriculture/Department of Health and Human Services Nutrition Education Committee for Maternal and Child Nutrition, *Cross-Cultural Counseling: A Guide for Nutrition and Health Counselors*, FNS-250 (Washington, D.C.: U.S. Government Printing Office, 1986), pp. 5, 32–33.

15. da Silva, "Hispanic Cultural Issues in the Health Care Setting," *Children's Health*, p. 7.

16. USDA/DHHS, *Cross-Cultural Counseling: A Guide for Nutrition and Health Counselors*, pp. 32–33.

17. Queen and Habenstein, *The Family in Various Cultures*, p. 426.

18. Fernando A. Guerra, "Hispanic Child Health Issues," *Children Today* 9 (September-October 1980): 19.

19. Marta Borbón Ehling, "The Mexican American (El Chicano)," *Culture and Childrearing*, A.L. Clark, ed. (Philadelphia: F.A. Davis, 1981), p. 195.

20. Celia Jaes Falicov, "Mexican Families," *Ethnicity and Family Therapy*, M. McGoldrick, J.K. Pearce, and J. Giordano, eds. (New York: Guilford, 1982), p. 138.

21. Ibid., p. 140.

22. Ibid., p. 135.

23. *Britannica World Data: Book of the Year 1986*, s.v., "Mexico."

24. Alberto C. Serrano, and Fortunato G. Castillo, "The Chicano Child and His Family," *Basic Handbook of Child Psychiatry*, p. 259.

25. Falicov, "Mexican Families," *Ethnicity and Family Therapy*, p. 138.

26. Serrano and Castillo, "The Chicano Child and His Family," *Basic Handbook of Child Psychiatry*, p. 259.

27. *Chicanos: Social and Psychological Perspectives*, quoted in *Extracting Learning Styles from Social/Cultural Diversity: Studies of Five American Minorities*, L. Morris, ed. (Norman, Oklahoma: University of Oklahoma Press, 1986), p. 32.

28. *Encyclopaedia Britannica*, 1988, s.v., "Mexico."

29. Irene F. Abril, "Mexican-American Folk Beliefs: How They Affect Health Care," *MCN, The American Journal of Maternal Child Nursing* 2 (May/June 1977): 169.

30. Ibid., pp. 168–173.

31. da Silva, "Awareness of Hispanic Cultural Issues in the Health Care Setting," *Children's Health*, p. 6.

32. Ehling, "The Mexican American (El Chicano)," *Culture and Childrearing*, p. 199.

33. *Britannica World Data: Book of the Year: 1986*, s.v., "Mexico."

34. Axelson, *Counseling and Development in a Multicultural Society*, p. 84.

35. Arturo Morales Carrión, *Puerto Rico: A Political and Cultural History* (New York: Norton, 1983), p. 347.

36. Ibid., p. 344.

37. J.P. Fitzpatrick, *Puerto Rican Americans: The Meaning of Immigration to the Mainland* (Englewood Cliffs, New Jersey: Prentice-Hall, 1971), p. 83.

38. Nydia Garcia-Preto, "Puerto Rican Families," *Ethnicity and Family Therapy*, M. McGoldrick, J.K. Pearce, and J. Giordano, eds. (New York: Guilford, 1982), p. 164.

39. *Britannica World Data: Book of the Year 1986*, s.v., "Puerto Rico."

40. Lacay, "The Puerto Rican in Mainland America," *Culture and Childrearing*, p. 213.

41. Ruth L. LaVietes, "The Puerto Rican Child," *Basic Handbook of Child Psychiatry*, Joseph P. Noshpitz and I.N. Berlin, eds., Vol. I: *Normal Development* (New York: Basic Books, 1979), p. 267.

42. *Britannica World Data: Book of the Year 1986*, s.v., "Puerto Rico."

43. Axelson, *Counseling and Development in a Multicultural Society,* p. 83.

44. Garcia-Preto, "Puerto Rican Families," *Ethnicity and Family Therapy,* p. 169.

45. LaVietes, "The Puerto Rican Child," *Basic Handbook of Child Psychiatry,* p. 265.

46. Ibid., p. 265.

47. Elena Padilla, *Up From Puerto Rico* (New York: Columbia University Press, 1958), p. 126.

48. Ruth Watson Lubic, "The Puerto Rican Family," *Bulletin of the American College of Nurse-Midwives* 16 (November 1969): 104–110.

49. Garcia-Preto, "Puerto Rican Families," *Ethnicity and Family Therapy,* p. 168.

50. Carrión, *Puerto Rico: A Political and Cultural History,* p. 344.

51. Ibid., p. 170.

52. da Silva, "Awareness of Hispanic Cultural Issues in the Health Care Setting," *Children's Health Care,* pp. 6–7.

53. Lacay, "The Puerto Rican in Mainland America," *Culture and Childrearing,* p. 226.

54. LaVietes, "The Puerto Rican Child," *Basic Handbook of Child Psychiatry,* p. 266.

55. Guillermo Bernal, "Cuban Families," *Ethnicity and Family Therapy,* M. McGoldrick, J.K. Pearce, and J. Giordano, eds. (New York: Guilford, 1982), p. 191.

56. Ibid., p. 190.

57. Axelson, *Counseling and Development in a Multicultural Society,* pp. 86, 113.

58. Bernal, "Cuban Families," *Ethnicity and Family Therapy,* pp. 187–207.

BIBLIOGRAPHY

Abril, Irene F. "Mexican-American Folk Beliefs: How They Affect Health Care." *MCN, The American Journal of Maternal/Child Nursing* 2 (May/June 1977): 168–173.

Describes cultural ways, beliefs, and historical background of the major subgroups of Mexican Americans with emphasis on their attitudes toward health and illness. The author, a Mexican American nurse, states that folk beliefs and practices are largely dependent on education and extent of acculturation. Advocates open-mindedness and tolerance of cultural beliefs.

Anderson, Penny P., and Emily Schrag Fenichel. *Serving Culturally Diverse Families of Infants and Toddlers with Disabilities.* Washington, D.C.: National Center for Clinical Infant Programs, 1989.

Provides examples of family and childrearing tendencies in Hispanic American families. Discusses health, illness, and disability beliefs and practices. Suggests guidelines for family/professional interaction that are sensitive to Hispanic American values. Describes projects and organizations that serve the special needs of Hispanic Americans.

Axelson, John A. *Counseling and Development in a Multicultural Society.* Belmont, Calif.: Brooks/Cole, 1985.

Discusses demographics and history of Hispanic Americans. Examines migration history, family life, and values of Mexican Americans, Puerto Rican Americans, and Cuban Americans.

Bernal, Guillermo. "Cuban Families." *Ethnicity and Family Therapy.* M. McGoldrick, J.K. Pearce, and J. Giordano, eds. New York: Guilford, 1982. pp. 187–207.

Reviews the migration of Cubans to the United States, their cultural heritage, religious practices, value structure, and family structure. Offers case histories to illustrate the common problems encountered by Cuban families in the United States. Extensive bibliography.

Brigham Young University David M. Kennedy Center for International Studies. *CULTURGRAMS.* Provo, Utah: Brigham Young University Publication Services, 1990.

A series of brief pamphlets, updated yearly, which succinctly present information on "Customs and Courtesies," "The People," "Lifestyle," and "The

Nation" of over 100 countries. Culturgrams are available on Argentina, Bolivia, Brazil, Chile, Colombia, Costa Rica, Ecuador, El Salvador, Guatemala, Honduras, Mexico, Nicaragua, Panama, Paraguay, Peru, Puerto Rico, Uruguay, and Venezuela.

Buriel, Raymond. "Ethnic Labeling and Identity Among Mexican Americans." *Children's Ethnic Socialization: Pluralism and Development.* J.S. Phinney and M.J. Rotheram, eds. Newbury Park, Calif.: Sage, 1987, pp. 134–152.

Describes the origin of ethnic terms such as *Mestizo, Chicano, Mexicano, Latino,* and *Hispanic* as well as the reactions of people to these labels.

Canino, Ian A., and Glorisa Canino. "Impact of Stress on the Puerto Rican Family." *American Journal of Orthopsychiatry* 50 (July 1980): 535–541.

Examines the impact of stress, due to migration and poverty, on the family structure of the low-income Puerto Rican family. Cites problems such as unsafe playgrounds and streets in urban areas, the paucity of extended family and community support, and the changes in family structure and function that result from immigration.

Carrión, Arturo Morales. *Puerto Rico: A Political and Cultural History.* New York: Norton, 1983.

Establishes a balanced perspective of what Puerto Rico constitutes as a people, a cultural nationality, and a distinctive Caribbean entity. Written by Puerto Ricans for readers in the United States interested in the island's social, institutional, and cultural evolution. Chapter 16, "A Special Voice: The Cultural Expression," provides insight into the rich cultural spectrum of Puerto Rican life—its folklore, language nuances, traditions, and artistic expressions.

Comas-Díaz, Lillian. "Puerto Rican Espiritismo and Psychotherapy." *American Journal Orthopsychiatry* 51 (4) (October 1981): 636–645.

Describes *espiritismo* as a system of beliefs which consists of an invisible world populated by spirits which surround the visible world. The practice evolved from the works of a 19th century French spiritist and is an adaptive mechanism for coping with alien environments. Relates the *espiritismo* system to other traditional Puerto Rican cultural beliefs and provides case examples of its role in mental health practices. Expresses the belief that *espiritismo* should not be viewed as primitive thinking, avoidance of responsibility, or a sign of pathology but as an adaptive attempt at functioning.

Cortez, Carlos E. "Chicano Culture, Experience, and Learning," *Extracting Learning Styles from Social/Cultural Diversity: Studies of Five American Minorities.* L. Morris, ed. Norman: University of Oklahoma Press, 1986, pp. 29–39.

Summarizes some of the important studies of the relationship between Chicano culture and school learning. Addresses the relationship between Chicano school experience and future learning. Discusses Chicano students in terms of language, class participation, experiential learning, affective motivation, cooperative/competitive learning, and field sensitivity.

da Silva, Gabriele C. "Awareness of Hispanic Cultural Issues in the Health Care Setting." *Children's Health Care, Journal of the Association for the Care of Children's Health* 13 (3) (Summer 1984): 4–10.

Describes the diversity in cross-cultural behaviors and details Hispanic perceptions of health and disease, culture-specific ailments, and Hispanic folk health practices. References included.

Ehling, Marta Borbón. "The Mexican American (El Chicano)." *Culture and Childrearing.* A.L. Clark, ed. Philadelphia: F.A. Davis, 1981, pp. 192–209.

Addresses the history of Mexican Americans, the strong family structure, and the traditions associated with each stage of childhood. Includes references and a bibliography.

Falicov, Celia Jaes. "Mexican Families." *Ethnicity and Family Therapy.* M. McGoldrick, J.K. Pearce, and J. Giordano, eds. New York: Guilford, 1982, pp. 134–163.

Reviews Mexican history and migration patterns and cultural family patterns. Describes functional and dysfunctional patterns of adapting to the cultural transitions associated with immigration. Includes case examples and extensive reference list.

Garcia-Preto, Nydia. "Puerto Rican Families." *Ethnicity and Family Therapy.* M. McGoldrick, J.K. Pearce, and J. Giordano, eds. New York: Guilford, 1982, pp. 164–186.

Explains the many ways in which present-day Puerto Rican families can differ from one another. Provides information on the historical background, economy, family structure, and cultural values of Puerto Rico. Describes the Puerto Rican belief in spirituality, dignity of the individual, respect for authority, patterns of handling stress, and control of aggression. Also addresses the problems of migration and subsequent effect on family structure. Extensive references.

Guerra, Fernando A. "Hispanic Child Health Issues," *Children Today* 9 (September-October 1980): 18–22.

Focuses on the special health care needs of Hispanic American children and offers suggestions to health care providers and policy makers to ameliorate these problems. Guerra is a pediatrician and chairman of the American Academy of Pediatrics Committee on Community Health Services.

Harwood, Alan. "The Hot-Cold Theory of Disease: Implication for Treatment of Puerto Rican Patients." *Journal of the American Medical Association* 216 (1971): 1153–1158.

Clarifies the origin, the various classifications, the significance, and the treatment considerations of this complex concept. Dr. Harwood is a medical anthropologist who has written extensively about his experiences investigating medical and paramedical beliefs and practices in the largely Puerto Rican neighborhoods of the Bronx, New York.

Harwood, Alan, ed. *Ethnicity and Medical Care*. Cambridge, Mass.: Harvard University Press, 1981.

Describes cultural attitudes and folk beliefs toward health and illness. Chapters on "Mainland Puerto Ricans," "Mexican Americans," and "Haitian Americans" are especially relevant.

Hays-Bautista, David, Werner O. Schink, and Jorge Chapa. *The Burden of Support: Young Latinos in an Aging Society*. Palo Alto, Calif.: Stanford University Press, 1988.

Explores social and economic implications of the fast-growing Hispanic (primarily of Mexican origin) work force amidst an aging Anglo population. Highlights Latino problems in education, in business, and with government agencies.

Inclán, Jaime E., and D. Gloria Herron. "Puerto Rican Adolescents." *Children of Color: Psychological Interventions with Minority Youth*. J.T. Gibbs, L.N. Huang and Associates, eds. San Francisco: Jossey-Bass, 1989.

Addresses educational problems of Puerto Rican youth in this country as well as generational clashes between Puerto Rican parents and their children. Highlights the mental health problems of this population and how they are dealt with in a New York community.

Kumabe, Kazuye T., and Yvonne Bickerton. *Ethnocultural Factors in Social Work and Health Care: A Selected Annotated Bibliography.* Honolulu: University of Hawaii School of Social Work, 1982.

An extensive multidisciplinary collection of reference books, journals, and monographs covering the period between 1970 and 1981. Includes annotations relevant to the many aspects of Hispanic cultures.

Kumabe, Kazuye T., Chikae Nishida, and Dean H. Hepworth. *Bridging Ethnocultural Diversity in Social Work and Health.* Honolulu: University of Hawaii School of Social Work, 1985.

Discusses the historical factors that have shaped cultural patterns in Puerto Rico and contrasts rural life with urban living in the United states. Considers the strengths of Puerto Rican families. Provides case examples to illustrate Puerto Rican traditions and problems.

Lacay, Gloria. "The Puerto Rican in Mainland America." *Culture and Childrearing.* A.L. Clark, ed. Philadelphia: F.A. Davis, 1981, pp. 210–227.

Reviews the history and migratory experiences of Puerto Ricans to the mainland. Compares the traditional family with the family today. Describes with examples traditions and customs associated with each developmental stage. Explains ethnic health practices and beliefs, including dietary practices. References and a bibliography are included.

LaVietes, Ruth L. "The Puerto Rican Child." *Basic Handbook of Child Psychiatry.* J.P. Noshpitz and I.N. Berlin, eds. Vol. I: *Normal Development.* New York: Basic Books, 1979, pp. 264–271.

Explains how problems of poverty and migration, traditional and cultural family factors, and the influence of religion and spiritualism impact on the psychosocial development of the Puerto Rican child. Describes those situations and developmental stages which might characteristically create emotional disturbances. Focuses on the special needs of Puerto Rican youth in acculturation into American society while still maintaining ethnic individuality.

Lawson, Lauren Valk. "Culturally Sensitive Support for Grieving Parents." *MCN, The American Journal of Maternal/Child Nursing* 15 (March/April 1990): 76–79.

Describes family life, attitudes toward health and healing, and concepts of death and grief among Mexican Americans.

Lewis, Oscar. *La Vida*. New York: Random House, 1966.

A classic study of the structure and organization of Puerto Rican families. A unique glimpse into the life-styles of this ethnic group by a noted anthropologist.

Lieberman, Alicia F. "Culturally Sensitive Intervention with Children and Families." *Child and Adolescent Social Work Journal* 7 (1990).

Compares values of Anglos and Hispanics living in the United States: differing cultural orientations toward individualism and collectivism, differing personal qualities, and differing attitudes toward childrearing.

Lieberman, Alicia F. "Infant-Parent Interventions with Recent Immigrants: Reflections on a Study with Latino Families." *Zero to Three* 10 (April 1990): 8–11.

Reports on a study of mental health risk among recent Latino immigrants. Explores support systems traditionally available within the Latino community and how these have been disrupted by immigration.

Lubic, Ruth Watson. "The Puerto Rican Family." *Bulletin of the American College of Nurse-Midwives* 16 (4) (November 1969): 104–110.

A study of the lives of lower-socioeconomic Puerto Rican families in New York. Focuses on those facets of behavior and customs which affect the provision of quality maternity and newborn care. Dr. Lubic, a nurse, anthropologist, and educator, is Director of The Maternity Center in New York City.

Macdonald, Anne C. "Folk Health Practices Among North Coastal Peruvians: Implication for Nursing." *Image, The Journal of Nursing Scholarship* 13 (June 1982): 51–55.

Explores the connection between the Spanish interest in medicine and medicinal herbs with the Inca knowledge of herbs, medicine, magic, and rituals of curing. Defines and provides examples of the three realms of health beliefs: magical, emotional, and rational. Provides an understanding of the Hispanic concept of balance (hot/cold) as it affects nutrition and health practices.

Murillo, Nathan. "The Mexican American Family." *Chicanos: Social and Psychological Perspectives*. C.A. Hernandez, M.J. Haug, and N.N. Wagner, eds. St. Louis: Mosby, 1976, pp. 99–102.

Explores traditional characteristics of Mexican Americans and cites trends and problems that threaten the continuation of their ethnic and cultural traditions.

National Coalition of Advocates for Students. *New Voices: Immigrant Students in U.S. Public Schools.* Boston: National Coalition of Advocates for Students, 1988.

Calls attention to the diversity within the Hispanic American community and the unique educational needs of their children. A comprehensive research and policy report. Extensive bibliography.

National Coalition of Hispanic Health and Human Service Organizations. *Delivering Preventive Health Care to Hispanics: A Manual for Providers.* Washington, D.C.: National Coalition of Hispanic Health and Human Service Organizations, 1988.

Highlights traditional values of Hispanic families and emphasizes the pivotal role of the family in both prevention and provision of health care. Stresses the need for health care professionals to "be warm, friendly, and personal—to take an active role in the patient's life."

Orrego, Maria Elena, and Ann B. Barnett. "Serving the Newest Arrivals: A Model of Early Intervention for Central American Babies and Their Families." *Zero to Three* 10 (April 1990): 11–16.

Describes the experiences of a bilingual and bicultural family resource center serving Central American immigrant and refugee families. Details the unique problems faced by Hispanic immigrant women who are pregnant or new mothers—separation from traditional support networks and transition from life in rural Central America to an urban environment. Explains how culturally sensitive interventions are provided.

Padilla, Elena. *Up From Puerto Rico.* New York: Columbia University Press, 1958.

A classic study of the changes which Puerto Rican families undergo as they adapt to their new life-style in a New York slum. Captures the cultural conflict experienced by these ethnic immigrants as they confront the bureaucracy and the different values with which they must cope.

Queen, Stuart A., and Robert W. Habenstein. *The Family in Various Cultures.* 4th ed. Philadelphia: Lippincott, 1974.

Provides a comparative perspective on the variations of family life among the different Hispanic cultures. Explains the influence of the Spaniards, the Mayans, the Aztecs, and the Toltecs, all of which were advanced cultures. Focuses on the strengths inherent in Hispanic traditions and contrasts these characteristics with those of the Anglo society.

Ramirez, Oscar. "Mexican-American Children and Adolescents." *Children of Color: Psychological Interventions with Minority Youth.* J.T. Gibbs, L.N. Huang, and Associates, eds. San Francisco: Jossey-Bass, 1989.

Explores the cultural conflict between traditional values of Latino parents and contemporary Anglo society values and how this tension often leads to anxiety and substance abuse among Hispanic youth.

Randall-David, Elizabeth. *Strategies for Working with Culturally Diverse Communities and Clients.* Washington, D.C.: Association for the Care of Children's Health, 1989.

Reviews the cultural values and behaviors of Haitians and Hispanics/Latinos. Provides specific information on variances, stressors, family structure, religion, health, illness, communication styles, and time orientation. Includes bibliography lists for Haitians, Hispanics/Latinos, Cuban Americans, Mexican Americans, and Puerto Ricans. Also lists organizations that serve these populations.

Rodriguez, Clara E. *Puerto Ricans: Born in the U.S.A..* Boston: Unwin Hyman, 1989.

Profiles Puerto Ricans living in the United States since the end of World War II, primarily those in New York City. Concentrates on four topics: race, education, housing, and work. Characterizes Puerto Ricans as a unicultural, multiracial, integrated group entering a multiethnic, biracial, segregated society. Draws upon examples from literature as well as personal experience.

Ruiz, R.A. "Cultural and Historical Perspectives in Counseling Hispanics." *Counseling the Culturally Different: Theory and Practice.* D. Sue, ed. New York: Wiley, 1981.

Reviews the unique aspects of the various Hispanic cultures and provides guidelines for professional intervention strategies based on cultural traditions.

Serrano, Alberto C., and Fortunato G. Castillo. "The Chicano Child and His Family." *Basic Handbook of Child Psychiatry.* J.P. Noshpitz and I.N.

Berlin, eds. Vol. I: *Normal Development.* New York: Basic Books, 1979, pp. 257–263.

Highlights the significance of language, customs, and culture on the development of the Mexican American child. Differentiates the childrearing patterns between Anglo and Mexican American families. Discusses the influence of folk medicine. Explores language development and academic performance of the Chicano child. Extensive reference list.

Totter, R.T. "Folk Remedies as Indicators of Common Illnesses: Examples from the United States." *Journal of Ethnopharmacology* 4 (1981): 207–221.

Contains an extensive list of popular home remedies, including ingredients, that are commonly used by Hispanics. List was compiled in the lower Rio Grande Valley but is not limited to Mexican American remedies.

Turnbull, H. Rutherford, III, and Ann P. Turnbull. *The Latin American Family and Public Policy in the United States: Informal Support and Transition into Adulthood.* Lawrence: University of Kansas Department of Special Education and Bureau of Child Research, 1987.

The report on a study for the World Rehabilitation Fund which explores (1) the Latin American family and its adaptations, coping strategies, and use of informal support in maintaining within the family a child or adult with a disability; and (2) the Latin American family and its traditions, attitudes, and behaviors with respect to the transition of the member with a disability from adolescence to adulthood.

Valle, K., and W. Vega. *Hispanic Natural Support Systems.* State of California Department of Mental Health, 1980.

Describes the natural support systems occurring in the Latino community, particularly the support network of Latina women: the *comadre* (peer who serves as confidante and provider of emotional and practical support) and *madrina* (woman selected by the parents to be "co-mother" to the infant and provide maternal guidance).

United States Department of Agriculture/Department of Health and Human Services. *Cross-Cultural Counseling: A Guide for Nutrition and Health Counselors.* No. FNS–250. Washington, D.C.: U.S. Government Printing Office, 1986.

Provides general guidelines for counseling people of diverse cultures. Contains specific information on relevant sociocultural issues affecting Hispanic Americans. Includes bibliography and reference lists.

BLACK CULTURES

It is perhaps incorrect to speak of "black cultures." "Black" is not a culture; it is a race. The term "black cultures" (as used in the United States) usually refers to descendants of Africans who were brought as slaves to America and to the Caribbean. The cultural heritage of blacks residing in the United States is more accurately identified as "Afro-American" or "African American." That term differentiates the descendants of Africans, who were brought to the United States as slaves, from descendants of Africans in other parts of the world, such as the Caribbean and South America.[1] Blacks who reside in (or who descend from families reared on) the islands of the Caribbean are more appropriately termed "West Indian" or "Caribbean" blacks.

In this chapter "black cultures" will be used as a collective term encompassing the many subgroups of African Americans and Caribbean blacks; while they share a common African heritage, there are differences among them resulting from the environmental experiences they encountered after emigration. Traditional traits which are shared by these cultures are presented first, providing a general frame of reference for understanding black children and their families. African Americans and Caribbean blacks are then profiled according to family structure, childrearing practices, religion, values, language, health care, and education.

A hallmark of black cultures is the strong, often complex kinship network inherent among them. According to the anthropologist Francis Hsu, there is a very real correlation between kinship and life-styles. Dr. Hsu has divided societies into four types, based on kinship patterns: (1) The majority of Oriental peoples (excluding Moslems and Hindus of India); (2) Western peoples of European origin; (3) Hindus in India and Moslems of the subcontinent; and (4) Africans south of the Sahara. The Oriental society is based on a kinship pattern of mutual dependency, emphasizing a father-son relationship; Western society is rooted on self-reliance, with a strong husband-wife relationship; Hindu and Moslem societies are based on a supernatural reliance, with a dominant mother-son relationship. The majority of Africans south of the Sahara constitute a society which is characterized by a kinship pattern of mutual dependence together with the emphasis on a brother-to-brother relationship, with minimal worship of ancestors.

Other distinctive features of this type of society, as seen from Hsu's anthropological perspective, are the conditioning of the individual to be inherently competitive; a present-time orientation; lack of a written language. Rulers in these societies maintain direct contact with their subjects, but they must exact obedience and awe from them to maintain their power, which is fostered by many taboos and restrictions. A systematic theology does not exist, and religion ranges from simple animism to personified gods. Racial and religious prejudice are almost non-existent, and there is a lack of missionary zeal. Religious mythology, including supernatural beings who are often related to ancestral spirits, is called upon to provide commonsense answers to concrete problems of daily life. There is a universal belief in witchcraft and sorcery. Witches are perceived as possessors of magic, witchcraft, influence, and power.[2]

An examination of African family life provides an understanding and appreciation of the rich cultural heritage that has survived among African Americans and West Indian and Caribbean blacks, despite the experience of slavery. African family life was based on (1) the kinship group and tribal survival, and (2) oneness of being and union with nature.[3] Marriage represented a union of families (not just individuals); these kinship bonds provided the basis of political, social, and economic organization within each tribal unit. Even land ownership was not by individuals, but by the tribal or family unit. A strong sense of shared loyalty prevailed.

Family structure was patriarchal in authority: great reverence was attached to the man's role as protector and provider for the family.[4] Family roles and relationships were otherwise flexible and interchangeable, promoting interdependence rather than reliance on specific members for specific tasks.[5]

Children were highly valued in African families and raised with considerable love and attention. They were seen as symbols of the continuity of life.[6] Grandmothers had a unique and honored role in the raising of children. Grandparents were seen as living links with the past, the source of family history, folklore, proverbs, and other traditional lore.[7]

An example of the important role of children in African culture is the tradition of "outdooring," the West African equivalent of a christening. According to Ghanaian ritual, the outdooring (representing the first time a baby is brought outside the house) is a family ceremony to celebrate God giving a precious gift—a baby. During the ceremony, a tribal chief chants prayers, intones the names of the baby's ancestors, requests that their spirits guide the child to a long and prosperous life, and spills a libation onto the ground in honor of the past chiefs and mothers. Three drops of water and three drops of liquor are placed on the baby's tongue "to teach the child the difference," and a coin is placed in the infant's hand "so he will learn to hold onto money."[8]

The influence of African attitudes toward health and illness is also notable:

> Health was viewed as being in harmony and union with nature. A long life was a sign of proper habits of living. Death after a fruitful life was seen as a natural process. Illness was a result of disharmony or disease. It was believed that illness was caused by evil spirits or demons acting on their own or on behalf of a living or dead soul. Conjure men and women, or voodoo doctors, were curers who specialized in magico-religious powers and the restoration of balance and harmony.[9]

Black cultures have strong roots in their African heritage. "There is a set of core values and behavior, which in its gestalt remains distinctively characteristic of and understood by a majority of Black people."[10] The African heritage of kinship bonds and role flexibility has withstood even the vicissitudes of slavery, and today remains a characteristic strength in black families.

There is no such entity as "the typical black family" any more than there is a "typical white family" or "typical Asian family." There are African American families and Caribbean black families of all socioeconomic levels, religious beliefs, occupations, and backgrounds. Each family is unique and must be considered in terms of its own heritage.

African Americans

Historically, black immigrants to America generally differed from other immigrant groups in that:

(1) Their country of origin had norms and values that were dissimilar to the Anglo-Saxon American way of life
(2) They represented a wide variety of tribes, each with its own traditions, language, and culture
(3) Initially, they came without women
(4) Most importantly, they came in bondage[11]

Subsequent diversity resulted from geographic residence, family values and life-style, education, socioeconomic status, and religious background. The effects of poverty and racism, and the life-style differences in the rural South versus the urban North are examples of disparate environmental influences that account for wide variations in "the black American family." Stressing the relationship between race and poverty, Small states that "[m]uch of the lifestyle and 'culture' designated as Black has been dictated by economics rather than choice."[12]

Pinderhughes has hypothesized that Afro-American ethnic identity is influenced by three cultural sources: (1) residuals from Africa, (2) identification with mainstream America, and (3) adaptations and responses to the "victim" system that is a product of racism, poverty, and oppression.[13]

Family Structure: Black family structure today among African Americans is heterogeneous. The extended family concept, reflecting a complex kinship network of blood and non-related persons, continues although most families are now nuclear in structure. Three generational families are not uncommon, as the elderly are usually cared for within the extended family network; grandmothers continue to play an especially significant role. Relatives tend to live in close proximity, providing a readily available support system for one another. Various people interchange roles, jobs, and family functions. As described by Small:

> Black families see nothing inherently wrong in leaving younger children in the care of older ones. Usually older

children are trained in child care by participation in basic family functions. Family position may be more significant than sex, and role distinction is not rigidly adhered to. Boys learn to cook and diaper babies, and girls learn to putty windows and repair iron cords. All learn how to deal with bill collectors, welfare workers and other "intruders."[14]

Fathers, regardless of income, expect recognition as the head of the family; their identity is tied to their ability to provide for their family. Mothers are "all sacrificing," the "strength of the family"; their identity is tied to their role as a mother.[15] The family unit, however it is configured, remains a basic source of strength.

The importance of family structure is reinforced in Axelson's profiles of black Americans according to three class structures: (1) the large number who are educated and assimilated into middle-class society, (2) poor blacks with a stable family structure and the potential for socioeconomic mobility, and (3) the black underclass, with unstable family structure, lack of job skills, and dependent on welfare.[16]

Childrearing: Children are generally loved and highly valued. Children, especially males, are seen as a special contribution to the family's existence in accordance with the African view of continuity of life;[17] they may also be seen as a measure of the parents' sexuality and maturity. A child's name often expresses ethnic pride in addition to giving a child his own identity. Nicknames are common. Grandmothers, older siblings and other kinfolk share in child-care responsibilities. In general, black mothers are more permissive than Anglo mothers in the feeding and weaning of their children.[18]

There is widespread concern about spoiling children. Physical punishment is often the accepted mode of discipline; parents consider it defensive training for survival in a hostile environment. This use of physical punishment may incorrectly be viewed as child abuse. It is important to consider discipline of African American children within a cultural context:

> African-American families have a strong belief in disciplining inappropriate behavior in children. The discipline administered may range from an "evil eye" (which conveys to the child that it is time to stop a behavior immediately), to threatening to punish, to "spanking"

(Anglo terminology) or "beating" (African-American terminology).[19]

In lower socioeconomic families, discipline is more likely to be harsh, preparing children for survival in a difficult environment. Variances in childrearing practices often reflect a family's socioeconomic status.

Children participate in most family activities. Action-oriented skills are encouraged. Adolescence starts early. Traditionally, males are socialized to be strong, aggressive, and independent; females are socialized to be self-sufficient and helpful to others in the family.

Children whose parents are unable to care for them are "informally adopted" by others, whether related or not. This tradition of taking in and raising other children is most commonly seen in extended families in the rural South and in the inner cities.

Religion: African-Americans are affiliated with a wide diversity of religions: Baptist, African Methodist, Jehovah's Witness, Church of God in Christ, Seventh Day Adventist, Pentecostal, Nation of Islam, numerous other Islamic sects, Presbyterian, Lutheran, Episcopal, and Roman Catholic. Religion plays a central role in the lives of black families; it is stable and organized. The black church meets a variety of needs: conserver of morals, strengthener of family life, and final authority on right and wrong. Through the church, blacks are able to obtain a sense of recognition, develop leadership abilities, release emotional tension, and socialize.[20] Many prominent black leaders have come from the ranks of ordained ministers.

The Black Muslim movement, a black nationalist group generic to America, blends religious and anti-integrationist beliefs. Its members, identifying with the ancient lost tribe, Shabazz, replace Western norms with Mohamadan ones:

> . . . members are required to give up vices such as overeating, drinking, using narcotics, and fornication, which their leaders say were foisted on blacks by their white masters. Women are taught homemaking and are expected to obey their husbands.[21]

The present American Muslim Mission seeks to end ideas of black nationalism and integrate with worldwide Islamic traditions.[22]

Values: African heritage as well as experiences in America are reflected in the cultural values of African Americans. Kinship, group loyalty, mutual support and aid, compassion, and adaptability are highly valued. Family and church are esteemed as sources of strength, consistency, and identity. Family problems and personal relationships are not freely discussed with outsiders. Time orientation varies along socioeconomic lines: Poorer families tend to be present-time oriented, while middle- and upper-class families tend to be future oriented.

Language/Communication Style: Many black Americans speak with a culturally distinctive dialect, black English, which differs from "standard English" in intonation, diction, inflection, structure, and form. It is characterized by dropping final consonants, omitting the verb "is" in the present tense, and using singular nouns for plural objects. Black English is often used in conjunction with "standard English" and/or in specific ethnic situations.

"Rapping" is another unique style of communication that is especially popular among black adolescents. "Rapping" has been described as:

> [a] fluent and lively way of talking, characterized by a high degree of personal style through which the speaker intends to draw attention to himself or some aspect of himself that he feels is attractive or carries weight with his crowd.[23]

Rapping involves considerable skill with vocabulary; it is similar in its complexity to the Cockney rhyming slang of old London. Rap music is especially popular among young blacks.

Attitudes Toward Health: Traditional African beliefs strongly influence the perception of health as related to the degree of harmony or discord in one's body, mind, and spirit. Some African Americans equate a healthy body with a balance of hot and cold humors. There are many folk beliefs about the quality and character of the blood (considered "hot"). There is a strong belief that serious illness can be avoided. Self-care and folk medicine are quite prevalent, especially where health care services are not affordable, convenient, or sensitive to the needs of the black community. Health beliefs are closely related to religious beliefs. The laying on of hands and rooting (derived from voodoo) are considered healing practices for some; others believe in healing by means of mystic (supernatural) phenomena, psychological support, and herbal remedies. Many rely upon prayer for the prevention and treatment of illness; some perceive illness as punishment for sins.

Specific health problems of black children include high rates of infant mortality, sickle-cell anemia, and elevated lead levels. Many of these and other health problems in the black community are related to poverty.

Attitude Toward Work and Education: Education and academic achievement are valued, yet the learning process for many black children is hindered by social and economic problems. A counterschool culture exists in low-income black (and other) neighborhoods where academic success is devalued; education is not perceived as a means of improving one's life.

There are ongoing controversies over theories that black children learn differently because of their different cultural background; each side charges racism. Some studies indicate that African American children utilize inferential reasoning in preference to deductive or inductive reasoning and tend to approximate space, number, and time in preference to complete accuracy. Differences in communication style—the use of black English versus standard English, and a "spiral" style of storytelling (skipping around among apparently unrelated topics) versus a "linear" style (proceeding clearly from one event to the next)—compound the issue. It is incorrect, however, to infer that a child's linguistic performance accurately represents that child's linguistic competence; it may only indicate a lack of abstract terminology:

> ... the direction of dependence between language and cognition is still undetermined. However, it is no longer considered possible to extrapolate cognitive patterns directly from specific linguistic patterns ... if a language or form of language is found to lack a unitary term for a certain phenomenon, this does not indicate ... its speakers are unaware of the phenomenon or that they cannot deal with it when it occurs.[24]

Black families have traditionally stressed a strong work orientation; this is one of the major strengths of the black family.[25] Poor blacks (men and women) are more likely to work than their white counterparts; young blacks enter the labor market at earlier ages than their white counterparts.[26] Black unemployment remains a major economic and social problem, particularly among adolescent males.

Caribbean Blacks

West Indian blacks share a common ancestry with African Americans; they also represent a distinctive cultural subgroup (or subgroups) quite different from American blacks. Most of these differences have evolved because of circumstances of history and environment. Caribbean blacks are a heterogeneous group; their differences are a reflection of the cultures that settled the West Indies—British, French, Spanish, and Dutch. Those in the British West Indies, for example, took on British traditions as a framework for their lives:

> Completely cut off from their own cultural roots, these black West Indians were molded into a new kind of culture, centered on the high-minded values of 19th century Britain—a simple Christian faith, respect for the law and education, a belief in hard work, a love of cricket, the monarchy and all things British.[27]

Emancipation of West Indian blacks occurred earlier than emancipation of blacks in America. As British West Indian slaves were freed, they were permitted to become true heads of their families, landowners, and economically independent. The black landowners became the black upper class, while the illegitimate black children of white plantation owners, the mulattos, formed the middle class. The first West Indian blacks who migrated to the United States (during the nineteenth century) were predominantly middle-class mulattos from the British-owned islands, many of whom were educated and skilled. Later immigrants (especially during the period from 1940 to 1978) were primarily adult, well educated, and skilled. Usually one family member migrated first and became established. Many women came alone, as it was often easier for them to secure employment. The new arrivals stayed with relatives who had immigrated earlier; other family members were sent for later. They developed their own support systems.[28]

The majority of West Indians migrated to the United States at the turn of the century, were relatively poor and uneducated, settled around the New York City area, and took menial jobs. The socioeconomic success of their descendants, similar to contemporary ethnic Europeans, is attributable to "hard work, vocational upgrading, conscientious thrift, and education."[29] West Indian blacks avoided the devastation and disorganization of the Civil War and Reconstruction period (suffered by American blacks) and subsequent dependent status. Consequently, they have maintained a distinct social self-identity and group solidarity.[30]

Because of their diverse experiences with independence and racial discrimination, American blacks and Caribbean blacks have developed different and separate ethnic identities. American blacks have a lengthy history of being an oppressed minority group who came here against their will. Caribbean blacks, on the contrary, have immigrated voluntarily to the United States. They were neither minorities nor oppressed on their islands; consequently, they are less apt to harbor a sense of racism and white dominance. Caribbean blacks emigrate for educational and occupational opportunities (and in the case of Haiti, to escape oppressive political regimes); they immigrate legally and illegally to the United States. In contrast, many American blacks (particularly those of lower socioeconomic status) tend to be present oriented, consider themselves hopeless victims of racism and poverty, and perceive the future with negativism. West Indians tend to be future oriented and have a stronger sense of control over their destiny.

Caribbean blacks have primarily settled along the east coast of the United States. They are proportionately few in number, representing only 1 percent of the total American black population.[31] Many have started small businesses. There is also a strong homeowner ethos; the expression "buy house" became symbolic of establishing a toehold in the mainstream society. Relations with American blacks can be strained for a variety of reasons. Caribbean blacks have a strong sense of ethnic identity and may resent being categorized indiscriminately along with all other blacks or Hispanics. They will often identify themselves as "British" or "West Indian" rather than "black"; their life-style is more similar to white or black middle-class Americans than to inner-city blacks. They have established their own self-help organizations, integrated into the existing society, and maintained ties with their homelands. American blacks often complain that Caribbean immigrants are willing to take menial jobs at low wages, lowering the standard for all blacks. Many American blacks resent what they consider a lack of commitment on the part of Caribbean blacks to civil rights and other black issues; Caribbean blacks do not always see these as "their" concerns.

The acceptance of immigrant groups by the host country is often determined by the availability of jobs and housing and by who on the economic ladder feels threatened (with displacement) by their presence. Those blacks from the British West Indies who immigrated to England in the 1950s encountered much discrimination. They were the "coloured" minority, discriminated against in jobs and housing. The subsequent closing of Britain's doors to black commonwealth nations in 1962 contributed to an increase in the immigration of Caribbean blacks to the United States. Prior to that influx, Caribbean immigrants integrated into black or Hispanic communities without many ethnic distinctions. As their numbers increased, ethnic Caribbean neighborhoods evolved.

It is important to recognize the broad diversity among West Indian immigrants. They come from Haiti, Jamaica, and the Dominican Republic, from Grenada, Barbados, and the Bahamas, from Trinidad, Tobago, and other island nations such as St. Vincent and the Grenadines. Cuba, Puerto Rico, Panama, Guyana, and Curaçao are sometimes included in a broader usage of the term "Caribbean blacks." These immigrants are different from each other, island by island, by reason of ethnicity, education, economic status, and to some degree, language.

Haitian Americans constitute a unique subgroup among Caribbean blacks. They are the most recent black immigrants to the United States, escaping a history of violence and repressive dictatorships and a devastated economy. These recent immigrants primarily come from a poor, rural background.

While Haitian Americans share an African heritage and many cultural similarities with other blacks, they differ from other Caribbean blacks in language, religious beliefs, and certain cultural values. In appearance, they are darker skinned than other black Americans. These differences can cause special problems:

> Haitian students find themselves in particularly difficult circumstances. Viewed as Blacks by White students, they suffer from discrimination on the basis of their race. Viewed as "foreigners" by Black students, they are frequently rejected on the basis of their culture.[32]

Family Structure: In all Caribbean black cultures, families are closely knit although the traditional extended, multigenerational family of the past is less likely to prevail. Family format now often varies according to social status: large, extended families predominate in the lower socioeconomic groups, while nuclear families are more common among upper- and middle-class groups. Marriage has a high status and is often postponed until economically feasible. The husband's primary role is that of economic provider; the wife's is childrearing.[33] There is little or no stigma attached to having a child outside of marriage, especially in lower socioeconomic groups; they believe that producing a child proves a male's virility and a female's desirability. Socially and economically, there is a wide disparity between the upper and lower classes in the islands.

Among Haitian Americans, parental control usually extends into adulthood—even to the selection of a marriage partner and the choice of occupation. The role of the mother tends to be influential; she is seen as a stabilizing force and a significant voice in family decision-making. Parental authority is generally respected and accepted without question.[34]

There is a strong bond between mothers and sons; sons are doted on regardless of their sibling position. This closeness continues even after the son's marriage; sons are expected to take care of their mothers. "Child lending" is an acceptable practice of sending school-aged children to live with extended family members.[35]

Childrearing Practices: Traditionally, among Caribbean blacks, children are highly valued and considered an essential part of marriage. A warm and loving relationship exists between parents and children. The mother assumes primary responsibility for child care; a mother who works may have her children live with grandmothers or other relatives. Parents often sacrifice for the betterment of their children, who are then expected to feel a strong sense of obligation to their families. Family elders, especially grandparents, are revered. Children are taught to respect their elders, not to talk back or to disagree with older persons. Spankings are the primary form of punishment and are often accompanied by scoldings or "tongue lashings." Girls are raised to be obedient; assertiveness is discouraged. Domestic training is emphasized. Traditionally, socialization with boys is closely supervised. Boys are socialized to be responsible. Achievement and education are emphasized.[36]

Religion: Most West Indians are Christian. All denominations are represented, with the majority belonging to the Anglican

(Episcopal), Roman Catholic, Baptist, Methodist, and Seventh-day Adventist churches. Women and children constitute the majority of churchgoers. Religious education is commonly included in school curricula on the Caribbean islands.

Religious beliefs are a source of support and problem solving to West Indians. Folk beliefs are also strong. Practitioners of *obeah* (witchcraft) are sought for consultation in crisis situations. The islands have a small but significant following in a variety of cults. Religious worship in Haiti, regardless of denomination (Catholic, Protestant, or voodoo) is vigorous, physical, and energy-consuming.[37] Voodoo and religious cults that involve ritual slaughter of animals are often practiced in Haiti. Voodoo is the religion of 80 percent of the six million Haitians in the world, one million of whom live in the United States and Canada. It is an animistic religion, which believes in one God over all (*"le bon dieu"*) and many lesser gods (*loas*), some of whose origins can be traced back to Africa. Voodoo supports reverence for ancestors and nature and involves elaborate ceremonies. The word "voodoo" is derived from the African word *vu-DU*, meaning spirit, or family of spirits. People who practice voodoo are said to "serve" the spirits.

Values: Caribbean blacks are characteristically law abiding, church going, hard working, and cheerfully optimistic. Their closely knit family life is their basic source of strength. The preservation of traditions is fostered. Thriftiness is valued, especially saving for a home or business. West Indians value family obligations, upward mobility, and helping other co-ethnics; they are proud and self-sufficient. Greetings and courtesies tend to be rather formal, yet their music, celebrations, and other social interactions are outgoing and lively. Many West Indians have a casual "soon come" attitude about time. Haitians, unlike most other Caribbean blacks, come from a bargaining culture similar to that of the Middle East.

Color distinction, as a value, still exists among some Caribbean blacks:

> American Blacks tend to define people as either Black or White. West Indians, in contrast, make three distinctions: Black (or Negro), colored and White. The lighter you are, the closer you are to the European end of the continuum and the higher your status in Caribbean society.[38]

Language: While English predominates, the language of many West Indians reflects the history of their particular island—English, French or Spanish. Those from the British West Indies speak with the traditional accent of British English. French is the official language of Haiti, but its use is limited to the upper classes. Creole is the language of most Haitians while *Patois*, a Creole dialect, is widely spoken in rural areas of Jamaica. Creole is a blend of French vocabulary and African grammar; it is primarily a spoken, rather than a written language. Spanish language and words of Spanish origin are used on several Caribbean islands.

Music and rhythm are an integral part of communication style in the Caribbean; they are an important form of expression. The distinctive varieties of Caribbean music, while sharing West African roots, reflect the wide cultural mix of the islands. There is the *merengue* of Dominica; the *salsa* of Cuba and Puerto Rico; the *calypso* of Trinidad; and the *reggae* of Jamaica. The steel-drum band, characteristically associated with Caribbean music, is of recent vintage. Steel-drum music dates back only to World War II, when Trinidad was a refueling stop for battleships; the empty oil drums began to add to the traditional drumming known as *tamboo bamboo*—rhythms that had been played on bamboo sticks to accompany carnival.

Attitude Toward Health: West Indians are generally stoical about pain and suffering and are reluctant to seek outside help. They prefer to turn to family elders, their local pastor, and/or folk medicine, such as witchcraft. Among Haitians, blood is considered the medium of bodily and spiritual disease; serious illnesses are believed to be caused by irregularities in the blood system.[39]

The diet of Caribbean blacks is typical of the diet in warm countries—spicy. Each island/ethnic group has its own specialties. The diet is usually well balanced and often includes rice and beans, seafood, chicken, meat, and tropical fruits. Rum is a favorite alcoholic beverage.

Attitude Toward Work and Education: Education is highly valued as a tool of upward mobility. There is a strong work ethic, reflective of their European heritage. In the New York City area, Caribbean immigrants are well represented in nursing, in restaurants, domestic skill jobs, in the taxi industry, and in high level positions within many city institutions and agencies.

The importance of education and work may cause some Caribbean black parents to misinterpret the procedures and processes of special education programs in United States schools. A typical Haitian response is eloquently expressed by the Director of the Center for Haitian Child Development, City College of New York:

> Placing Haitian children who are not seriously or severely impaired in segregated programs is in conflict with Haitian culture; not because there is an inability on the part of parents to accept that their children may have problems, but because it is felt that these problems can be remedied or compensated for. The Haitian parent would rather have, and be proud of, a child who has good academic skills, but in the event that this is not the case, the parent would like to see that other skills be encouraged and nurtured. In this way, the child can still become a productive and self-sufficient member of society.[40]

The similarities and the differences between African Americans and Caribbean blacks provide a unique study of a broad culture that originated from a similar (perhaps the same) heritage and subsequently evolved under very different environmental circumstances into different cultural subgroups/ethnic groups. It reinforces the importance of exploring migration history in cross-cultural assessment. To understand an African-American child or a Caribbean black child, it is essential to utilize a family systems perspective—to consider that child in terms of family *and* environment.

NOTES

1. Elaine Pinderhughes, "Afro-American Families and the Victim System," *Ethnicity and Family Therapy*, M. McGoldrick, J.K. Pearce, and J. Giordano, eds. (New York: Guilford, 1982), p. 108.
2. Francis L.K. Hsu, "Kinship and Ways of Life: An Exploration," *Psychological Anthropology: Approaches to Culture and Personality*, F.L.K. Hsu, ed. (Homewood, Ill.: Dorsey, 1961), pp. 400–456.
3. Betty Greathouse and Velvet G. Miller, "The Black American," *Culture and Childrearing*, A.L. Clark, ed. (Philadelphia: F.A. Davis, 1981), p. 71.

4. Robert Staples, *Introduction to Black Sociology* (New York: McGraw-Hill, 1976), p. 114.

5. W.W. Nobles and G.M. Nobles, "African Roots in Black Families: The Social-Psychological Dynamics of Black Family Life and the Implications for Nursing Care," *Black Awareness: Implications for Black Patient Care*, D. Luckoft, ed. (New York: American Journal of Nursing, 1976), p. 8.

6. Staples, *Introduction to Black Sociology*, p. 115.

7. Ronald Staples, *The Black Woman in America: Sex, Marriage, and the Family* (Chicago: Nelson-Hall, 1973).

8. "Ghanaians Celebrate New Babies and One Another," *New York Times*, 27 August 1990, p. B5.

9. "Cultural Health Traditions: a Black Perspective," *Providing Safe Nursing Care for Ethnic People of Color*, quoted by Greathouse and Miller, *Culture and Childrearing*, p. 72.

10. Paulette Moore Hines and Nancy Boyd-Franklin, "Black Families," *Ethnicity and Family Therapy*, M. McGoldrick, J.K. Pearce, and J. Giordano, eds. (New York: Guilford, 1982), p. 84.

11. Staples, *Introduction to Black Sociology*, p. 113.

12. Willie V. Small, "The Neglect of Black Children," *Child Abuse, Neglect and the Family Within a Cultural Context*. DHEW Publication No. (OHDS) 78-30135) (Washington, D.C.: U.S. Government Printing Office, 1978), p. 14.

13. Pinderhughes, *Ethnicity and Family Therapy*, p. 108.

14. Small, *Child Abuse, Neglect and the Family Within a Cultural Context*, p. 14.

15. Hines and Boyd-Franklin, *Ethnicity and Family Therapy*, p. 88.

16. John A. Axelson, *Counseling and Development in a Multicultural Society* (Belmont, Calif.: Brooks/Cole, 1985), p. 73.

17. Staples, *Introduction to Black Sociology*, p. 133.

18. Greathouse and Miller, "The Black American," *Culture and Childrearing*, p. 81.

19. Personal correspondence (Justine Strickland) cited by Penny P. Anderson and Emily Schrag Fenichel, *Serving Culturally Diverse Families of Infants and Toddlers with Disabilities* (Washington, D.C.: National Center for Clinical Infant Programs, 1989), p. 10.

20. Staples, *Introduction to Black Sociology*, pp. 166-169.

21. *The People's Almanac*, quoted in John A. Axelson, *Counseling and Development in a Multicultural Society*, p. 74.

22. Axelson, *Counseling and Development in a Multicultural Society*, p. 74.

23. Greathouse and Miller, *Culture and Childrearing*, pp. 85-86.

24. S.H. Houston, "A Re-examination of Some Assumptions About the Language of the Disadvantaged Child," *Progress in Child Psychiatry and Child*

Development, S. Chess and A. Thomas, eds. (New York: Brunner-Mazel, 1971), pp. 233–250.

25. Robert B. Hill, *The Strengths of Black Families* (New York: National Urban League, 1971), pp. 5–8.

26. Greathouse and Miller, *Culture and Childrearing,* p. 78.

27. Christopher Booker, "Failure of a Promised Land," *The London Telegram,* March 28, 1987.

28. Janet Brice, "West Indian Families," *Ethnicity and Family Therapy,* M. McGoldrick, J.K. Pearce, and J. Giordano, eds. (New York: Guilford, 1982), pp. 124–125.

29. Axelson, *Counseling and Development in a Multicultural Society,* p. 74.

30. Thomas Sowell, "Three Black Histories," *American Ethnic Groups,* T. Sowell, ed. (Washington, D.C.: The Urban Institute, 1978), pp. 47–49.

31. Axelson, *Counseling and Development in a Multicultural Society,* p. 74.

32. National Coalition of Advocates for Students, *New Voices: Immigrant Students in U.S. Public Schools* (Boston: National Coalition of Advocates for Students, 1988), p. 61.

33. Brice, "West Indian Families," *Ethnicity and Family Therapy,* pp. 128–129.

34. Elizabeth Randall-David, *Strategies for Working with Culturally Diverse Communities and Clients* (Washington, D.C.: Association for the Care of Children's Health, 1989), p. 53; and Axelson, *Counseling and Development in a Multicultural Society,* p. 76.

35. Brice, "West Indian Families," *Ethnicity and Family Therapy,* pp. 128–129.

36. Ibid., pp. 128–129.

37. Axelson, *Counseling and Development in a Multicultural Society,* p. 76.

38. M. Garvey, *The Consequences of Class and Color,* quoted in Brice, "West Indian Families," *Ethnicity and Family Therapy,* p. 126.

39. Randall-David, *Strategies for Working with Culturally Diverse Communities and Clients,* p. 54.

40. Maryse Roumain, quoted in *New Voices: Immigrant Students in U.S. Public Schools,* p. 55.

BIBLIOGRAPHY

Anderson, Penny P., and Emily Schrag Fenichel. *Serving Culturally Diverse Families of Infants and Toddlers with Disabilities.* Washington, D.C.: National Center for Clinical Infant Programs, 1989.

Presents examples of characteristic "tendencies" of African American families concerning childrearing, illness and disability, communication and interactional patterns.

Axelson, John A. *Counseling and Development in a Multicultural Society.* Belmont, Calif.: Brooks/Cole, 1985.

Reviews the history of African Americans and West Indian blacks. Describes characteristics of three classes of blacks in present day society: (1) those who have assimilated into middle-class society; (2) poor blacks; and (3) black underclass. Discusses religious beliefs, including Black Muslims.

Berry, Gordon Lavern, and Joy Keido Asamen. *Black Students: Psychosocial Issues and Academic Achievement.* Newbury Park, Calif.: Sage, 1989.

Argues that academic achievement for black students is influenced not only by circumstances found in the individual or family and school settings but by a whole host of factors. Social and economic environments, the development of the self-concept, peer pressure, personal attributes such as resources, skills and motivation—these are among the many factors contributing toward a person's ability to achieve academically. *Black Students* brings together current research to address these factors from a variety of perspectives and covers the full educational cycle from kindergarten through the college years.

Billingsley, Andrew. *Black Families in White America.* Englewood Cliffs, N.J.: Prentice-Hall, 1968.

Describes and defines three major types of contemporary black families: nuclear, extended, and augmented. Presents data that refute the widely held concept that structure of the family determines the functioning of its members; two-parent families are not necessarily stable, nor are single-parent families necessarily disorganized and unstable.

Billingsley, Andrew. "Family Functioning in the Low-Income Black Community." *Social Casework* 50 (1969): 563–572.

A series of studies of childrearing patterns and family life among low-income black families are cited to dispel common stereotypes and negative generalizations of the black family. Lower-class blacks are divided into the working non-poor, the working poor, and the non-working poor and the distinct patterns of family structure at each level are described.

Boyd-Franklin, Nancy. *Black Families in Therapy: A Multisystems Approach.* New York: Guilford, 1989.

Addresses aspects of the black experience such as extended family systems, informal adoption, cultural and political values, and religious or spiritual orientation. Explores the issues faced by different socioeconomic groups among black families, including poor families, two-parent and single-parent families, middle-class families, and upper-middle-class families. Advocates a "multisystems" approach to treatment incorporating the individual, the family, extended family, church, community, and social services.

Brice, Janet. "West Indian Families." *Ethnicity and Family Therapy.* M. McGoldrick, J.K. Pearce, and J. Giordano, eds. New York: Guilford, 1982, pp. 123–133.

Reviews the historical heritage, migration, and demographics of the British West Indian family. Discusses the cultural distinctions between British West Indian families and American black families, primarily in a mental health context.

Comer, James P., and Alvin F. Poussaint. *Black Child Care.* New York: Simon and Schuster, 1975.

A guide to the emotional and psychological development of black children in America, written by two black child psychiatrists. Addresses identity problems of infancy, preschool, school, and adolescence. Suggests ways for black parents to deal with problems of prejudice and racism. Provides an understanding of the developmental issues facing black families. Includes a suggested reading list.

Ellison, Christopher. "Family Ties, Friendships, and Subjective Well-being Among Black Americans." *Journal of Marriage and the Family* 52 (May 1990): 298–310.

Explores the close extended-kin relations among lower-class blacks which persist even among upwardly mobile black families. Cites the exchanges of goods and services as an example of an adaptive reaction to deprivation.

Gary, Lawrence E., ed. *Black Men.* Newbury Park, Calif.: Sage, 1981.

Examines the black man's demographics, his relationships with women and family, his psychological and social coping strategies, and his role in major institutions—school, church, social welfare, and the legal system. Interdisciplinary content counterbalances previously held assumptions and myths.

Gibbs, Jewelle Taylor, Larke Nahme Huang, and Associates. *Children of Color: Psychological Interventions with Minority Youth.* San Francisco: Jossey-Bass, 1989.

Provides guidelines for understanding, recognizing, and successfully treating the psychological problems of minority children and adolescents. Chapter 4, "Black American Children," by LaRue Allen and Shayda Majidi-Ahi, explains how poverty, racism and discrimination can shape a black child's personality. Chapter 6, "Black American Adolescents," by Jewelle Taylor Gibbs, shows how extreme poverty and inadequate living conditions make black adolescents more vulnerable to drug and alcohol abuse and susceptible to increased levels of hostility and depression.

Greathouse, Betty, and Velvet G. Miller. "The Black American." *Culture and Childrearing.* A.L. Clark, ed. Philadelphia: F.A. Davis, 1981, pp. 68–95.

The authors, black nurses, review the historical background (pre-slavery, slavery, and post-slavery periods), family structure and strengths, childrearing (early infancy, middle years, and adolescence), and health care implications for black Americans. The comprehensive information is drawn from extensive reference sources.

Hale, Janice. *Extracting Learning Styles from Social/Cultural Diversity: Studies of Five American Minorities.* L. Morris, ed. Norman: University of Oklahoma Press, 1986, pp. 7–27.

Discusses past and present research on how black children learn, and what can be done to educate them more effectively. Traces norms and childrearing practices of African-Americans to West Africa and considers this distinctive subculture, implicating teaching-learning styles and cognitive development.

Hale-Benson, Janice E. *Black Children: Their Roots, Culture, and Learning Styles.* Baltimore: Johns Hopkins, 1986.

Describes the influence of African heritage on African American children from anthropological, sociological, psychological, and historical perspectives. Contrasts the cognitive styles, family life, and patterns of play of black and

Anglo children. Advocates educational practices that are more sensitive to the learning styles of African American children.

Haley, Arthur. *Roots.* Garden City, N.Y.: Doubleday, 1976.

This popular book (and television mini-series) poignantly portrays the richness of African culture and the vicissitudes of slavery. The author's tale of the search for his family's roots is related in a manner that evokes understanding and respect for the heritage of black Americans.

Hanna, Judith Lynne. "Race Relations: Ideals and Children's Realities." *The Brown University Child Behavior and Development Letter* 4 (April 1988): 4–6.

Report on a study of the problematic inter-racial experiences of children in desegregated schools. Discusses the causes of counterschool culture in low-income populations. Suggests positive approaches for promoting positive interracial relations, such as individual and classroom counseling.

Harel, Zev, Edward A. McKinney, and Michael Williams. *Black Aged: Understanding Diversity and Service Needs.* Newbury Park, Calif.: Sage, 1990.

Demonstrates that the black community is among the poorest of ethnic communities in levels of health, income, and quality of housing for its aged. Assesses the state of America's black aged and analyzes policies and programs.

Hill, Robert B. *The Strengths of Black Families.* New York: National Urban League, 1971.

In researching the adaptive strengths of black families, Hill cites five characteristics—strong kinship bonds, strong work orientation, adaptability of family roles, strong achievement orientation, and strong religious orientation—as the strengths that have enabled black Americans to survive and advance in spite of racism and poverty.

Hines, Paulette Moore, and Nancy Boyd-Franklin. "Black Families." *Ethnicity and Family Therapy.* M. McGoldrick, J.K. Pearce, and J. Giordano, eds. New York: Guilford, 1982.

Dispels the notion that "all blacks fit into one mold." Describes the diversity that exists among black families and communities as determined by a complex interplay of variables. Profiles black families within a cultural and societal context and an understanding of their strengths. Urges other therapists to treat black families utilizing such an ecostructural approach. Includes case study examples and references.

Hsu, Francis L.K. "Kinship and Ways of Life: An Exploration." *Psychological Anthropology: Approaches to Culture and Personality*. F.L.K. Hsu, ed. Homewood, Ill.: Dorsey, 1961, pp. 400–456.

Asserts that a very real correlation exists between kinship and ways of life. Categorizes societies according to their patterns of kinship. Highlights the societal structure of Africans, explaining the origins and the implications of the common heritage of black Americans and Caribbean blacks.

Huff, C. Ronald, ed. *Gangs in America: Diffusion, Diversity, and Public Policy*. Newbury Park, Calif.: Sage, 1990.

Focuses on the historical and cultural perspectives of gangs, defines and measures gang violence, and compares and contrasts black gang membership with that of other ethnic and racial groups.

Kochman, Thomas. *Black and White Styles in Conflict*. Chicago: University of Chicago Press, 1981.

Examines the diversity between black and white communication styles. Explores the controversy concerning the use of black English.

Lincoln, C. Eric, and Lawrence H. Mamiya. *The Black Church in the African-American Experience*. Durham, N.C.: Duke University Press, 1990.

Examines the role of the black church as the hub of traditional black life. Reviews the history and development of black churches, their complexity, variety, and rich religious traditions. Researches the religious experiences of the African American people and the role of preaching, music, and women in those experiences.

McAdoo, Harriette Pipes, ed. *Black Families*. 2nd ed. Newbury Park, Calif.: Sage, 1988.

Addresses the historical and theoretical conceptualizations of black families; demographic, economic, mobility, and educational patterns; male-female relationships; and family policy and advocacy. Part IV, "Socialization within African-American Families," contains chapters dealing with parenting and family issues.

McAdoo, Harriette Pipes, and John L. McAdoo, eds. *Black Children: Social, Educational, and Parental Environments.* Newbury Park, Calif.: Sage, 1985.

Presents empirical research that African American children develop a duality for their existence and that in order to be fully functional, they must develop skills to do well simultaneously in two different cultures, black and non-black. Explores the meaning of this duality in socioeconomic, educational, parental, and internal environments.

National Coalition of Advocates for Students. *New Voices: Immigrant Students in U.S. Public Schools.* Boston: National Coalition of Advocates for Students, 1988.

Provides firsthand comments from immigrant children, their parents, teachers, and others involved in helping them adjust to a new culture and its educational system. Addresses the unique problems of Haitian children.

Norton, Dolores G. "Understanding the Early Experience of Black Children in High Risk Environments: Culturally and Ecologically Relevant Research as a Guide to Support for Families." *Zero to Three* 10 (April 1990): 1–7.

Utilizes an anthropological framework to understand support patterns for mothers and children in the inner city. Cites research on the differences in patterns of parent-child, social, emotional, and linguistic interaction. States that black families, isolated in the inner city and separated from major societal institutions and resources, may not be able to teach their children the "rules and tools" for success in the larger society.

Ogbu, John. "Origins of Human Competence: A Cultural Ecological Perspective." *Child Development* 52 (1982): 413–429.

Classifies minorities into three types: autonomous, immigrant, and castelike. Ogbu views African Americans as a castelike minority—a group incorporated into an existing social system involuntarily and permanently. Black Americans have an ascribed status that was not entered into by choice but by legal and extralegal forces.

Patterson, Orlando. *Die the Long Day.* New York: William Morrow, 1972.

Contrasts growing up black in the West Indies and growing up black in the United States. Examines the theme of survival during slavery among black peoples of the New World diaspora, especially as it affects personal interactions. Author is a professor of sociology at Harvard.

Phinney, Jean S., and Mary Jane Rotheram, eds. *Children's Ethnic Socialization: Pluralism and Development.* Newbury Park, Calif.: Sage, 1987.

Deals with the impact of ethnicity on preschool and elementary-age children, middle childhood, and adolescence. Discusses what ethnicity means to children at each stage of development, how they see themselves, and how others see them in relation to their ethnic group membership. Describes the developmental processes by which black children acquire their behaviors, perceptions, values, and attitudes.

Pinderhughes, Charles. "Black Personality in American Society." *The Black American Reference Book.* M. Smythe, ed. Englewood Cliffs, N.J.: Prentice-Hall, 1976.

Cites the factors that have prevented African Americans from having a unified culture and from integrating into the American mainstream: (1) victimizing, (2) the cutoff from African culture, (3) the coercive slave culture, (4) the unpredictability of life after emancipation, (5) urbanization, and (6) political events of the 1960s.

Pinderhughes, Elaine. "Afro-American Families and the Victim System." *Ethnicity and Family Therapy.* M. McGoldrick, J.K. Pearce, and J. Giordano, eds. New York: Guilford, 1982.

Hypothesizes that the conflicting value systems of African Americans (African American, mainstream American, and "victim") can create maladaptive behaviors. Victimization can cause behavior based on immediate gratification of need; this is in conflict with the future orientation of mainstream America. African American families must be bi-cultural, able to function in two worlds.

Randall-David, Elizabeth. *Strategies for Working with Culturally Diverse Communities and Clients.* Washington, D.C.: Association for the Care of Children's Health, 1989.

Highlights the diversity of black cultures in America. Lists the principal stressors affecting black Americans. Describes important cultural values and behaviors and suggests appropriate intervention strategies which respect those cultural values. Considers the Haitian culture separately, in spite of similarities to African American culture.

Rodgers-Rose, La Frances, ed. *The Black Woman.* Newbury Park, Calif.: Sage, 1980.

Analyzes the black woman, her relationship to the black man, family, community, the political and educational systems, and the economy. Contributors are all black women.

Scheinfeld, Daniel R. "Family Relationships and School Achievement Among Boys of Lower-Income Urban Black Families" *American Journal of Orthopsychiatry* 53 (January 1983): 127–143.

Explores the processes through which family life influences the academic achievement of children of urban, lower-income black children. Finds that mothers of high achievers emphasize self-motivation and "active, learning engagement with the world," while mothers of low achievers emphasize constraint, isolation, and adult control. Study also considers effects of a hostile environment on family interaction.

Slaughter, Diana T., ed. *Black Children and Poverty: A Developmental Perspective*. New Directions for Child Development Series, no. 42. San Francisco: Jossey-Bass, 1988.

Addresses the impact of culture and community (cultural beliefs and attitudes) on family and child-rearing; the relationships between culture and language socialization; the identity development of children; and cognitive development. Extensive references.

Small, Willie V. "The Neglect of Black Children." *Child Abuse, Neglect and The Family Within a Cultural Context*. DHEW Publication No. (OHDS) 78-30135. Washington, D.C.: U.S. Department of Health, Education, and Welfare, 1978, pp. 14–15.

Contends that the determination of child neglect is complicated by cultural differences. States that within an oppressed minority status in society, abusive language and behavior is often the only way a black adult can establish authority over children and adolescents.

Sowell, Thomas. "Three Black Histories." *American Ethnic Groups*. T. Sowell, ed. Washington, D.C.: The Urban Institute, 1978, pp. 7–64.

Describes and differentiates three distinct subgroups of blacks in the United States: (1) "free persons of color," (2) emancipated slaves and their descendants, and (3) those blacks who migrated from the West Indies.

Sowell, Thomas. *Markets and Minorities*. New York: Basic Books, 1981.

A black economist's perspective of the economic lot of the nation's ethnic and racial minorities—what it is today and why, and how it can (and cannot) be improved. Demolishes widespread myths about the nature of discrimination in economic life. Describes how and why government efforts in minimum-wage laws, housing regulations, and affirmative action have been unsuccessful. A provocative look at the relationship between economics and the social problems of minorities.

Spencer, Margaret B., Geraldine K. Brookins, and Walter R. Allen, eds. *Beginnings: The Social and Affective Development of Black Children.* Hillsdale, N.J.: Lawrence Erlbaum Associates, 1985.

Describes the purpose of *Beginnings* as "to redefine how black children and their families are treated in the literature." Addresses issues of social competence, identity, and family. States need for research on interactions between class and culture in black life; implications of changing family structure, bio-psycho-social factors in black child development; and ecological determinants of black child development.

Spurlock, Jeanne, and Leonard E. Lawrence. "The Black Child." *Basic Handbook of Child Psychiatry.* J.P. Noshpitz and I.N. Berlin, eds. Vol. I: *Normal Development.* New York: Basic Books, 1979, pp. 248–257.

Reviews the rich African heritage of black children, the psychological sequelae of slavery on development, family patterns, the impact of poverty, the impact of "blackness" on development, and resultant behavioral manifestations. Discusses misconceptions concerning language development and cognitive ability in the black child.

Stack, C.B. *All Our Kin: Strategies for Survival in a Black Community.* New York: Harper and Row, 1975.

Emphasizes the strengths in kinship patterns of American blacks. States that the black urban family is "an organized, tenacious, active, lifelong network."

Staples, Robert. *Introduction to Black Sociology.* New York: McGraw-Hill, 1976.

A comprehensive history of the evolution of the black family. Describes the kinship bonds, gender roles, and status of marriage in tribal Africa; the effects of slavery on family life; family functioning in the post-slavery era; and contemporary black family life.

Steele, Shelby. *The Content of Our Character: A New Vision of Race in America.* New York: St. Martin's Press, 1990.

Addresses the issue of victimization, which Steele states is a primary source of power for blacks; it is the basis of demand for redress. Believes that victims carry an "inferiority anxiety" which tells them there is less opportunity than actually exists.

Steele, Shelby. "Ghettoized by Black Unity." *Harper's* 280 (May 1990): 20–23.

Asserts that while racism still exists, it is not what is holding back America's black people; that the specter of racism has become a crippling fixation of blacks, a way to avoid dealing with real problems. Steele is a black professor of English and a controversial writer and commentator on racial issues.

Thompson, Leonard. *A History of South Africa*. New Haven: Yale University Press, 1990.

Traces the cultures of the country's original inhabitants, destroying misconceptions about Africans being unproductive, uncompetitive, or generally "uncivilized." Although the book's main theme is apartheid (its rise and gradual demise), it offers a documented history of African traditions.

United States Department of Agriculture/Department of Health and Human Services. *Cross-Cultural Counseling: A Guide for Nutrition and Health Counselors*. FNS-250. Washington, D.C.: U.S. Government Printing Office, 1986.

In addition to general guidelines for cross-cultural counseling, this booklet describes the unique sociocultural issues that affect black Americans (and other minorities), such as access to adequate health care and dietary practices. Recommends a selected bibliography.

Washington, Valora, and Velma LaPoint. *Black Children and American Institutions: An Ecological Review and Resource Guide*. New York: Garland, 1988.

Examines the family, schools, social services, child welfare, criminal justice system, and physical and mental health services with which black children interact. Brief essays followed by an annotated bibliography and a list of national organizations which advocate for and promote the development of black children.

Wolf, Ann Marie. "A Personal View of Black Inner-City Foster Families." *American Journal of Orthopsychiatry* 53 (January 1983): 144–151.

Relates the experience of a white, middle-class medical student living in a black inner-city neighborhood. Describes the special form of extended family that flourished in her neighborhood, "taking her in" because she was seen as a young person needing assistance. Cites the strengths of family ties in the black inner-city culture and their practice of informal adoptions. Advocates for white agencies serving this population to understand, respect, and utilize this bond of kin and this willingness to nurture and raise young children.

EUROPEAN CULTURES

The impact of European history, geography, economics, and religion on modern-day American culture—and therefore on child development—requires an understanding of the cultural heritage of the many Americans who immigrated here around the turn of the century. It calls for the study of traditional as well as contemporary European cultures, especially the latter's welfare policies, such as those of socialism in Scandinavia, which is demonstrating innovative ways to provide preventive health care, adequate day care, early childhood education and supportive services to foster family stability. The customs and traditions of Europe reflect many countries, each with its unique cultural and historical heritage; they also reflect many ethnic regions, such as Alsace, Bavaria, and Northern Ireland.

These early immigrants to the United States brought with them the customs and traditions of their respective cultural and ethnic groups; many of the values and customs which are considered "American" actually have European origins. Christmas rituals and festivities, for example, include a number of European customs: Santa Claus, a synthesis of the Dutch *Sint Nikolaas*, the English Father Christmas, the German *Kris Kringle*, the Italian *Befana*, and the Russian *Babouschka*; the carols, yule log, and mistletoe of England; the Christmas tree and Advent wreath of Germany; and the Nativity plays of Belgium. Similarly, many wedding customs reflect European traditions: bridal showers and rehearsal dinners originated in Holland; the white wedding gown and tiered wedding cake from England; and tossing the bridal bouquet from France.

This chapter will explore both the traditional and contemporary characteristics of various European cultures: the traditional ones because they are often considered to be the basis of Western or "mainstream American" culture; the contemporary policies because they provide a look at alternative child welfare policies and their implications. Accordingly, the representative cultures of Germany, the Scandinavian countries (with emphasis on Sweden), and the United

Kingdom (with emphasis on England), will be profiled in detail. Significant cultural and ethnic traditions of other European countries will also be selectively reviewed.

While there are distinct differences among the many European countries, there are common characteristics as well. In Hsu's categorization of societies according to kinship patterns, the majority of Western people (European and European descent) exhibit "self-reliance on the part of the individual which is rooted in the supremacy of the husband-wife axis at the expense of all other relationships."[1] This husband-wife relationship is strongest in the United States, weakest in Eastern Europe.

Other relevant traits/patterns of European cultures, according to Hsu, are the nuclear family and the encouragement of individualism and creativity. Religion is monotheistic (often with a missionary zeal) and religious prejudice is common (e.g., history of religious wars). There is an attitude toward right versus wrong and reward versus punishment that tends to be absolute. Intergenerational conflict is common. Government is usually in the form of national states, highly organized, either extremely authoritarian or democratic.[2]

Europe has been referred to as "preeminently the homeland of white people."[3] Historically, European nations have been divided by cultural traditions, religion, and language rather than by geography.[4] Religion, particularly, has played a crucial role in European history. Most of Europe, except for the Islamic areas in the Balkan and southeast regions, is Christian. The primary branches of Christianity—Catholicism, Protestantism, and Orthodoxy—are linked with Latin, German, and Slavic cultures, respectively. In Europe, ethnic consciousness is closely related to religion and ethnic minorities often survive more because of their religion than because of their language:

> In Ireland, Catholicism acts as a shield against English assimilation, and in Finland, Estonia, and Latvia, Protestantism is a fortress against Russification.... The faithfulness to Rome of the Hungarians and Poles is a consequence of their particular devotion to Latinity....[5]

Many of the symbols and religious practices of Europe that exist today in Europe have evolved from an agricultural life-style. Some pre-Christian ideas (e.g., pagan, magic) also persist; religious rituals associated with the solstices reflect prehistoric times. Folk rituals associated with Catholic traditions (e.g., the cult of saints, the nativity crib) are rarely seen in regions that are predominantly Protestant.

A notable variance also exists between urban and rural life-styles in Europe. This "contrast between urban industrial civilization and traditional ethnic culture" represents a "sociocultural dualism" that has long divided Europe and involves differences in life-style, communication style, and socialization practices.

Traditional cultural patterns have disappeared more rapidly in west central Europe than in the eastern, northern, and southern regions. There appears to be a coincidence between economic and cultural geography. If one considers west central Europe (roughly, the area between Paris, London, Amsterdam, and Frankfurt) as the most economically developed, the further one moves away from this center of development, the more one can expect the standard of living to decline and traditional cultural elements to increase. "The geography of material poverty coincides with the geography of ethnic traditionalism."[6] Strongholds of ethnic traditionalism remain in islands such as Iceland, the Faeroes, and the Hebrides, the Channel Islands, Corsica, Sicily, Malta, the Greek archipelago, and mountain/moorland areas such as the Scottish Highlands, the Pyrenees, and the deltas of the Danube and Po rivers.

The many wars and the political and economic upheavals in Europe have resulted in migrations from country to country, usually westward, toward the economically strong countries:

> One of the most remarkable examples of the influence of the westward trend of population groups on social morphology is the orientation of the various class districts in the large European capitals. Residential and fashionable districts in Moscow, Berlin, Budapest, Vienna, Rome, Paris, London, and other cities are invariably situated in the "west end," whereas almost everywhere the "east end" is the slummy district.[7]

These same wars, the political upheaval, and economic problems were the reasons for the large European immigration to the United States, which was perceived as "the land of opportunity and of freedom." These European immigrants represented diverse countries of origin, religions, languages, educational levels, occupations, and life-styles, value systems, etc. The European immigrants represent diverse migration histories, both prior and subsequent to their arrival in the United States. A consideration of the variables discussed in Chapter IV provides a framework for understanding the broad diversity of European immigrants.

The following brief profiles are intended to provide a broad overview of selected European cultures. Distinctive features of the country/region are presented, as these distinctions often contribute to the genesis of cultural traits. Traditional characteristics most likely to be observed (to some degree) in descendants of that country's emigrants are highlighted. Even though cultural differences become more diffuse with each succeeding generation, there remains a powerful mainstream tradition.[8] Intergroup variability, socioeconomic factors, and other contemporary influences must be considered as well. Cultural configurations *have* changed and continue to change in Europe and worldwide. The influence of European cultures (however varied and varying) on child development practices in the United States is unmistakable.

Brief Profile of Germany

In many ways Germany exemplifies the "old world" tradition of childrearing; it also illustrates the many differences that can occur in even a relatively small country, due to geographical differences (rural, industrial, farm, or seaport); political differences (East-West); religious differences (Catholic-Protestant); and ethnic/regional distinctions (e.g., Bavaria, Swabia).

Family Structure: Traditionally, the father is the head of the household while the mother's responsibility is *Kinder, Kuche,* and *Kirche* (children, kitchen, and church). Women are expected to be hardworking and dutiful; a clean house and a neat, well-groomed family are important. Mothers of young children do not generally work outside of the home unless a grandmother or other close relative is available to provide child care. Increasingly, businesses are establishing "mothers' hours" permitting women to work while the children are in school. Holidays, such as Christmas, are celebrated primarily in the home, are rich in tradition, and feature home-made gifts.

Families are small and nuclear, yet often in close proximity to relatives. Family life generally reflects German society, which is basically authoritarian, highly structured, and formal. The sense of family and family life is strong, almost sacred; mutual support and loyalty are emphasized. Population density is very high, but a boundary of privacy is maintained between family and community. A distinction is made between business and personal friends, and families of politicians are not in the public eye.

Childrearing Practices: Children are highly valued in German families. At present, there are many government incentives which support and promote family stability during the childbearing years: cash allowances for each child (increasing in amount with each successive child); health care (based on a scheme of sickness insurance); paid maternity leave for fathers and mothers (or outside assistance during the post-partum period, if necessary); special entitlements for nursing mothers. A six-week paid leave prior to delivery is optional; an eight-week paid post-partum leave is required; and an unpaid maternity leave for six months is then available. Five days of parental sick leave per year are also available. Despite these arrangements, the birth rate is low, and a matter of national concern.

Children are traditionally raised in an atmosphere of structure and high expectations. They are taught to be obedient, respectful, and responsible; they are expected to be polite, well-behaved, and to assist with family chores. A sense of self-sufficiency is fostered within the family. Social activities (business, community, religious, recreational) often include all generations, especially the children.

Teenagers are less likely to drive in Germany than in the United States: automobiles and petrol (gasoline) cost considerably more, parking is limited, and public transportation is excellent. Formal instruction in a driving school is a prerequisite for a license. Motorcycles or motor scooters are popular. As in much of Europe, there is a strong prohibition against driving after drinking.

Religion: The population in western Germany is almost equally divided between Catholics and Protestants. Catholicism is more common in the South and West; its followers tend to be more traditionally oriented, and guided by church authority. Protestants (primarily Lutherans) live mostly in the North and East; their followers emphasize individual responsibility and conscience. Not many Germans attend church regularly. Religious freedom is guaranteed to all.

Values: Germans have an intense sense of pride in their work, their family, and their country. Neatness, precision, and punctuality are traditional German values. Public displays of affection, grief, anger, or other emotions are discouraged. Germans tend to be formal, restrained, and reserved; handshaking and the use of titles are common.

There is a traditional work ethic of thoroughness, solid craftsmanship, attention to detail, skill, diligence, and industriousness. *Lebensraum* (space for living) and the privacy of family life are preserved by fences, shrubbery, walls, and closed doors. There is a great appreciation for the arts, literature, and nature at all socioeconomic levels. Little class consciousness is evidenced.[9] Germans value health, youth, energy, high spirits, sexual vigor, efficiency at work, and self-sufficiency. They are law-abiding citizens with a strong sense of justice. Many transit systems, for example, operate on the honor system (for payment).

Language: The official language is *Hochdeutsch* (high German), with the many regional dialects reflecting historical and traditional divisions. English is widely used and is taught to all school children.

Health: Germans are health conscious; illness is avoided because it fosters dependency. Health spas (*bads*) are popular. Cardio-vascular illness is a major concern; the typical diet is high in carbohydrates, fatty meats, and salt. Cigarette smoking is very popular in Germany, as in most of Europe. Increasingly, there is concern over the environment and its long term effect on health. Exercise, particularly hiking, is widely enjoyed by people of all ages. Medical and health services are of high quality.

Education: Education is highly prized in Germany. Schooling is free and compulsory to at least age fourteen; students follow different educational tracts according to their academic and vocational aptitude and interest. There is much pride in both high technology and "old-world" craftsmanship; apprenticeships are common. In (formerly) East Germany, polytechnical schools, physical training, and athletics were stressed. In Germany, social status is based on one's level of education as much—if not more so—than one's wealth; the titles *Herr Doktor*/*Herr Professor* are especially prestigious. Bookstores are very popular; illiteracy is virtually nonexistent.

Other Significant Data: During the war years, the observance of German customs and traditions diminished among Americans of German descent. In the resurgence of universal ethnic pride, these customs are now re-emerging. German foods, festivals (e.g., Oktoberfest), and language study are becoming more prevalent.

Germany is basically a homogeneous society. Foreigners (mainly an outgrowth of workers brought in to aid in rebuilding a post-war Germany) constitute less than 5 percent of the population. Most of these residents are Turks, Yugoslavians, Italians, Greeks, Danes, and Pakistanis; the relationship between ethnic and non-ethnic Germans can be tenuous.

West Germany (the Federal Republic of Germany) enjoyed one of the highest standards of living in the world. Even East Germany (the German Democratic Republic) enjoyed a standard of living higher than that of other Communist countries. Life-styles have varied in the two Germanys due to differences in politics and economics. Now that German reunification has become a reality, additional changes in life-style can be expected.

Brief Profile of Sweden and Scandinavia

The Nordic region consists of three monarchies (Denmark, Norway, and Sweden), two republics (Finland and Iceland), and three autonomous territories (the Faeroes, Greenland, and Aland). These countries are, in general, sparsely populated, with high concentration in urban centers. They are highly industrialized, and the standard of living is high, as well as reasonably distributed among various socioeconomic groups. In general, the work week is short and unemployment is low.

The Scandinavian countries are basically homogeneous in people, cultural traditions, language, environment, and social and economic conditions. Their socialistic welfare policies are designed to integrate and include the entire population, rather than target resources at particular problem groups. Sweden and Norway have small indigenous Lapp populations.

Family Structure: Close family ties and loyalties are very important in Sweden, even though family unity is not emphasized as much as in the past. The home is considered a place for intimacy, reduced demands, and greater permissiveness than the outside world; it is an important place for socialization and for feelings of belonging and closeness.

Sweden is a very egalitarian nation, and women are actively involved in all aspects of society. Family policy (ideologies involving the public provision of pre-school care) is a leading political issue. Public child care in Sweden includes care of small children of pre-school age and after-school activities. The aim is to provide children with a stimulating and secure environment while at the same time giving men and women equal opportunities to combine gainful employment with family life.[10]

Over 90 percent of all mothers work outside the home, approximately half of them part time; Swedish women have the highest employment rate in the Western world. Child allowances are generous and tax free. However, parental insurance, which entitles the mother or father to stay at home for a year after childbirth at 90 percent salary, is subject to income tax. There is a similar "special parental benefit" for either parent to stay home and care for an ill child. The average family size is the lowest in the world, and the divorce rate is high.

The liberal abortion policy has not led to an increase in abortions or to abortion being used as a substitute for contraception. On the contrary, since implementation of the Abortion Act (1975), the abortion rate has remained more or less constant, and there has been a marked decrease in the number of teenage pregnancies and teenage abortions.[11]

Most people in Sweden under age twenty live with their parents. During the last twenty years, the inclination for starting a family has diminished among young people; most young families are childless. Young couples with children find themselves in a tight economic situation in spite of liberal social welfare policies. Children's needs are accorded top priority, and parents feel it is important that their children not be worse off than other people's.[12]

Norwegian family structure is also egalitarian; family size is small, and the divorce rate is low. Danish families are close-knit and stable; there are many common-law marriages. Icelandic families are small, close and mutually dependent; the father is generally the head of the household.

Childrearing Practices: Children, child care, and child development are priority issues in Scandinavia: there is both an economic and a psychological investment in children. Social welfare policies promote high standards of health, education, and support for families. Infant mortality is the lowest in the world, and high quality health, developmental, and special needs services are available to all who need them. Child care services (which recognize individual differences) are extensively available; the majority of women work outside the home. There are generous parental leave policies for fathers as well as mothers.

In spite of a recognizably low infant mortality rate, Swedish parents still tend to view pregnancy and early infancy as a very vulnerable time. Expectant parents customarily put off the purchase of "baby things" till the infant's safe arrival. The parental insurance period is welcomed and provides reassurance that the parents themselves will be available to care for the infant during this vulnerable period. Parent education information is widely available and earnestly followed.[13]

In Sweden, society as a whole takes very good care of its children. Buses and subways accommodate baby carriages and strollers; this overt example of a culture valuing its children is seen in many European countries. Fathers are very involved in the raising of their children. Swedish parents consider it important to foster the development of their child's individuality.

Among adolescents, music, dancing, and sports are very popular. Smoking has decreased in the last decade. High taxes on liquor discourage drinking. Swedish youth organizations are responsible for most recreational activities and are an important part of adolescent life. Young people from upper-class backgrounds are more likely to belong to youth organizations than those from middle-class or working-class backgrounds.[14]

Religion: Sweden, like most of Europe, is a highly secular society. Most Swedes belong to the Evangelical Lutheran Church, which is state supported; most are casual church attenders. Finland has two state churches: the Evangelical Lutheran Church of Finland and the Orthodox Church of Finland. Most Finns belong to the Lutheran Church, although there are small groups of Roman Catholics, Jews, Muslims, and Protestants. In Iceland, most people belong to the state church, the Evangelical Lutheran Church; a small percentage belongs to the Lutheran Free Church, other Protestant churches, or the Roman Catholic Church. Most Norwegians belong to the Evangelical Lutheran Church. The Evangelical Lutheran Church is the national church of Denmark. Like their fellow Scandinavians, few Danes attend church regularly.

Values: The Scandinavians tend to be quiet and unassuming, patient themselves, and offended by impatience in others. Their honesty, hospitality, and helpfulness are proverbial. Scandinavians value punctuality, egalitarian ideals, hard work, and are extremely proud of their land and the achievements of their culture. Swedes traditionally possess a calm, cool, critical disposition; they tend to be formal and reserved. Swedes value their homes, animals, and nature; a summer home in the country is highly desirable.

In traditional Norwegian families, the husband controls the finances and the discipline; the wife is responsible for communication and socialization within the extended family network. Within that network, assistance may be offered but not requested. Children are expected to be considerate, responsible, and obedient, without sacrificing their innate individuality. It is traditional for the eldest son to take over the family farm. Norwegians value independence, hard work and being *kjekk* (courageous, positive, humorous, and strong). American physicians are often amazed at the stoicism, the health, and longevity of their Norwegian patients.

Finns are noted for their strong, introverted character. Children's rights are a vital issue in Finland. The Danes impart great importance to the individual, and the individual's right (even that of a child) to make decisions for himself. Icelanders are proud of their classless society (it is a population with virtually no crime); they judge others on the basis of their ability rather than their station in life. Myths which extol ancient gods, warriors, and the triumph of good over evil are common in Scandinavian folklore. These myths are often a key to understanding traditional Nordic traits.

Language: English is widely taught and spoken in Scandinavia. In Sweden, the national language is Swedish, an old North Germanic tongue related to Danish, Norwegian, and Icelandic. The Norwegian language has two forms: Bokmal (the official written language, a dialect heavily influenced by Danish) and Nynorsk (or Landsmal, a language constructed of various Norwegian dialects). Nynorsk (or *Nyorsk,* New Norwegian) is spoken mainly in southern and western Norway, while Bokmal is used in the eastern part of the country and in the towns. Icelandic is an ancient Scandinavian language, the oldest living language in Europe. Danish is a Scandinavian dialect with a distinct guttural quality. Finnish is totally different from the other Scandinavian languages. It belongs to the Finno-Ugrian language group, found in eastern Europe and western Siberia. The Lapps have their own language, Lappish.

Health: Social-welfare systems which include compulsory health insurance are a major factor in the provision of high level health care services in the Scandinavian countries. Another interesting feature is that in Scandinavia, nurses are primarily responsible for the content and continuity of health care with physicians serving as a "second line of defense."[15] Home visiting by nurses, especially to provide maternal and child health services, is a prominent feature of the health care systems throughout Europe. Scandinavia is no exception, except for those regions where the population is extremely rural and sparse. Prevention and health education are priorities; health surveys are common. There is also a strong commitment of support and services for the disabled. In Sweden, this concern for the disabled dates back to the sixteenth century. The Swedish movement of disabled people consists largely *of* and not just *for* the disabled; they consider this an important distinction. Every effort is made to totally integrate disabled persons of all ages into the community. In the Swedish view, a handicap is not looked upon as a characteristic of a person with a disability caused by injury or illness but a relationship between the person and the environment; it shifts the handicap from the individuals to their environment, thus preventing a disability from becoming a handicap.

Health problems evident in the Scandinavian countries are alcoholism, suicide, drug abuse, smoking, and the medical problems of immigrants. Some of the problems are believed to be related to the long, harsh winters and periods of extended darkness which are a result of the extreme northern location.

Education: Education is a major priority in Scandinavia with literacy rates of 99 percent to 100 percent. In Norway, schooling is compulsory from ages seven to fourteen; in Iceland, from seven to fifteen (and students must know how to swim to graduate from grammar school); in Denmark, from seven to sixteen; and in Finland, for at least nine years.

In Sweden, the public school system provides a comprehensive program from age seven to sixteen, an integrated upper secondary school designed to accommodate all sixteen year olds, a system of municipal adult education for all adults, and a higher education system open to all who qualify. This is in addition to pre-school education. There is also an extensive educational program for immigrant children and adults. A home language program aims to encourage such children to take pride in and retain their mother tongue, in addition to learning

Swedish. There is an emphasis on intercultural and multicultural teaching in the schools.[16]

In Finland, play, work, and teaching are the cornerstones of early childhood education. There is a serious educational aspect to day care and kindergarten. Pre-schools motivate children to ask, observe, and experiment to create readiness for later learning, but do not explicitly teach reading and addition. Corporal punishment and other humiliating treatment are specifically outlawed.[17]

Other Significant Data: Sweden is one of the richest countries in the world and is heavily industrialized; some of the industries are aggressively capitalistic even though the country is socialistic. Taxes are high and over 50 percent of the country's budget is allocated to social-welfare programs. Poverty is practically non-existent in Sweden or in any of the Scandinavian countries, and most people are middle class.

In Iceland it is customary to address people by their first name, regardless of title. A man's last name is the possessive of his father's first name, followed by *son* (e.g., Jensson). Women do not change their name after marriage; their last name is the possessive form of their father's first name, followed by *dotter*. Descriptive nicknames, such as "Leif the Lucky" are commonly used.

Iceland is an active volcanic island with more hot springs than any other country in the world. Its climate is moderated by the warm Gulf Stream. In contrast to a popular misconception, there are no Eskimos in Iceland. Denmark is the smallest and the flattest of the Scandinavian countries. Approximately 70 percent of its land area is agricultural, yet less than 5 percent of the people are employed in agriculture.

Brief Profile of England and the United Kingdom

The United Kingdom of Great Britain and Northern Ireland is made up of the four countries of England, Wales, Scotland, and Northern Ireland. The people of Wales, Scotland, and Northern Ireland, though they regard themselves as British and part of the United Kingdom, tend to cherish their own separate histories, traditions, and different characters.

Family Structure: English families are traditionally small, tightly knit, and often closed to outsiders. Family structure is basically nuclear and patriarchal; families tend to live where work and housing are available, even if distant from relatives. Family relationships are often reserved and unemotional. The formal Sunday dinner of roast beef and Yorkshire pudding is an old-fashioned tradition.

Within England, there are regional and socioeconomic variances in family structure and function. Family life in a major cosmopolitan center, such as London, is quite different from that in the rest of England. To judge English life-style by London is as skewed as judging American life-style by New York City. England still retains many vestiges of a class society. Many middle- and lower-income families (almost a quarter of the population) live in council housing, built and subsidized by local government. There is a growing middle class that has evolved since the war and with changing political leadership. The cost of living and taxes are high, and many wives work in order to maintain a higher standard of living.

In Welsh families, the father is usually the decision-maker, although the mother's role is also influential; families tend to be very close. In Scotland, clans are now mainly symbolic. Scottish families are generally close-knit yet independent. Extended family relationships are more apt to exist in Wales and Scotland than in England. In Northern Ireland, the father is the undisputed head of the family and traditionally not actively involved in household or childrearing duties. The role of women is nevertheless influential, though often conservative. The divorce rate is very low.

In the United States, the acronym WASP (White Anglo-Saxon Protestant) is often attributed to British-Americans, especially those descendants of early immigrant families. As in their countries of origin, family life varies according to religion, socioeconomic status, and geographic residence (region of country, urban/rural). Migration experiences (en route and within the United States) also play a significant role:

> Domestic migration has been crucial in the formation of British-American family culture and in the evolution of the major regional patterns. British-American families today can be divided into two broad groups: (1) descendants of those who stayed put in New England and in the South, evolving old regional subcultures and strong

family identification with a locality and (2) descendants of the predominantly Mid-Atlantic migrants who moved to the Midwest, and then perhaps on again, until, for some Western families, they became identified with the process of moving.[18]

Childrearing: Historically, childrearing practices changed along with economic, religious, social, and political changes in England (e.g., Puritanism, the Industrial Revolution, the Victorian era). Contemporary English childrearing does not differ substantially from that in America. Childrearing in England stresses discipline, politeness, and consideration of adults. Peer relationships are significant. There is strong interest in scientific and modern methods of childrearing, perhaps in compensation for the lack of advice and support from extended families. British families, whether in the United Kingdom or the United States, believe in raising children to be independent and responsible. Developmental stages and transitions (e.g., going off to school, getting married) are taken in stride and considered as normal events rather than occasions for involved celebrations. Welsh families, however, place great importance on rites of passage from one developmental stage to the next: there is much folklore associated with pregnancy and birth. English parents have many choices in child care: play groups, nursery schools, infant schools, family day care and "child-minders." The government provides maternity leave as well as a maternity grant and a family allowance.

Religion: More than half of the population of the United Kingdom nominally belongs to the Church of England, the Anglican church, while less than 10 percent belong to the Catholic church. The Church of Scotland is Presbyterian, but there is also a substantial Roman Catholic minority. Most Welsh are members of the independent chapels or the Church of Wales (Anglican); there is also a Roman Catholic minority. Northern Ireland is predominantly Protestant, a source of major conflict with the Republic of Ireland. England also has a variety of Methodist and Presbyterian sects, such as Quakers and Baptists, as well as sizable numbers of Jews and Moslems. Most British are somewhat apathetic toward organized religion.

Values: Manners and "proper" behavior are important to the British, as is the Protestant work ethic; hard work is equated with virtue. There is a strong sense of volunteerism and caring for one's fellow man. A goal for many English families is a "detached" house (as opposed to a "council" semi-attached or row house) with room for a garden. The English love of flowers and animals is legendary. They have a strong future orientation and sense of responsibility. The British are justly proud of their cultural heritage (art, literature, and music), their government, and their legal system. The queen and monarchy are revered.

British Americans value individualism, self-reliance, self-sufficiency, and self-control. They often have difficulty expressing emotional feelings, as characterized by the British saying "Keep a stiff upper lip!" They have a strong future orientation for individual achievement. Above all, they value work; hard work is equated with virtue.[19]

The Scottish people are noted for their innate courtesy, their critical and independent nature, and the ability to relentlessly persevere. There are variances, mostly attitudinal, in different regional and socioeconomic groups. The people of Northern Ireland value sincerity and honor: when they give their word or make a verbal promise, they keep it. They also treasure the beauties of nature. Keeping one's word is also important to the Welsh people, who are philosophical in nature. There is also a traditional appreciation for singing, especially hymns and folk music. Writers, poets, musicians and dramatists are greatly admired; there is a strong cultural element to Welsh nationalism.

Language: The official language, English, is often referred to as "The Queen's English" to distinguish it from American English: there are some differences between the two in pronunciation, meaning, and usage of words. Within the United Kingdom, there are many regional dialects; in England there are also socioeconomic speech variances (see page 14). Gaelic, an ancient Celtic language, is spoken in the Highlands and the many offshore islands of Scotland. In Wales, Welsh and English are both official languages. Welsh is used as the medium of instruction in some schools and in some radio and television programs.

Health: Britain is famed for its system of health and social services, often referred to as a "welfare state." Although there are often long waits for elective procedures, the quality of services is high. Maternal and child health care are free, and there are generous benefits for childbearing families, including preventive and educational services. The British diet often includes fatty foods, meats and dairy products high in cholesterol, and many sweets. Consequently, the incidence of cardio-vascular disease and dental caries tends to be high.

Education: The British school system differs from that of other European countries by having a public educational system coexisting with a private sector ("public schools"). These "public schools" are primarily in England and are often criticized as being socially divisive. Education is free and compulsory from ages five to sixteen. Higher education is available to all on the basis of merit. Performance in school exams is an important factor in determining choice of career and job prospects. Adult education is widely available and attended. There is virtually no illiteracy in Britain.

In Northern Ireland, children attend either Catholic or Protestant schools. Children ages four-and-a-half to eleven attend primary school. At age eleven, all students take an exam which determines whether they prepare for a university education, a profession, or a trade.

Other Significant Data: The proper term for residents of Scotland is Scots, not Scotch; Scotch is a whisky. It is also an error to consider Scotland, Wales, and Northern Ireland as part of England; they are each a separate country, jointly comprising the United Kingdom. There has been some racial tension in Britain with West Indian, Indian, Pakistani, and other immigrant groups; housing, welfare, and employment issues are often the cause. In Northern Ireland, the existing climate of ethnic-religious hostilities is an issue that may affect personality development. The standard of living in Britain is somewhat lower than in the United States.

Pertinent Data on Other European Cultures

Ireland: The Republic of Ireland (Eire) occupies most of the island of Ireland, which it shares with Northern Ireland, but is not part of the United Kingdom. In spite of its history of multiple invasions and colonization, Ireland remains a country with little racial and ethnic diversity. Tradition is very important to the Irish. The Irish are known for their humor, their wit, their good nature, and their optimism. The Roman Catholic church plays a central role in family life-style. Families are large, maintain close ties, and often reside near one another. Family reunions traditionally celebrate holidays as well as events marking developmental transitions. Irish family life stresses consanguinity (blood descent) and sibling loyalty. In the traditional Irish family, the role of the woman is subservient to that of her husband, and children are taught to be subordinate, obedient, and respectful. Gender roles are somewhat rigid, and alcoholism is higher than in other cultures. Economic problems were the cause of massive Irish emigration—almost half the population—in the last century.[20]

France: French families are traditionally small, close-knit, hardworking, and home-loving. Discipline is strict, but tempered with love. The French judge success by level of education, reputation of family, and financial status. Most are Roman Catholic, are deeply rooted in tradition, yet do not actively practice Catholicism. Folk traditions and festivals have preserved a variety of regional customs. The French value individualism and freedom of expression.

The present state of child care in France reflects how highly children are valued. As in most of Europe, child-care services, 80 percent state funded, are intended for children in all strata of society, not merely targeted for poor children or those at risk. The system is a blend of child care, education, and health services based on free full-day preschool programs, subsidized day-care centers, and licensed care in private homes for infants and toddlers. Preschool programs (noncompulsory) serve nearly 90 percent of French children three to five years old and offer language arts, exercise, crafts, and play. The system also features intensive training and adequate compensation for teachers and other caregivers, a free preventive health program for all young children, and concern about the architecture and safety of day-care centers.[21]

Italy: The Italian family is noted for strong, traditional ties. There are some regional variations in language and traditions, but the devotion to family and children is a national trait. The Italian family, as in other Latin cultures, is an extended family. The extended family network includes aunts, uncles, cousins, *gumbares* (old friends and neighbors), and godparents. *La via vecchia* (the old way) symbolizes a value system that emphasizes protecting the family. The father is the undisputed head of the family, the mother its heart. Children are raised to be obedient and dependent on family; socialization is according to gender. There is a special pride in home ownership, a symbol of the family, and of independence; the family table is the center of all activity. There is a marked reluctance to leave one's home and family; family solidarity is more urgent than education or work.

Italian immigrants to the United States came primarily from southern Italy. Their economy (and the population) was poorer than in the industrial North; the people relied on farming, were less educated, and more fatalistic in their outlook on life.[22] In contrast to the Irish, most Italians view the Church as a source of drama and ritual, rather than as a source of authority. They adhere to the Roman Catholic church because it stands for tradition, family, and community.[23]

Education is free and compulsory from ages six to fourteen. The high cost of education at the trade and university levels, however, effectively limits higher education to a privileged elite. It is a country of great social and economic difference. Over one-third of the country's population emigrated in search of work between the late nineteenth and late twentieth centuries. Many came to the United States; some for a few years, most for life.[24]

Certainly, there have been significant contributions to "mainstream" American culture by other European countries and ethnic groups. A review of each one is beyond the scope of this book and is not to be interpreted as a lack of recognition of the contribution of each. Some of these are noted in the selected annotated bibliography at the end of this chapter. The Ellis Island Immigration Museum is recommended as a unique resource on the European cultures.

A wide diversity of cultures and ethnic groups exists in Europe, often within the borders of a single country. An appreciation of the diversities, the values, and the customs is vital to understanding how European immigration affected life-styles and childrearing practices in the United States. It affords an insight into European history and heritage and to the traditions which those immigrants have transmitted to subsequent generations. Yet it is not a study of "the old ways" alone that is beneficial. Present programs and policies in Europe are deserving of consideration by all concerned with the health, education, and welfare of children.

NOTES

1. Francis L.K. Hsu, ed., "Kinship and Ways of Life: An Exploration," *Psychological Anthropology: Approaches to Culture and Personality* (Homewood, Ill.: Dorsey Press, 1961), pp. 400–456.

2. Ibid.

3. *Encyclopaedia Britannica,* 1988, s.v. "Europe," p. 649.
4. Ibid., p, 668.
5. Ibid., p. 668.
6. Ibid., p. 669.
7. Ibid., p. 669.
8. Ann L. Clark, "Childrearing in Matrix America," *Culture and Childrearing,* A.L. Clark, ed. (Philadelphia: F.A. Davis, 1981), p. 37.
9. Hinda Winawer-Steiner and Norbert A. Wetzel, "German Families," *Ethnicity and Family Therapy,* M. McGoldrick, J.K. Pearce, and J. Giordano, eds. (New York: Guilford, 1982), pp. 247–268.
10. Lillemor Melsted, "Swedish Family Policy and the Election this Autumn," *Current Sweden,* no. 361. The Swedish Institute, May 1988.
11. The Swedish Institute, "Family Planning in Sweden," *Fact Sheets on Sweden,* FS 73 k Vn, August 1986.
12. The Swedish Institute, "Facts and Figures about Youth in Sweden," *Fact Sheets on Sweden,* FS 88c Ohfb, December 1986.
13. Barbara Welles-Nystrom, "Parenthood and Infancy in Sweden," *Parental Behavior in Diverse Societies.* New Directions for Child Development Series, no. 40, R.A. LeVine, P.M. Miller, and M. Maxwell West, eds. (San Francisco: Jossey-Bass, 1988), pp. 76–77.
14. Ibid.
15. Lennart Kohler and Gunborg Jakobsson. *Children's Health and Well-Being in the Nordic Countries.* Clinics in Developmental Medicine no. 98. (London: Mac Keith Press, 1987).
16. *An Intercultural Approach in Teaching and Teaching Materials* (Stockholm: Swedish Nation Board of Education, 1987).
17. Lewis P. Lipsitt. "Child Care is a Thing of Today," *The Brown University Child Behavior and Development Letter* 5 (August 1989): 8.
18. David McGill and John K. Pearce. "British Families," *Ethnicity and Family Therapy,* M. McGoldrick, J.K. Pearce, and J. Giordano, eds. (New York: Guilford, 1982), pp. 460–461.
19. Ibid.
20. *Encyclopaedia Britannica,* 1988 ed., s.v., "Ireland."
21. Gail Richardson and Elisabeth Marx, *A Welcome for Every Child: How France Achieves Quality in Child Care—Practical Ideas for the United States* (New York: The French-American Foundation, 1989).
22. Marie Rotunno and Monica McGoldrick, "Italian Families," *Ethnicity and Family Therapy,* M. McGoldrick, J.K. Pearce, and J. Giordano, eds. (New York: Guilford, 1982), p. 340.
23. Ibid., p. 345.
24. *Encyclopaedia Britannica,* 1988 ed., s.v., "Italy."

BIBLIOGRAPHY

Adams, Paul L. "The WASP Child." *Basic Handbook of Child Psychiatry*, J.P. Noshpitz and I.N. Berlin, eds. Vol. I: *Normal Development*. New York: Basic Books, 1979, pp. 283–290.

Describes the childrearing practices of "WASP" (white Anglo-Saxon Protestant) families such as individualism, ethnocentrism, class distinction, self-worth, strong work ethic, accountability, civic responsibility, and patriotism. Stresses that all Protestants are not alike, that they vary on theological, regional, and class lines. Clarifies the differences among the various Protestant sects, the denominations, and the ecclesiastical groups.

Allen, James Paul, and Eugene James Turner. *We the People: An Atlas of America's Ethnic Diversity*. New York: Macmillan, 1988.

Provides a definitive study of the internal migration patterns of European (and other) immigrants within the United States. More than just demographics, this book includes maps and analyses of where (and why) various ethnic groups have settled.

Archdeacon, Thomas J. *Becoming American, An Ethnic History*. New York: Free Press, 1983.

Chronicles the immigration history of Europeans to the United States— why they came, how they came, where they came from, and where they settled.

Bernardo, Stephanie. *The Ethnic Almanac*. Garden City, N.Y.: Dolphin/Doubleday, 1981.

Examines the customs and traditions of the various ethnic groups in the United States, many of whom are of European origin.

Berry, Eric. *The Land and People of Finland*. Rev. ed. Portraits of the Nations Series. New York: Lippincott, 1972.

Reports on the traditions and life-style of the Finns, people who enjoy nature and are very proud of their country and its social and economic achievements. Describes the Finnish people as strong and introverted in character. In addition to the (state) Lutheran Church, there are small groups of Catholics, Protestants, Jews, Muslims, and even shamanistic cults who believe in animism.

Berry, Eric. *The Land and People of Iceland*. Rev. ed. Portraits of the Nations Series. New York: Lippincott, 1972.

A compilation of information about the traditions, customs, and values of Icelanders. Discusses those unique characteristics, such as the traditional naming of children and the Viking influence, that distinguish the culture of Iceland from its Scandinavian neighbors.

Bryant, Andrew. *The Italians: How They Live and Work*. New York: Frederick A. Prager, 1968.

Describes the mixture of heritage and dialects that comprise the Italian life-style. Cites the devotion to family and children, to regions and cities, the lack of aggression, the affability, the genuine interest in other people, the sensitivity to art, beauty, creativity, and inventiveness, and a sunny, outward attitude toward life as traditions characteristic of Italians.

Carew, Dorothy. *The Netherlands*. A Nations Today Book. New York: Macmillan, 1965.

Characterizes the Dutch people (from an anonymous quote) as "the discoverers of the family, the individual, and the private house." Lists the traditional values of the Dutch as love of freedom, devotion to duty, hard work, a sense of order, respect for others, patience, enjoyment of beauty, and the ability to turn misfortune into advantage.

Childs, David, and Jeffrey Johnson. *West Germany: Politics and Society*. London: Croom Helm, 1981.

Portrays the current life-style in Germany and how it is influenced by regional, religious, geographical, occupational, and gender differences. Describes the German society as still basically authoritarian. Cites two major factors—the weight of history and acute self-criticism in contact with outsiders—as responsible for changes in attitude in the post-war period.

Clark, Ann L. "Childrearing in Matrix America." *Culture and Childrearing*. A.L. Clark, ed. Philadelphia: Davis, 1981, pp. 37–54.

Focuses on the manner in which the dominant American culture rears its young and how these parenting practices have evolved from other cultures, primarily European.

Dahlberg, Inger Sigfridsson. *Immigrant Pupils in the School for Mentally Retarded in Sweden: An Interim Report on a Development Program in*

Process. Stockholm: National Swedish Board of Education, Information Section, 1985.

Reviews and analyzes problem areas in the education of mentally retarded immigrant pupils and proposes further research and development of curricula. The section on "Personality Development of the Mentally Retarded Immigrants" is particularly noteworthy; it focuses on the significance of how the family and the home-culture view a child's handicap. Report also provides examples of the level of commitment and services for handicapped immigrant children in Sweden.

Davey, Thomas. *A Generation Divided: German Children and the Berlin Wall.* Durham, N.C.: Duke University Press, 1987.

Reports on the emotional and cognitive feelings of loyalty and/or alienation of children (on both sides of the Berlin wall) toward their nation. Compiled by interviews, direct observation, interpretation of drawings, and talks with teachers and families.

Encyclopaedia Britannica, Macropaedia: Knowledge in Depth, 15th Edition, 1988.

Presents objective synopses of countries. Reviews not only the history and geography of each country but also information such as: Patterns of Settlement; Migration; Population Distribution; Major Language Patterns; Demographics; Races; Language; and Components of Societies. In addition to providing detailed knowledge about the countries of Europe, includes an extensive section on Europe in general (Volume 18), broadly describing the people, languages, cultural and ethnic patterns. Updated yearly.

Encyclopaedia Britannica, Micropaedia: Ready Reference, 15th Edition, 1988.

Similar in style and content to the *Macropaedia: Knowledge in Depth* multi-volume series listed above, *Micropaedia* provides a shorter, more concise, yet reliable reference source.

Gartler, Marion, Caryl Roman, and George L. Hall. *Understanding France.* Understanding Your World Series. River Forest, Ill.: Laidlaw, 1965.

Describes the outstanding characteristics of the French as hardworking and home loving. Examines the childrearing customs in families that are primarily small and close knit. Traces the educational system and the various religions in France.

Gianakoulis, Theodore. *The Land and People of Greece.* Portraits of the Nations Series. New York: Lippincott, 1972.

States that the traditions that have been handed down for centuries are still the basis of everyday life. Little, if any, differences are found in culture, language, and religion regardless of location. Reports that "Philotimo" ("philo" = loving; "timi" = honor) is the most distinctive trait of Greeks.

Halldén, Gunilla. *Parental Belief Systems and Time: Parents' Reflections on Development and Child Rearing.* Stockholm: Department of Education, University of Stockholm, October 1988.

A paper presented at the third European Conference on Developmental Psychology, Budapest, Hungary, June 15–19, 1988. Halldén states that parental belief systems concerning children's development and needs are culturally related and are transmitted from one generation to the next. Reports on a study of parental ideas about development and parenting in a small community in southern Sweden.

Herz, Fredda M., and Elliot J. Rosen. "Jewish Families." *Ethnicity and Family Therapy.* M. McGoldrick, J.K. Pearce, and J. Giordano, eds. New York: Guilford, 1982, pp. 364–392.

Focuses on family patterns, values, gender roles, parent-child relationships, and life-cycle rituals in exploring the demographic and historical roots of Jews in America. Explains the similarities and the differences among Sephardic (Spanish) Jews, Western European (primarily German) Jews, and Eastern European (Russian, Polish, etc.) Jews.

Kobayashi, Noboru, and T. Berry Brazelton, eds. *The Growing Child in Family and Society: An Interdisciplinary Study in Parent-Infant Bonding.* Tokyo: University of Tokyo Press, 1984.

Explores international variations in child-rearing patterns. Includes research studies and national concerns involving children in West Germany, England, Sweden, France, and Hungary. Compares social welfare, educational, and medical policies, with emphasis on maternity leave policies, day care, and maternal working patterns.

Kohler, Lennart, and Gunborg Jakobsson. "Children's Health and Well-Being in the Nordic Countries." *Clinics in Developmental Medicine No. 98.* London: Mac Keith Press, 1987.

Reports on the demographics of child morbidity and mortality in the Scandinavian countries. Also compares the social welfare systems, describes the problems, and discusses prevention strategies.

Lambert, Wallace, and Otto Klineberg. *Children's Views of Foreign Peoples*. New York: Meredith, 1967.

Focuses on children growing up in regions of the world, such as Northern Ireland, East and West Berlin, and Poland, where political and religious conflict are commonplace. Describes how children in these circumstances are forced to come to terms early with political and moral reality, and to learn early *what* and *who* works for and against them.

Lengyel, Emil. *The Land and People of Hungary*. Portraits of the Nations Series. New York: Lippincott, 1965.

Details the influence of invasion and occupation by Russia, Germany, the Tartars, Austrians, and Turks. Describes and explains the uniqueness of the Hungarian language. Also addresses the priorities in the Hungarian education system.

Lipsitt, Lewis P. "Child Care is a Thing of Today." *The Brown University Child Behavior and Development Letter* 5 (August 1989): 8.

An editorial focusing on the economic and psychological investment of Scandinavian countries in their children. Specifically extols the Finnish system of early childhood education and their child welfare policy.

Loder, Dorothy. *The Land and People of Spain*. Rev. ed. Portraits of the Nations Series. New York: Lippincott, 1972.

Explains the cultural variances that exist among regional groups, such as the Catalans, the Basques, and the Moors. Describes the class system, the values, and the importance of family names. Presents a historical perspective of the Spanish educational system.

Lynch, James. "Multiethnic Education in Europe: Problems and Prospects." *Phi Delta Kappan* 64 (1983): 566–579.

Chronicles the factors contributing to multicultural education in Europe. Highlights the demographic patterns of settlement across Europe by people of differing customs and languages.

McGill, David, and John K. Pearce. "British Families." *Ethnicity and Family Therapy.* M. McGoldrick, J.K. Pearce, and J. Giordano, eds. New York: Guilford, 1982, pp. 457–479.

Presents an historical review of English, Scottish, and Scotch Irish immigrants to the United States. Explains how varied British American families have become due to factors such as migration experience, religious differences, urban/rural and regional differences, and socioeconomic status. Elaborates on the traditional values of English families.

McGoldrick, Monica. "Irish Families." *Ethnicity and Family Therapy.* M. McGoldrick, J.K. Pearce, and J. Giordano, eds. New York: Guilford, 1982, pp. 310–339.

Provides a paradigm of historical Irish traits for understanding Irish American families. Examines such characteristics as the unifying force of the Catholic church, verbal talent, humor, alcoholism, and family life-style.

Melsted, Lillemor. *Current Sweden: Election Year '88: Swedish Family Policy and the Election This Autumn.* Roger Tanner, trans. Stockholm: Swedish Institute, 1988.

Provides a rare "behind the scene" look at the history, ideology, and problems of supportive pre-school services in Swedish culture. This report "is directly bound up with the massive expansion over the past two decades in the ranks of working mothers."

Midelfort, C.F., and H.C. Midelfort. "Norwegian Families." *Ethnicity and Family Therapy.* M. McGoldrick, J.K. Pearce, and J. Giordano, eds. New York: Guilford, 1982, pp. 438–456.

Reviews Norwegian history and values and provides insights into the dualistic nature of the Norwegian culture, religion, and folklore. States that many of the characteristics described also apply to Swedish and Danish families; differences are primarily attributable to historical circumstances and to geography.

Miller, C. Arden. *Maternal Health and Infant Survival.* Washington, D.C.: National Center for Clinical Infant Programs, 1987.

Analyzes the medical and social services for pregnant women, newborns, and their families in ten European countries: Belgium, Denmark, France, Federal Republic of Germany, Ireland, Netherlands, Norway, Spain, Switzerland, and the United Kingdom. This study is aimed at influencing policy and practice in the United States. It is also valuable in providing a cross-cultural examination of European traditions associated with child welfare.

Mindel, Charles H., and Robert W. Haberstein, eds. *Ethnic Families in America: Patterns and Variations.* New York: Elsevier Scientific, 1976.

Examines a variety of ethnic families/groups, including many with European roots: Polish, Italian, Irish-Catholic, Greek, Amish, Franco-American, French-Canadian, Jewish, and Mormon. Focuses on the structure and functioning of their family life as well as on their social and cultural heritage.

Moen, Phyllis. *Working Parents: Transformations in Gender Roles and Public Policies in Sweden.* Madison: University of Wisconsin Press, 1989.

Analyzes the conflicts and pressures faced by parents of young children in Sweden. Finds that single mothers face increased stresses and that gender inequity persists in spite of public policies which are intended to promote gender equity.

Mondykowski, Sandra M. "Polish Families." *Ethnicity and Family Therapy.* M. McGoldrick, J.K. Pearce, and J. Giordano, eds. New York: Guilford, 1982, pp. 393–411.

Provides a review of Polish history as a context in which to understand Polish culture and ethnic traditions. Describes the emphasis on family solidarity and religious faith and how these values have impeded rapid acculturation in America.

Moritza, Everett. "Portuguese Families." *Ethnicity and Family Therapy.* M. McGoldrick, J.K. Pearce, and J. Giordano, eds. New York: Guilford, 1982, pp. 412–437.

Identifies the traditional attitudes, beliefs, and practices of Portuguese culture, and its effect on childrearing practices of Portuguese American immigrants. Reviews the history of Continental Portugal and the Azores, attributing Portuguese fatalism to environmental difficulties.

Mueller, Thomas, and Thomas Espenshade. *The Fourth Wave.* Washington, D.C.: Urban Institute Press, 1985.

Describes the great waves of European migration to the United States in the nineteenth and twentieth centuries. Reports on the characteristics of immigrants from Germany, Britain, Ireland, Italy, and Scandinavia and how the immigrants varied in each wave.

New, Rebecca Staples. "Parental Goals and Italian Infant Care." *Parental Behavior in Diverse Societies.* New Directions for Child Development Series, no. 40. R. A. LeVine, P.M. Miller, and M.M. West, eds. San Francisco: Jossey-Bass, 1988, pp. 51–63.

Examines the goals and childrearing practices of Italian parents. Illustrates the role of culture in maintaining practices that are no longer serving an obvious adaptive function.

Olmsted, Patricia P., and David P. Weikart, eds. *How Nations Serve Young Children: Profiles of Child Care and Education in 14 Countries.* Ypsilanti, Mich.: High/Scope Press, 1989.

Contains national profiles of early childhood care and education in Belgium, Germany, Finland, Hungary, Italy, Portugal, and Spain. Deals with a range of national child care policies. Many of these policies are currently undergoing reevaluation and change. Reflects findings of an ongoing international study investigating "the nature, quality, and effects of the experiences of children prior to formal schooling." This study is being conducted by the (IEA) International Association for the Evaluation of Educational Achievement, a nongovernmental, nonprofit organization of research institutions in 45 countries.

Owen, Trefor M. *Welsh Folk Customs.* Cardiff: National Museum of Wales, 1978.

Chronicles the unique customs of Wales, such as those associated with stages in the life cycle, especially birth and death. Describes the many superstitions and astrological beliefs associated with pregnancy. Reviews other traditional customs in Wales, such as the importance of godparents and the practice of giving of "love spoons" at time of betrothal.

Payer, Lynn. *Medicine and Culture: Varieties of Treatment in the Unites States, England, West Germany, and France.* New York: Henry Holt, 1988.

Explores transcultural views of the human condition, concepts of health and disease, and approaches to medical practice. Focuses on cultural biases in medical sciences and how this determines the type and method of service delivery.

Pfeiffer, Christine. *Poland: Land of Freedom Fighters.* Minneapolis, Minn.: Dillon Press. 1984.

Offers a view of the valued customs and traditions of Polish life, such as the strong sense of family, the importance of education and religion, and the pride in celebrating "Polishness" in conversation, songs, poetry, dance, plays, art, essays, and speeches.

Richardson, Gail, and Elisabeth Marx. *A Welcome for Every Child: How France Achieves Quality in Child Care—Practical Ideas for the United States*. New York: The French-American Foundation, 1989.

Examines the preschool and child care system in France. Reports on a two-year project conducted by 14 child care experts from the United States. Discusses issues such as maternity leave, training and supervision of caregivers, and salaries for child care professionals. Describes how French policy on child care was developed and how it is financed.

Richman, Amy L., R.A. LeVine, R.S. New, G.A. Howrigan, B. Welles-Nystrom, and S.E. LeVine, "Maternal Behavior to Infants in Five Cultures." *Parental Behavior in Diverse Societies*. New Directions for Child Development Series, no. 40. San Francisco: Jossey-Bass, 1988, pp. 81–96.

Examines the demographic, socioeconomic, and cultural contexts of infant care in Italy and Sweden, as well as in three non-European societies.

Rodén, Gunilla. *Handicapped Immigrant Preschool Children in Sweden*. Stockholm: National Swedish Board of Education, Information Section, 1985.

A report on how services are provided in accordance with the law of 1968. Details the process by which these children—and their families—are integrated into Swedish society. Several case studies illustrate service effectiveness. Of particular interest is the section on "mother tongue-language activity."

Rotunno, Marie, and Monica McGoldrick. "Italian Families." *Ethnicity and Family Therapy*. M. McGoldrick, J.K. Pearce, and Joseph Giordano, eds. New York: Guilford, 1982, pp. 340–363.

Focuses on the character and family patterns of southern Italians and the implications of these patterns for American families of Italian heritage. Examines the historical, psychological, and sociological background of *la via vecchia* (the old way), a value system organized primarily around protecting the family.

Swedish Institute. *Fact Sheets on Sweden*. New York: The Swedish Information Service, 1988.

A series of fact sheets produced as part of the Swedish information service abroad. Intended for reference purposes, these fact sheets are available in a wide range of subjects from Government and Politics to Social Issues. Fact sheets relevant to this chapter include, "Immigrants in Sweden," "Primary and Secondary Education in Sweden," "Child Care in Sweden," "Facts and Figures about Youth in Sweden," and "The Health Care System in Sweden."

Swedish National Board of Education. *An Intercultural Approach in Teaching and Teaching Materials*. Roger Tanner, trans. Stockholm: Swedish National Board of Education Information Section, 1987.

Indicates different ways of utilizing the multicultural reality of school life and presents ideas on how to develop an intercultural approach to teaching and the use of teaching materials. The corresponding Swedish version provides illustrated examples of ways in which the content, materials, and methods for teaching different subjects can be based on all pupils' experience.

Thernstrom, S., A. Orlov, and O. Handlin, eds. *Harvard Encyclopedia of American Ethnic Groups*. Cambridge, Mass.: Harvard University Press, 1980.

Provides detailed information on the many European ethnic groups who settled in the United States. Each chapter discusses the customs and traditions of the various ethnic groups at length.

U.S. Department of State, Bureau of Public Affairs. *Background Notes*. Washington, D.C.: U.S. Department of State, Public Communications Office, March 1990.

Unique series of brief, authoritative pamphlets (approximately 170) on selected countries and geographic entities of the world (except U.S.) and international organizations. Series is updated every two years. Provides concise information on the history, geography, culture, government, politics, economy, and travel tips. *Background Notes* available on Belgium, Czechoslovakia, F.R.G. (West Germany), D.R.G. (East Germany), Greece, Hungary, Italy, Netherlands, Norway, Poland, Portugal, Romania, Spain, Sweden, Switzerland, and the United Kingdom.

Welles-Nystrom, Barbara. "Parenthood and Infancy in Sweden." *Parental Behavior in Diverse Societies*. New Directions for Child Development Series, no. 40. R.A. LeVine, P.M. Miller, and M.M. West, eds. San Francisco: Jossey-Bass, 1988, pp. 75–80.

Explores the experience of parenthood and infant care in Sweden, with emphasis on those features that distinguish it from parental experience elsewhere. Notes that urban parents in Sweden are more apt than their counterparts in other countries to look to medical science and government for guidance in matters of reproduction and child care.

Welts, Eve Primpas. "Greek Families." *Ethnicity and Family Therapy."* M. McGoldrick, J.K. Pearce, and J. Giordano, eds. San Francisco: Jossey-Bass, 1982, pp. 269–288.

Focuses on four key elements of the Greek culture: (1) The mercurial and paradoxical nature of the people; (2) The tremendous pride in individual achievement and the self-concept of individualism; (3) The importance of honor; and (4) The rigid definition of family roles.

Winawer-Steiner, Hinda, and Norbert A. Wetzel. "German Families." *Ethnicity and Family Therapy.* M. McGoldrick, J.K. Pearce, and J. Giordano, eds. San Francisco: Jossey-Bass, 1982, pp. 247–268.

Discusses those aspects of German cultural and familial heritage such as *Lebensram* (space for living) that are related to internal and external survival factors. Another characteristic trait of German heritage is emotional restraint. Examines German family life, family patterns, life cycle issues, the work ethic, and the emphasis on education. Explains the origins of diversity among Germans.

Winwar, Frances. *The Land and People of Italy.* Rev. ed. Portraits of the Nation Series. Philadelphia: Lippincott, 1972.

Describes how the various regions of Italy differ from one another. Portrays the Italians as intensely religious people who traditionally excel at trades of skill and creative intelligence, music, and the creation of jewelry and furniture.

Wohlrabe, Raymond, and Werner Krusch. *The Land and People of Portugal.* Portraits of the Nation Series. Philadelphia: Lippincott, 1963.

Portrays the Portuguese culture as a fusion of races. Cites their friendly and patient nature which differs from the quick and often violent-tempered personality of their Spanish neighbors. Notes the love of fun, and the colorful fairs and festivals that are so prevalent in Portuguese culture.

AUTHOR INDEX

A.B.C. Task Force, 55
Abril, Irene F., 183n, 185
Abu-Saad, Huda, 107n, 108
Ackerman, Nathan W., 37n, 38
Acock, Alan C., 20, 38
Adams, Paul L., 20, 242
Aldrich, Howard, 91
Allen, James Paul, 83, 242
Allen, Walter R., 220
Allport, Gordon W., 48, 54n
Anderson, Penny P., 20, 38, 82n, 108, 148n, 151, 182n, 185, 210n, 212
Andres, Francis D., 38
Anthony, E. James, 39
Aquino, Consuelo J., 150n, 151
Archdeacon, Thomas J., 242
Asamen, Joy Keido, 212
Axelson, John A., 20, 48, 54n, 108, 150n, 151, 181n, 183n, 184n, 185, 199, 210n, 211n, 212

Baca, Leonard, 17n, 109, 182n
Banfield, Beryle, 54n,
Barnett, Ann B., 191
Barnsteiner, Jane H., 39, 55
Baron, Richard, 107n, 109
Barrett, Richard A., 20
Bartlett, Elsa, 112
Benedek, Therese, 39
Benedict, Ruth, 148n
Bennis, Warren, 82n
Berg-Cross, Linda, 39, 83
Bernal, Guillermo, 184n, 185
Bernardo, Stephanie, 83, 149n, 242

Berry, Eric, 242, 243
Berry, Gordon Lavern, 212
Bestman, E., 107n
Bickerton, Yvonne, 114, 189
Billingsly, Andrew, 212
Blakeslee, Sandra, 18n
Block, B., 89
Bond, Lynne A., 39
Booker, Christopher, 211n
Bourne, E., 59
Bowen, Murray, 39, 42
Bowette, T.R., 84
Boyd-Franklin, Nancy, 210n, 213, 215
Boyle, Joyceen S., 19n, 21
Bransford, Louis A., 17n, 109, 151, 182n
Brazelton, T. Berry, 25, 27, 149n, 155, 245
Brembeck, Cole S., 109
Brice, Janet, 211n, 213
Brim, Orville G., 9, 18n
Brislin, Richard W., 55, 57, 84
Bronfenbrenner, Urie, 20
Brookins, Geraldine K., 220
Brotherson, Mary Jane, 34, 37n, 44
Brown, Ina Corrine, 8, 18n, 75, 82n, 84
Brown, Marie Scott, 55
Bryant, Andrew, 243
Buckley, W., 32, 37n
Buriel, Raymond, 186

Canino, Glorisa, 186
Canino, Ian A., 186
Caplan, Gerald, 37n

Caplan, Nathan, 150n, 152
Carew, Dorothy, 243
Carlin, Jean E., 148n, 152
Carrión, Arturo Morales, 183n, 184n, 185
Carter, E.A., 40
Castillo, Fortunato G., 182n, 183n, 192
Chapa, Jorge, 188
Char, Evelyn L., 149n, 152
Childs, David, 243
Chin, Ann-ping, 63, 82n, 149n, 152
Chin, Jean Lau, 153
Church, Alexandria, 54n
Church, Joseph, 54n
Clair, Jeffrey M., 20, 38
Clark, Ann L., 21, 84, 109, 241n, 243
Clark, Margaret, 107n
Cole, M., 109, 148n, 153
Coles, Robert, 85
Comas-Diaz, Lillian, 186
Combrinck-Graham, Lee, 40, 110
Comer, James P., 21, 110, 213
Cormican, J.D., 84, 110
Cortez, Carlos E., 187
Cutler, Robert S., 54n

Dahlberg, Inger Sigfridsson, 243
Darling, Rosalyn Benjamin, 44, 90
da Silva, Gabriele C., 107n, 111, 182n, 183n, 184n, 185
Davey, Thomas, 244
Davidson, Dana H., 107n, 119, 160
Davis, Larry E., 119
Deal, Angela, 40
Delgado, M., 111
Derman-Sparks, Louise, 55, 111
Dixon, Terrence, 22
Doi, Takeo L., 149n, 153
Doyle, Glen Caspers, 43
Dugan, T.F., 85
Dundes, Alan, 10, 18n
Dung, Trinh Ngoc, 153

Dunst, Carl, 40
Duvall, Evelyn M., 40

Edwards, Carolyn Pope, 22
Ehling, Marta Borbón, 182n, 187
Eisenberg, Leon, 114
Ellison, Christopher, 213
Erickson, R.V., 113, 155
Espenshade, Thomas, 248

Fairservis, Walter A., Jr., 148n, 149n, 153
Falicov, Cecelia Jaes, 183n, 187
Farb, Peter, 17n, 38n
Fenichel, Emily Schrag, 20, 38, 82n, 108, 149n, 151, 182n, 185, 210n, 212
Ferrari, Michael, 111
Fersh, Seymour, 154
Fishman, Joshua, 85, 107n
Fitzpatrick, J.P., 175, 183n
Flaherty, Mary Jean, 85, 111
Fogel, Alan, 22
Fox, Renee, 107n
Freeman, David S., 41, 56
Friedman, Alma S., 41
Friedman, David Belais, 41
Friedman, W.J., 22
Frost, Robert, 34, 37n

Galinsky, Ellen, 41
Gallagher, James J., 22
Garcia-Preto, Nydia, 183n, 184n, 187
Gardner, Howard, 154
Gartler, Marion, 244
Gartner, Alan, 112
Garvey, M., 211n
Gary, Lawrence E., 214
Gay, J., 148
Geertz, Clifford, 23
Gianakoulis, Theodore, 245
Gibbs, Jewelle Taylor, 112, 154, 214
Gillis-Donovan, Joanne, 39, 55

Author Index

Gilmore, David D., 23
Ginsburg, Sol W., 112
Giordano, Grace P., 18n
Giordano, Joseph, 18n, 26, 88, 112, 115
Glazer, Nathan, 18n, 23
Glick, J., 148n
Good, Byron, 114
Goodenough, Ward, H., 7, 18n
Greathouse, Betty, 107n, 209n, 210n, 214
Greeley, Andrew M., 24, 37n, 85, 108
Grinker, Roy R. Sr., 37n
Grosso, Camille, 154
Guerin, Philip J., 56
Guerra, Fernando A., 182n, 188
Gussler, Judith, 86

Habenstein, Robert W., 157, 158, 182n, 191n, 248
Hale-Benson, Janice E., 214
Haley, Arthur, 215
Hall, Edward T., 17n, 24, 53, 54n
Hall, George L., 244
Hall, William S., 112–113
Halldén, Gunilla, 245
Handlin, O., 251
Hanna, Judith, Lynne, 215
Harel, Zev, 215
Haring, Douglas, G., 155
Harkness, Sara, 29
Harrington, Charles, 24
Harris, Marvin, 24, 56
Harwood, Alan, 86, 182n, 188
Hays-Bautista, David, 188
Helmreich, William, 47, 54n
Henry, Jules, 41
Hepworth, Dean H., 17n, 26, 57, 86, 107n, 114, 156, 189
Herron, D. Gloria, 188
Herz, Fredda M., 245
Hill, Robert B., 211n, 215
Hill, Walker H., 109

Hines, Paulette Moore, 210n, 215
Hinkle, L.E., 67, 82n
Hite, Shere, 25
Hoang, G.N., 113, 155
Hoffman, Lois Wladis, 82n
Honey, John, 15, 19n
Honigman, John J., 25
Houston, S.H., 210n
Howard, A., 56–57
Howrigan, G.A., 250
Hsu, Francis L.K., 18n, 25, 195–196, 209, 216, 224, 240n
Huang, Larke Nahme, 112, 154, 214
Huff, C. Ronald, 113, 155, 216
Hughes, Alva T., 112
Hughes, Helen Macgill, 37n
Hunt, J. McVicker, 113

Inclán, Jaime E., 188

Ja, Davis Y., 148n, 159
Jackson, K.T., 42
Jakobsson, Gunborg, 241n, 245
Janosik, Ellen H., 43, 116
Jelliffe, D.B., 113
Johnson, Jeffrey, 243

Kantor, David, 42
Karplus, Zipi, 18n
Keen, Michael, E., 57
Kerr, Michael, 42, 57
Khoa, L.X., 155
Kim, Susie, 150n, 155
Kleinman, Arthur, 114
Klinebery, Otto, 246
Kluckhohn, Clyde, 7, 8, 18n, 25
Kobayashi, Noboru, 25, 149n, 155, 245
Kochman, Thomas, 216
Kohler, Lennart, 241n, 245
Kramer, Rita, 42
Krusch, Werner, 252

Kumabe, Kazuye T., 17n, 26, 57, 86, 107n, 114, 156, 189

Lacay, Gloria, 182n, 183n, 184n, 189
La Du, Elizabeth Bjorkman, 150n, 156
Lambert, Wallace, 246
Landis, D., 57
Lane, Karen, 17n, 109, 182n
LaPoint, Velma, 221
LaVietes, Ruth L., 183n, 189
Lawrence, Leonard E., 220
Lawson, Lauren Valk, 26, 42, 115, 156, 189
Lee, Evelyn, 149n, 156
Lee, L., 160
Lee, Shu-ching, 157
Leghorn, Lisa, 87
Lehr, William, 42
Lengyel, Emil, 246
Leninger, Madeline, 58
Lester, Barry M., 27
LeVine, Robert A., 87, 250
LeVine, S.E., 250
Lewis, Jerry M., 42
Lewis, Oscar, 190
Leyn, Rita Bayer, 150n, 157
Lieberman, Alicia F., 26, 43, 58, 82n, 87, 115, 190
Liem, Linda Diep, 150n, 159
Liem, Nguyen Dang, 150n, 159
Lin, Mei-Yuan (Wang), 149n
Lincoln, C. Eric, 216
Linton, Ralph, 89, 18n, 45, 46, 54n
Lipsky, Dorothy Kerzner, 112
Lipsitt, Lewis P., 241, 246
Loder, Dorothy, 246
Lubic, Ruth Watson, 184n, 190
Lucas, Martin, 22
Lynch, James, 246

McAdoo, Harriette Pipes, 216, 217
McAdoo, John L., 217

Macdonald, Anne C., 190
McGill, David, 241n, 247
McGoldrick, Monica, 18n, 26, 40, 58, 88, 115, 241n, 247, 250
McKinney, Edward A., 215
McLeod, Beverly, 157
McNeil, Marian, 149n
Maheady, Donna C., 88
Mahoney, Maureen A., 21
Mamiya, Lawrence H., 216
Markides, Kyriakos S., 43
Marx, Elisabeth, 241n, 250
Mead, Margaret, 88, 100, 107n
Meleis, Afaf Ibrahim, 88, 115
Melson, Gail F., 22
Melsted, Lillemor, 241n, 247
Mercer, Ramona T., 43
Midelfort, C.F., 247
Midelfort, H.C., 247
Miller, Brent C., 40
Miller, C. Arden, 115, 247
Miller, Jean R., 43, 116
Miller, Patricia M., 87
Miller, Velvet G., 107n, 209n, 210n, 214
Mindel, Charles H., 157, 248
Miner, Horace, 54n, 58
Minuchin, Salvador, 44
Moen, Phyllis, 248
Mondykowski, Sandra M., 248
Monrroy, L, 89
Moore, Robert B., 54n
Moritza, Everett, 248
Morris, Lee, 116, 157, 183n
Moynihan, Daniel Patrick, 18n, 22
Mueller, Thomas, 248
Murillo, Nathan, 190

Nakane, Chie, 149n, 158
National Coalition of Advocates for Students, 58, 89, 116, 158, 191, 211n, 217

Author Index

National Coalition of Hispanic Health and Human Service Organizations, 182n, 191
National Institute of Mental Health, 158
New, Rebecca Staples, 249, 250
Nichols, Elizabeth G., 43
Nishida, Chikae, 17n, 26, 57, 86, 107n, 114, 156, 189
Nobles, G.M., 210n
Nobles, W.W., 210n
Nolte, Dorothy Law, 19n
Norton, Delores G., 27, 217
Nugent, J.Kevin, 27

Offer, Daniel, 27
Ogbu, John, 18n 217
Ohsawa, Lima, 149n
Olmstead, Patricia P., 89, 116, 158, 249
Olson, D.H., 38n
Opler, Marvin K., 27
Orlov, A., 251
Orque, Modesta S., 89
Orrego, Maria Elena, 191
Owen, Trefor M., 249

Padilla, A.M., 181n
Padilla, Elena, 177, 184n, 191
Papp, Peggy,, 37n
Parker, Katherine, 87
Patterson, Orlando, 217
Payer, Lynn, 117, 249
Peak, Lois, 107n, 117
Pearce, John K., 26, 88, 115, 241n. 247
Pendagast, Eileen G., 56
Pfeiffer, Christine, 249
Phinney, Jean S., 59, 89, 117, 218
Pinderhughes, Charles, 218
Pinderhughes, Elaine, 198, 209n, 210n, 218
Poussaint, Alvin F., 213

Queen, Stuart A., 158, 182n, 191

Ramey, Craig T., 22
Ramirez, Oscar, 192
Ramsey, Patricia G., 117
Randall-David, Elizabeth, 28, 54n, 90, 118, 148n, 150n, 159, 192, 211n, 218
Rautenberg, Ellen L., 118
Reidy, Joseph, 28
Richardson, Gail, 241n, 250
Richman, Amy L., 250
Rodén, Gunilla, 250
Rodgers-Rose, La Frances, 218
Rodriguez, Clara E., 192
Roman, Caryl, 244
Roosens, Eugeen E., 28
Rosen, Eliot J., 245
Rotheram, Mary Jane, 59, 89, 117, 218
Rotunno, Marie, 241n, 250
Roumain, Maryse, 211n
Ruiz, R.A., 181nm 192

Sagan, Leonard A., 118
Santoli, Al., 90, 118
Sapir, Edward, 15, 19n
Satir, Virginia, 82n
Scheinfeld, Daniel R., 219
Schwartzman, Helen B., 28
Schweder, R., 59
Scott, R., 56
Seligman, Milton, 44, 90
Selye, H. Ned, 14, 19n, 28, 90
Serrano, Alberto C., 182n, 183n, 192
Sharp, D., 148n
Shink, Werner O., 188
Shon, Steven P., 148n, 159
Shorter, E., 44
Slaughter, Diana T., 219
Small, Willie V., 198, 210n, 219
Sodetani-Shibata, Aimee Emiko, 148n, 159

Sorrell, Leila, 88, 115
Sowell, Thomas, 211n, 219
Spencer, Margaret B., 220
Spindler, George D., 29
Spurlock, Jeanne, 220
Stack, C.B., 220
Staples, Robert, 210n, 220
Staples, Ronald, 210n
Staub, Ervin, 54n
Steele, Shelby, 220
Steinberg, Stephen, 29, 66, 74, 82n, 90
Stern, Phyllis Noerager, 159
Stevenson, Harold W., 30
Stiffman, Arlene Rubin, 119
Stone, Elizabeth, 11, 18n, 29
Strickland, Justine, 210n
Stringfellow, Lorraine, 150n, 159
Sue, Derald W., 119, 159
Summers, Jean Ann, 34, 37n, 44
Super, Charles M., 29
Suro, Roberto, 182n
Sussman, Marvin B., 111
Swedish Institute, 241n, 250

Takaki, Ronald, 160
Thernstrom, S., 251
Thomasma, E.R., 160
Thompson, Leonard, 221
Tobin, Joseph J., 107n, 119, 160
Tong, Benjamin R., 160
Totter, R.T., 193
Traver, Nancy, 108n, 119
Trivette, Carol, 40
Tsui, Ming, 161
Turnbull, Ann P., 34, 37n, 44, 112, 193
Turnbull, H. Rutherford III, 193
Turner, Eugene James, 83, 242
Tyler, Edward B., 17n

U.S. Department of Agriculture/Department of Health and Human Services, 30, 82n, 91, 107n, 119, 120, 148n, 182n, 193, 221

Valle, K., 193
Vega, W., 193
Vold, Edwina Battle, 117

Wagner, Barry M., 39
Wagner, Daniel A., 30, 120
Waldinger, Roger, 91
Wang, Sung-hsing, 149n
Ward, Robin, 91
Warson, Samuel, 41
Washington, Valora, 221
Weikart, David P., 89, 116, 158, 249
Welles-Nystrom, Barbara, 241n, 250, 251
Welts, Eve Primpas, 252
West, Mary Maxwell, 87
Wetzel, Norbert A., 241n, 252
White, M.I., 87
Whiting, Beatrice B., 14, 19n, 30
Whiting, John W.M., 14, 19n, 30
Williams, Leslie R, 117
Williams, Michael, 215
Wilson, Paul A., 108n
Winawer-Steiner, Hinda, 241n, 252
Winwar, Frances, 252
Wohlrabe, Raymond, 252
Wolf, Ann Marie, 221
Wolfenstein, Martha, 88
Wu, David Y.H., 107n, 119, 160

Yeatman, G.W., 150n
Young, Michael, 30

Zborowski, Mark, 59, 120

TITLE INDEX

Aging and Ethnicity, 43
All Our Kin: Strategies for Survival in a Black Community, 220
American Ethnic Groups, 211n, 219
Anatomy of Dependence, The, 149n, 153
Annotated Bibliography on Refugee Mental Health, An, 158
Anthropological Perspectives on Child Development, 29
Anti-Bias Curriculum: Tools for Empowering Young Children, 55, 111
Applied Cross-Cultural Psychology, 55, 84
ASIA: Traditions and Treasures, 148n, 149n, 153

Background Notes, 251
Basic Concepts in Family Therapy: An Introductory Text, 39, 83
Basic Handbook of Child Psychiatry, 20, 28, 148n, 152, 183n, 189, 192, 220, 242
Becoming American: An Ethnic History, 242
Beginnings: The Social and Affective Development of Black Children, 220
Beyond Culture, 17n, 54n
Beyond the Melting Pot: The Negroes, Puerto Ricans, Jews, Italians, and Irish of New York City, 18n, 23
Black and White Styles in Conflict, 216
Black Aged: Understanding Diversity and Service Needs, 215
Black American Reference Book, The, 218
Black Awareness: Implications for Black Patient Care, 210n
Black Child Care, 213
Black Children and American Institutions: An Ecological Review and Resource Guide, 221
Black Children and Poverty: A Developmental Perspective, 18n, 219
Black Children: Social, Educational, and Parental Environments, 217
Black Children: Their Roots, Culture, and Learning Styles, 214
Black Church in the African American Experience, The, 216
Black Families, 216
Black Families in Therapy: A Multisystems Approach, 213
Black Families in White America, 212
Black Men, 214
Black Sheep and Kissing Cousins: How Our Family Stories Shape Us, 18n, 29

Black Students: Psychosocial Issues and Academic Achievement, 212
Black Woman, The, 218
Black Woman in America: Sex, Marriage, and the Family, The, 210n
Boat People and Achievement in America, The, 150n, 152
Bridging Ethnocultural Diversity in Social Work and Health, 17n, 26, 57, 86, 107n, 114, 156, 189
Burden of Support: Young Latinos in an Aging Society, The, 188

Chicanos: Social and Psychological Perspectives, 183n, 190
Child Abuse, Neglect and the Family Within a Cultural Context, 23, 210n, 219
Child in Our Times: Studies in the Development of Resiliency, 85
Child Development and International Development: Research-Policy Interfaces, 120
Childhood Disability and Family Systems, 111
Childhood in Contemporary Cultures, 88
Children in Family Contexts: Perspectives on Treatment, 40, 110
Children of China: Voices from Recent Years, 82n, 149n, 152
Children of Color: Psychological Intervention with Minority Youth, 112, 154, 188, 192, 214
Children of Six Cultures: A Psycho-Cultural Analysis, 19n, 30
Children's Ethnic Socialization: Pluralism and Development, 59, 89, 117, 186, 218
Children's Health and Well-Being in the Nordic Countries, 241n
Children's Views of Foreign Peoples, 246
Chrysanthemum and the Sword: Patterns of Japanese Culture, The, 148n
Consequences of Class and Color, 211n
Content of our Character: A New Vision of Race in America, The, 220
Counseling and Development in a Multicultural Society, 20, 54n, 54, 108, 150n, 151, 160, 181n, 183n, 184n, 185, 210n, 212
Counseling the Culturally Different: Theory and Practice, 119, 192
Cows, Pigs, Wars, and Witches: The Riddles of Culture, 56
Crabgrass Frontier - The Suburbanization of the United States, 42
Creating Ethnicity: The Process of Ethnogenesis, 28
Cross-Cultural Counseling: A Guide for Nutrition and Health Counselors, 30, 82n, 91, 107n, 119, 148n, 161, 182n, 193, 221
Cultural Background of Personality, The, 18n, 54n
Cultural Backgrounds of the Indochinese People, 160
Cultural Challenges to Education: The Influence of Cultural Factors in School Learning, 109
Cultural Conceptions of Mental Health and Therapy, 59
Cultural Context of Infancy, The, 27
Cultural Context of Learning and Thinking: An Explanation in Experimental Anthropology, 109, 148n, 153

Title Index

Cultural Diversity and the Exceptional Child, 17n, 109, 151, 182n
Cultural Perspectives on Child Development, 30
Culture and Childrearing, 21, 55, 84, 107n, 109, 149n, 150n, 151, 152, 159, 160, 182n, 182n, 184n, 187, 189, 209n, 210n, 214, 241n, 243
Culture and Conduct: An Excursion in Anthropology, 20
Culture, Language and Society, 18n, 24
CULTURGRAMS, 151, 185
Current Research, Treatment, and Policy Issues, 44
Current Sweden, 241n, 247

Death of the Hired Man, The, 37n
Delivering Preventive Health Care to Hispanics: A Manual for Providers, 182n, 191
Developmental Psychology of Time, The, 22
Die the Long Day, 217
Diseases of Children in the Subtropics and Tropics, 113
Does Accent Matter? The Pygmalion Factor, 19n

Early Experience and the Development of Competence, 107n, 113, 117
Education and Cultural Process: Anthropological Approaches, 29
Enabling and Empowering Families: Principles and Guidelines for Practice, 40
Ethnic Almanac, The, 83, 150n, 242
Ethnic Entrepreneurs: Immigrant Business in Industrial Societies, 91
Ethnic Families in America: Patterns and Variations, 157, 248
Ethnic Issues in Adolescent Mental Health, 119
Ethnic Myth: Race, Ethnicity, and Class in America, The, 29, 82n, 90
Ethnic Nursing Care: A Multicultural Approach, 89
Ethnicity and Family Therapy, 18n, 26, 58, 88, 115, 148n, 149n, 156, 159, 183n, 184n, 185, 187, 209n, 210n, 211n, 213, 215, 218, 241n, 245, 247, 248, 250, 252
Ethnicity and Health Care, 118
Ethnicity and Medical Care, 86, 188
Ethnicity in the United States: A Preliminary Reconnaissance, 24, 37n, 108n
Ethno-Cultural Factor in Mental Health: A Literature Review and Bibliography, 18n
Ethnocultural Factors in Social Work and Health Care: A Selected Annotated Bibliography, 114
Extracting Learning Styles from Social/Cultural Diversity: Studies of Five American Minorities, 116, 157, 160, 187, 214

Fact Sheets on Sweden, 241n, 250
Families and Family Therapy, 44

Families in Transition, 39
Families of Handicapped Persons: Current Research, Treatment, and Policy Issues, 37n
Family Assessment, 42
Family Focused Care, 43, 116
Family in Various Cultures, The, 158, 182n, 191
Family Life Cycle: A Framework for Family Therapy, 40
Family Therapy: Theory and Practice, 39, 56
Fourth Wave, The, 248

Gangs in America: Diffusion, Diversity, and Public Policy, 113, 155, 216
Generation Divided: German Children and the Berlin Wall, The, 244
Georgetown Family Symposium Papers, 38, 57
Growing Child in Family and Society: An Interdisciplinary Study in Parent-Infant Bonding, The, 25, 149n, 150n, 155, 245
Growing Up in New Guinea, 107n

Handbook of Asian American/Pacific Islander Mental Health, 158
Handbook of Cross-Cultural Human Development, 56
Handbook of Intercultural Training: Area Studies in Intercultural Training, 57
Handbook of Korea, A, 149n, 154
Handicapped Immigrant Preschool Children in Sweden, 250
Harvard Encyclopedia of American Ethnic Groups, 251
Health in the Mexican-American Culture: A Community Study, 107n
Health of Nations: True Causes of Sickness and Well-Being, The, 118
Hispanic Natural Support Systems, 193
History of South Africa, A, 221
How Nations Serve Young Children: Profiles of Child Care and Education in 14 Countries, 89, 116, 158, 249
How's Your Family?: A Guide to Identifying Your Family's Strengths and Weaknesses, 42
Humankind, 17n, 38n
Human Race, The, 22

Immigrant Pupils in the School for Mentally Retarded in Sweden: An Interim Report on a Development Program in Process, 243
In Defense of the Family: Raising Children in America Today, 42
Influence of the Family: A Review and Annotated Bibliography of Socialization, Ethnicity, and Delinquency, The, 20, 38
Influences on Human Development, 21
Inside the Family: Toward a Theory of Family Process, 42
Intercultural Approach in Teaching and Teaching Materials, An, 241n, 251
Interpretation of culture, The, 23

Title Index

Introduction to Black Sociology, 210n, 220
Italians: How They Live and Work, The, 243

Japanese Society, 149n, 158

Kife: The Lives and Dreams of Soviet Youth, 108n, 119

Land and People of Finland, The, 242
Land and People of Greece, The, 245
Land and People of Hungary, The, 246
Land and People of Iceland, The, 243
Land and People of Italy, The, 252
Land and People of Portugal, The, 252
Land and People of Spain, The, 246
Latin American Family and Public Policy in the United States: Informal Support and Transition into Adulthood, The, 193
Latino Mental Health: A Review of the Literature, 181n
La Vida, 190
Learning About Peoples and Cultures, 154

Macrobiotic Cuisine, 149n
Maggie's American Dream, 21
Making of the Modern Family, The, 44
Malleability of Children, The, 18n, 22
Manhood in the Making: Cultural Concepts of Masculinity, 23
Markets and Minorities, 219
Marriage and Family Development, 40
Maternal Health and Infant Survival: An Analysis of Medical and Social Services to Pregnant Women, Newborns and their Families in Ten European Countries, with Implications for Policy and Practice in the United States, 115, 247
Medicine and Culture: Varieties of Treatment in the United States, 117, 249
Metronomic Society: Natural Rhythms and Human Timetables, The, 30
Mirror for Man: The Relation of Anthropology to Modern Life, 18n, 25
Modern Perspectives in Psychiatry, 27
Multicultural Education: A Source Book, 117

Nature of Prejudice, The, 54n
Netherlands, The, 243
New Voices: Immigrant Students in U.S. Public Schools, 58, 89, 116, 158, 190, 211n, 217

One Thousand Families: A National Survey, 38n
Oral History: Immigrants and Refugees in the U.S. Today, An, 90, 118
Ordinary Families, Special Children: A Systems Approach to Childhood Disability, 44, 90
Origins of Nurturance: Developmental, Biological, and Cultural Perspectives on Caregiving, 22
Our Kind, 24

Parental Behavior in Diverse Societies, 82n, 241n
Parental Belief Systems and Time: Parents' Reflections on Development and Child Rearing, 245
Parenthood: Its Psychology and Psychopathology, 39
Parenting Across the Life Span, 87
Patients and Healers in the Context of Culture: An Exploration of the Borderland Between Anthropology, Medicine, and Psychiatry, 114
People in Pain, 59, 120
People's Almanac, The, 210n
Peoplemaking, 82n
Personal Character and Cultural Milieu, 155
Personality Development in Children, 18n
Planning of Change, The, 82n
Poland: Land of Freedom Fighters, 249
Primitive Cultures, 17n
Progress in Child Psychiatry and Child Development, 210n
Promoting Social and Moral Development in Young Children, 22
Providing Safe Nursing Care for Ethnic People of Color, 210n
Psychiatrist's Views on Social Issues, A, 112
Psychodynamics of Family Life: Diagnosis and Treatment of Family Relationships, The, 37n
Psychological Anthropology and Education: A Delineation of a Field of Inquiry, 24, 216, 240n
Psychological Anthropology: Approaches to Culture and Personality, 18n, 25, 209n
Puerto Rican Americans: The Meaning of Immigration to the Mainland, 83n
Puerto Ricans: Born in the U.S.A., 192
Puerto Rico: A Political and Cultural History, 183n, 184n, 186

Resources for Early Childhood: An Annotated Bibliography and Guide for Educators, Librarians, Health Care Professionals, and Parents, 54n
Roots, 215
Roots of Evil: The Psychological and Cultural Origin of Genocide, The, 54n

Title Index

School Power: Implications of an Intervention Project, 110
Serving Culturally Diverse Families of Infants and Toddlers with Disabilities, 20, 38, 82n, 108, 148n, 151, 182n, 185, 210n, 212
Silent Language, The, 24
Six Stages of Parenthood, The, 41
Sociology and Modern Systems Theory, 37n
Strangers from a Different Shore: A History of Asian Americans, 160
Strategies for Working with Culturally Diverse Communities and Clients, 28, 54n, 90, 118, 148n, 150n, 159, 192, 211n, 218
Strengths of Black Families, 211n, 215
Stressful Life Events, 82n
Supporting Families with a Child with a Disability: An International Outlook, 112
Support Systems and Mutual Help, 37n

Tally's Corner: A Study of Negro Street Corner Men, 82n
Teaching Culture: Strategies for Intercultural Communication, 19n, 28, 90
Teenage World: Adolescents Self-Image in Ten Countries, The, 27
Things They Say Behind Your Back, The, 54n
To Open Minds: Chinese Clues to the Dilemma of Contemporary Education, 154
Towars a Unified Theory of Human Behavior, 37n
Transformations: The Anthropology of Children's Play, 28
Transitions in a Woman's Life: Major Life Events in Developmental Context, 43
Treating the Troubled Family, 38

Understanding Culture, 25
Understanding France, 244
Understanding Other Cultures, 18n, 82n, 84
Up From Puerto Rico, 184n, 191

Welcome For Every Child: How France Achieves Quality in Child Care—Practical Ideas for the United States, A, 241n, 250
Welsh Folk Customs, 249
West Germany: Politics and Society, 243
We the People: An Atlas of America;s Ethnic Diversity, 83, 242
Why Can't They Be Like Us?, 85
Woman's Worth: Sexual Economics and the World of Women, 87
Women and Love: A Cultural Revolution in Progress, 25
Working Parents: Transformations in Gender Roles and Public Policies in Sweden, 248

SUBJECT INDEX

Adolescence 35, 65; Black 201, 202; Filipino 95; German 227; Mexican 172
Adopted children 11, 166, 120
African American childrearing practices 16, 199–200; Education 101, 202;
    Family structure 77, 198–199; Health 73, 97, 201– 202;
    Language/communication style 101, 201, 202; Religion 97, 200; Values
    4, 77, 200–201. *See also* Black cultures.
African origin 65, 163, 176, 177, 178, 179, 180, 195, 197, 201, 203, 205, 207,
    208. *See also* Black cultures.
Alcohol consumption 13, 51, 75, 178, 200, 208, 227, 231. 233, 239
Aliens (illegal) 65–66, 164, 170, 204
American/Anglo (Mainstream) 11, 15, 16, 46, 47, 66, 74, 75, 76, 101, 102, 125,
    126, 129, 138, 165, 168, 172–173, 195, 199, 223, 224, 227, 235, 236,
    237, 238, 240
American Indian. *See* Native American.
Ancestor worship 12,124, 128, 130, 131, 134, 141, 143, 144, 106, 207
Animism 95, 123, 124, 125, 143, 146, 196, 207
Anthropology 4, 45–46, 52, 78, 101, 171, 195–196
Arab. *See* Middle East.
Asian cultures 96, 121–150; Bibliography 151–161; Profiles—of Cambodia
    144–145; China 130–132; Hong Kong 134–135; Japan 127– 129; Korea
    135–138; Laos 146–147; Philippines 140–142; Singapore 138–139;
    Taiwan 133; Thailand 139–140; Vietnam 144
Assessment of culture and ethnicity 61–91, 93, 209; Chart 79–81
Assimilation/acculturation 61, 65, 76, 79, 93, 100, 125, 126, 181, 199

Baptist Church 200, 207, 236
Belgium 223. *See also* European Cultures.
Birth 9, 51, 124, 126, 134, 136, 171, 227, 230, 236
Birth order 17, 127
Black cultures 4, 16, 73, 77, 95, 97, 101, 176, 178, 180, 195–211; Bibliography
    212–222; Profiles of African-Americans 198–202; Caribbean (West
    Indian) Blacks 203–209
Black English 201, 202
Black Muslims 200
"Boat people" 65, 104, 144

Body language 15, 69, 80; in Asian cultures 122; in Hispanic cultures 165
Brazil 80. *See also* Central and South America.
British. *See* England/United Kingdom.
Buddhism 13, 70, 121, 123, 128, 131, 133, 134, 136, 138, 139, 143, 144, 145, 146

Cambodia 94, 95, 121–127, 144–145, 146; Childrearing practices 44; Education 145; Family structure 144; Health 145; Language/communication style 145; Religion 144; Values 144– 145. *See also* Asian cultures.
Caribbean (West Indian) blacks 177, 180, 181, 195–198, 203–209, 238; Childrearing practices 206; Education 208–209; Family structure 205–206; Health 208; Language/communication style 208; Religion 206–207; Values 207, 208–209. *See also* Black cultures.
Catholicism 13, 70, 172, 176–177, 179, 180, 200, 201; in Asia 140, 141, 143; in England/United Kingdom 236, 238; in Europe 224, 225; in Finland 231; in France 239; in Germany 226, 227; in Ireland 238; in Italy 240
Central America/South America 163–171, 179–181, 195; Childrearing practices 180, 181; Family structure 180–181; Health 180–181; Language/communication style 180; Religion 180; Values 179, 180, 181. *See also* Hispanic cultures.
Childrearing practices 6–7, 52, 62, 71–72, 77, 81, 240. *See also* specific cultural/ethnic groups.
"Chicano" 174. *See also* Mexican-American.
Chile 180. *See also* Central and South America.
China (mainland China) 64, 94, 104, 121–127, 130–132, 135, 136, 140, 146; Childrearing practices 63, 101, 123, 130–131; Education 101–102, 132; Family structure 130; Health 131–132; Language/communication style 102, 131; Religion 124, 131; Values 101–102, 131. *See also* Asian cultures.
Christianity 13, 128, 131, 133, 134, 136, 138, 139, 141, 142, 203, 206, 224
Colombia 94, 180. *See also* Central/South America.
Communication style/language 4, 14–15, 16, 45, 46, 53, 67, 68–70, 80, 93, 94, 95, 101, 102, 104; in Asian cultures 122, 126, 131–133, 134, 138, 139, 141, 143; in Black cultures 196, 198, 201, 202, 205, 208; in European cultures 224, 225, 228, 229, 232, 233, 237, 239; in Hispanic cultures 163, 165, 167, 169, 170, 180
Competition, competitiveness 13, 14, 48, 72, 77, 80, 101; in Asian cultures 129, 133, 135, 141, 143; in Black cultures 196; in Hispanic cultures 165, 169
Confucianism 13, 121, 122, 123, 124, 127, 128, 129, 133, 134, 136, 143
Costa Rica 94. *See also* Central/South America.
Country of origin 63–64, 64, 79, 180
Cross-cultural 12, 14, 71, 125, 209

Subject Index

Cuba 94, 103, 163, 164, 179, 205, 208. *See also* Hispanic cultures.
Cultural sensitivity 53, 62, 69, 73, 78, 81, 93–96, 201
Culture, assessment of 61–91, 79–81 (chart), 125; Definitions of 3–5, 62, 195; Understanding one's own 45–59

Death/dying 70, 124, 176, 177
Denmark 229–234. *See also* Scandinavia.
Dependency 9, 35, 68, 71–72, 77, 80, 96; in Asian cultures 121, 128, 137, 140, 141, 142, 146, 147; in Black cultures 195, 196, 199, 200, 203, 204; in European cultures 228, 230, 232, 235, 236, 237, 239; in Hispanic cultures 167, 169, 170, 171, 174, 176
Dietary practices/nutrition 4, 9, 12, 13, 53, 66, 74–76, 77, 81, 99–100; in Asian cultures 126–127, 129, 132, 133, 137, 138, 139–140,142, 143, 145, 147; in Black cultures 208; in European cultures 228, 229, 235, 237, 239; in Hispanic cultures 169, 175, 178, 181. *See also* Health in specific cultural/ethnic group.
Discipline 7–9, 12, 52, 71–72, 95, 104, 130; in Asian cultures 123, 130, 134, 140, 142, 144; in Black cultures 95, 199, 201, 206; in European cultures 224, 232, 234, 236, 239; in Hispanic cultures 166, 167, 171–172, 176. *See also* Childrearing practices in specific cultural/ethnic group and Guilt/shame.
Disabilities 62, 80, 96, 97; in Asian cultures 126, 134, 141–142; in European cultures 230, 233; in Hispanic cultures 97, 170

Ecuador 180. *See also* Central/South America.
Education 7, 9, 11, 13, 15, 16, 36, 51, 61, 62, 65, 66, 68–70, 73, 76, 79, 80, 93, 95, 98, 100–105, 105, 106; in Asian cultures 95–96, 101–103, 104, 123, 124, 125–126, 126–127, 128, 129, 130, 132, 133, 135, 137, 138, 139; in Black cultures 198, 199, 202, 203, 204, 205, 206, 207, 208, 209; in European cultures 228, 230, 231, 233, 234, 239, 240; in Hispanic cultures 103, 164, 169, 170, 171, 173, 174, 175, 176, 178, 180; in Soviet Union 104–105. *See also* Preschool education.
England and the United Kingdom 14–15, 135, 138, 201, 203, 204, 205, 208, 223, 224, 234–238; Childrearing practices 236; Education 14–15, 238; Family structure 235–236; Health 237; Language/communication style 14–15, 208, 237; Religion 236; Values 203, 226–237. *See also* European cultures.
Environment, influence of 5, 6, 7, 8, 12, 31, 35, 36, 46, 49, 62, 71, 100, 125, 134, 139, 147, 168, 175, 195, 198, 199, 200, 203, 209, 228, 229, 230, 233
Episcopal Church 200, 207; Anglican Church 236. *See also* Religion.
Ethnic neighborhood. *See* Neighborhood.
Ethnic pride 66, 93, 177, 199, 228

Ethnicity, assessment of 61–91; 79–81 (chart); Definitions of 3–6, 48, 62
Ethnocentrism 45–48, 53, 73, 77, 81, 105
European cultures 65, 75, 140, 163, 179, 195, 203, 207, 208, 223–241;
    Bibliography 242–252; Profiles—of England and the United Kingdom 234–238; France 239; Germany 226–229, Ireland 238–239; Italy; Sweden and Scandinavia 229–234
Evangelical Church 167, 172, 176; Evangelical Lutheran Church 231
"Evil eye" 10, 100, 169, 173, 177, 199

Family/family systems theory 31–45, 46, 49, 62, 67, 93, 99, 106, 147–148, 209;
    blended 67, 79; boundaries 32–34, 51, 93; composition 14, 49, 62, 67, 79; extended 33, 36, 66, 67, 71, 77, 79, 81, 95, 98; functions 34–35, 52, 77, 100–101; "ghosts" 33; ideologies 12, 51–52, 70–72, 79–81; life cycle stages 12, 33–36, 67–68, 79; nuclear 33, 67, 71, 77, 79; of origin 33, 45, 46, 49, 51–52; role in health/illness 73–74, 93, 94, 97, 98, 99; roles 33–36, 52, 63, 71, 72–73, 80, 93–94, 99; structure 32, 34–36, 77; subsystems 32–34, 36; toxic issues 51; triangles 32–33, 35
Fatalism 10, 13, 80, 97, 141, 165, 168, 169, 170, 240
Finland 224, 229, 231, 232, 233, 234. *See also* Scandinavia.
Folk beliefs/folklore 9–11, 73, 97–98; in Asian cultures 141, 143, 146, 165; in Black cultures 196, 207; in European cultures 224–225, 232, 236; in Hispanic cultures 165, 170, 171, 173, 176, 178
Folk medicine 66, 73, 74, 77, 97–98, 99, 100; in Asian cultures 132, 137, 141, 143, 147; in Black cultures 201, 208; in Hispanic cultures 168, 169, 170, 173, 178, 179, 181. *See also* Health in specific cultural/ethnic groups.
Food. *See* Dietary practices/nutrition.
Folk religions 98, 131, 134, 136, 170, 176, 201, 207
France 11, 143, 145, 165, 203, 208, 223, 239. *See also* European cultures.

Gender/sex roles 4, 15–17, 35, 36, 64, 72, 73, 75, 76, 77, 80, 81, 94, 101, 102, 103; in Asian cultures 123, 124, 127, 129, 130, 135, 136, 140, 142, 144, 145, 146; in Black cultures 195, 197, 199, 200, 202, 203, 206, 207; in European cultures 226, 227, 230, 231, 232, 234, 235, 239; in Hispanic cultures 165, 166, 167, 170, 171, 172, 174, 175, 176, 178, 180
Generalizations 70, 95, 171
Genogram 49–52; example of 50
Germany 223, 224, 226–229; Childrearing practices 12, 16, 227; Education 228; Family structure 226–227; Health 228; Language/communication style 12, 179; Religion 227; Values 12, 16, 165, 228. *See also* European cultures.
Ghana 197. *See also* Black cultures.

Subject Index

Godparents 52, 98; in Asian cultures 140; in European cultures; in Hispanic cultures 166, 168, 170, 171

Grandparents 11, 51, 52, 63, 102; in Asian cultures 123, 126, 127, 143; in Black cultures 196, 198, 199, 206; in European cultures 226; in Hispanic cultures 166, 175

Guilt/shame 7, 12, 13, 17, 94, 97; in Asian cultures 122, 123, 131, 140, 141, 145; in Hispanic cultures 170, 172. *See also* Discipline.

Haiti 10, 195–197, 204, 205, 206, 207, 208, 209. *See also* Caribbean blacks.
Hawaii 103, 127
Handicapped Children. *See* Disabilities.
Health, perceptions of 9, 12, 46, 62, 73–74, 74–76, 80, 94, 96–100. *See also* Illness.

Health care 66, 73–74, 74–76, 80, 96–100; Practices and beliefs in Asian cultures 126–127, 129, 131–132, 133, 134, 137, 138, 139– 140, 141– 142; in Black cultures 197, 201–202, 208; in European cultures 223, 228, 233, 237, 239; in Hispanic cultures 168– 169, 170, 171, 173, 177, 178, 180–181

Herbalism 70, 74, 98, 99, 100, 140, 141; in Asian cultures 126, 137, 143; in Black cultures 201, 204, 205; in Hispanic cultures 167, 169, 170, 173, 177. *See also* Folk medicine.

Hinduism 10, 138, 195

Hispanic cultures 12, 70, 73, 74, 94, 98, 99, 100, 140, 163–241; Bibliography 242–252; Profiles—of Central and South America 179–181; Cuba 179; Mexico 171–174; Puerto Rico 174–179

Hmong 95–96, 121–127, 146, 147. *See also* Cambodia and Laos in Asian cultures.

Holidays/festivals, celebration of 5, 52, 70, 80; in Asian cultures 124, 132; in European cultures 223, 226, 229, 238, 239; in Hispanic cultures 165

Holistic medicine 96, 169, 179, 181
Home visits (by professionals) 52, 67, 72, 133, 233
Honduras 180, *See also* Central/South America.
Hong Kong 121–127, 134–135. *See also* Asian cultures.
"Hot" and "cold" humors/theories 73–74, 74–76, 97, 99–100, 168–169, 170, 178, 201.

Iceland 225, 229–234. *See also* Scandinavia.
Illness, cause of/perceptions of 5, 11, 12, 62, 73, 75, 80, 96–100; in Asian cultures 124, 126, 129, 142, 143; in Black cultures 197, 201, 208; in European cultures 228–233; in Hispanic cultures 168–169, 170, 173, 177, 178. *See also* Health.

Immigrants/immigration 62, 64–66, 66, 67, 69, 76, 79, 96, 98, 100, 103, 104; in Asian cultures 121, 126, 127, 137, 138, 146, 147; in Black cultures 195,

198, 203, 204, 205, 208, 209; in European cultures 223, 225, 226, 233, 235–236, 238, 239, 240; in Hispanic cultures 164, 170, 174, 175, 177, 179, 181
India 10, 74, 138, 139, 144, 145, 195, 238. *See also* Moslem and Hindu.
Indians, Native American (North America) 10, 12, 69, 97, 100, 101, 163; Spanish/Hispanic 163–164, 178, 180
Infant mortality 63, 73, 145, 147, 202, 230, 231
Interpreters, use of 93, 105
Interviewing 52, 93–94, 94
Iran 12, 95. *See also* Middle East.
Ireland 172, 224, 238; Northern Ireland 223, 234–238. *See also* European cultures.
Islam 144, 200, 224. *See also* Religion.
Italy 223, 229, 239, 240. *See also* European cultures.

Jamaica 205, 208. *See also* Caribbean blacks.
Japan 46, 64, 94, 121–127, 127–129, 136, 145; Childrearing practices 127–128; Education 101–102, 102–103, 129; Family structure 127; Health 129; Language/communication style 129; Religion 70, 124, 128; Values 101–102, 102–103, 128–129. *See also* Asian cultures.
Jehovah's Witnesses 172, 200
Judaism 13, 70, 75, 231, 236

Khmer 95–96, 144, 145. *See also* Cambodia.
Kindergarten. *See* Preschool.
Kinship 77, 175, 195, 196, 197, 198, 199, 200, 224.
Korea 94, 106, 121–127, 135–138; Childrearing practices 136; Education 137; Family structure 135; Health 137; Language 137; Religion 124; Values 136–139. *See also* Asian cultures.

Language. *See* Communication style/language.
Laos 95–96, 121–127, 146–147. *See also* Asian cultures.
Latino. *See* Hispanic cultures.
Learning styles 68–70, 93, 100–105, 125–126, 202. *See also* Education.
Lutheran Church 200, 227, 231; Evangelical Lutheran 231; Lutheran Free Church 231

"Melting pot" 47
Methodist Church 236
Mexico 94. 163–171, 171–174; Childrearing practices 171–172; Education 104, 173; Family structure 171; Health 97, 173; Language/communication style 173; Religion 172; Values 172. *See also* Hispanic cultures.
Middle East 10, 12, 16, 100, 207

Subject Index

Misconceptions/misinterpretations 15, 47, 64, 69, 70, 78, 79, 93, 94, 95, 97, 104, 105, 165, 173, 181, 209, 234
Mormon Church 13
Moslem/Muslim religion 10, 133, 138, 139, 141, 195, 200. 231, 236
Mulatto 203
Multicultural 93, 234
Music 15, 102–103; in Black cultures 201, 207, 208; in European cultures 231, 237; in Hispanic cultures 165, 178, 179
Myths, cultural 8, 141, 196, 232; family 10–11; stories 8, 9–11, 52, 101, 103, 202

Name, significance of 49, 51, 62–63, 79; in Asian cultures 127, 128, 131, 135, 136, 142, 143, 146; in Black cultures 197, 199; in European cultures 234; in Hispanic cultures 163, 171, 180
Nationality 47, 64
Neighborhood 14, 35, 53, 66, 79, 140, 168, 225, 235; Ethnic 8, 52, 66, 79, 202, 205
Nicaragua 180. *See also* Central/South America.
Norway 229, 230, 232, 233. *See also* Scandinavia.
Nutrition. *See* Dietary practices/Nutrition and health.

Occupation 11, 13, 16, 35, 66, 71, 73, 76, 77, 79, 80, 81; in Asian cultures 125, 136–137; in Black cultures 197, 198, 199, 203, 204, 206, 208; in Hispanic cultures 174–175; in European cultures 225, 228, 238

Pain, cultural response to 69, 99; in Asian cultures 126; in Black cultures 208
Pakistan 144, 229, 238
Parenting practices/parenthood 32, 33, 34, 35, 36, 51, 63, 71–72, 80, 99, 101, 102, 103, 104. *See also* Parenting practices in specific cultural/ethnic groups.
Pentecostal Church 172, 176, 200
Personality development 3–30, 51, 70, 71–72. 80, 134, 177, 238
Philippines 121–127, 140–142, 163; Childrearing practices 95, 140; Education 142; Family structure 140–141; Health 73, 141–142; Language/communication style 141; Religion 141, 143; Values 95, 141. *See also* Asian cultures.
Play 6, 14, 72, 104, 131, 176, 234, 236, 239
Politics/political affiliation 13, 35, 65, 70–71; in Asian cultures 142, 147; in Black cultures 196, 204; in Hispanic cultures 164, 174, 174, 180, 181; in European cultures 225, 226, 227, 229, 230, 235, 236; in Hispanic cultures 164, 174, 180, 181
Portugal 180. *See also* European cultures.
Prejudice 33, 47–48, 76, 77, 81, 196, 229, 238. *See also* Race/race relations.

Prenatal care/childbearing 9, 35, 75, 76, 100, 130
Preschool education/day care 101–103,104–104; in Asian cultures 127, 140; in European cultures 223, 230, 234, 236, 239; in Hispanic cultures 178. *See also* Education.
Protestant Church 13, 136, 141, 167, 176, 180, 207, 224, 226, 227, 231, 235
Puerto Rico 94, 95, 163–171, 174–179, 181, 205, 208; Childrearing practices 97, 176; Education 178; Family structure 174; Health 94–95, 97, 178; Language/communication style 178, Religion 97, 98, 176–177; Values 97, 106, 177–178. *See also* Hispanic cultures.

Quaker Church 236

Race/race relations 5, 36, 47, 63–64, 76, 138, 178, 179, 195, 196, 198, 204, 205, 238. *See also* Prejudice.
"Rapping" 201
Religion/religious beliefs and practices 7, 9, 12–13; in Asian cultures 13, 70, 94, 95, 98, 121–125, 128, 131, 133, 134, 136, 138, 139, 141, 143, 144, 146; in Black cultures 97, 196, 200, 201, 206, 207; in European cultures 223–224, 225, 226, 227, 230, 231, 235, 236, 238, 239, 240; in Hispanic cultures 70, 94, 97–98, 167–168, 172, 176–177, 179, 180. *See also* specific denominations.
Rites of Passage 16, 72
Russia. *See* Soviet Union.

Santaría 177, 179
"Saving face" 7, 122, 144, 146
Scandinavian countries 64, 223, 229–234; Childrearing practices 12, 95, 230–231; Education 233–234; Family structure 229–230; Health 233; Language 232; Religion 231; Values 12, 231–232. *See also* European cultures.
Scotland 225, 234, 235, 236, 237, 238. *See also* England/United Kingdom.
Shamanism 97, 124, 136, 137
Shame. *See* Guilt/shame.
Shintoism 70, 123, 124, 128
Siblings 9, 11, 17, 36, 52, 140, 171, 196, 206, 238
Singapore 121–127, 138–139. *See also* Asian cultures.
Social services, role/function 93, 95, 105, 106, 223, 229, 237; serving Asian clients 126–127; serving Hispanic clients 170
Socialization 4, 7–9, 16, 35, 71–72, 79, 80, 101, 104; in Asian cultures 134, 142, 144; in Black cultures 200, 206; in Hispanic cultures 172, 174, 176
Socioeconomic status 6, 12, 14, 16, 35, 36, 48, 49, 51, 62, 66, 72, 76, 81, 98, 101, 103, 104
Sorcery/witchcraft 10, 70, 97, 98, 143, 167, 169, 173, 196, 207, 208

Subject Index

South America. *See* Central America/South America.
Soviet Union 104, 105, 179
Spain 141, 142, 163, 164, 166, 168, 172, 174, 176, 178, 179, 181, 203, 208. *See also* European cultures.
Stereotypes 10, 47–48, 61, 77; Asian 147; Hispanic 171, 181
Strengths and weaknesses 77, 81; in Asian cultures 147; in Black cultures 197, 199, 200, 201, 202, 207; in Hispanic cultures 170, 181
Supernatural 74, 98, 141, 163, 173, 176, 177, 195, 196, 201
Superstitions 9–11, 173, 181
Support systems 33, 51, 66, 67, 73, 77,, 79, 80, 93, 99, 103; in Asian cultures 140; in Black cultures 198, 201, 203, 204, 207; in Hispanic cultures 166, 167, 170, 174, 181
Sweden 220–234. *See also* Scandinavia.
Switzerland 12. *See also* European cultures.

Taboo(s) 15, 74–75, 91, 196
Taiwan (Republic of China) 63, 104, 121–127, 133. *See also* Asian cultures.
Taoism 13, 123, 124, 128, 131, 134, 138, 143
Thailand 98, 121–127, 139–140, 145, 146. *See also* Asian cultures
Time orientation 10, 11–12, 13, 72; in Asian cultures 137; in Black cultures 196, 201, 204, 207; in European cultures 237

United Kingdom. *See* England and the United Kingdom and also the specific countries.
Uruguay 180. *See also* Central/South America.

Vietnam 94, 104, 121–127, 142–144, 145. *See also* Asian cultures.
Voodoo 197, 201, 207

Wales 234–238. *See also* England and the United Kingdom.
"WASP" 235
West Indies. *See* Caribbean.
Witchcraft. *See* Sorcery/witchcraft.

Yin and *yang* 75, 97, 124, 128, 131–132